Religion
and Power
in Morocco

Religion and Power in Morocco

Henry Munson, Jr.

Yale
University
Press
New Haven
and London

Set in Joanna by Marathon Typography Services, Inc., Durham, North Carolina. Printed in the United States of America by BookCrafters, Chelsea, Michigan.

Library of Congress Cataloging-in-Publication Data

Munson, Henry, 1946–
    Religion and power in Morocco / Henry Munson, Jr.
        p.   cm.
    Includes bibliographical references and index.
    ISBN 0-300-05376-2
    1. Islam and politics—Morocco.   2. Morocco—Politics and
government.   I. Title.
    BP64.M6M86   1993
    322'.1'0964—dc20   92-40202
                                                                        CIP

A catalogue record for this book is available from the British Library.

The paper in this book meets the guidelines for permanence and durability of the Committee on Production Guidelines for Book Longevity of the Council on Library Resources.

10   9   8   7   6   5   4   3   2   1

To the memory of my father

Contents

Preface

The relation between religion and power is invariably distorted when we focus exclusively on the overtly political aspects of religion or the overtly religious aspects of power. Without some idea of how a religion is understood by ordinary people in their everyday lives, we cannot begin to assess the political impact of the religious rhetoric of rulers and rebels. Conversely, if we restrict our attention to the overtly religious facets of power, we exaggerate their significance and ignore others—like force, fear, and the rage of people who cannot find work.

In this book, I have attempted to trace the evolution of the political role of Islam in Morocco on the basis of these assumptions. I focus primarily on a series of conflicts between rulers and rebels that exemplified the myth of the righteous man of God who dares to defy an unjust sultan. I use these conflicts and this myth as a way of understanding the religious and political structures in which they are embedded.

In *Religion and Power in Morocco*, I cover many of the topics discussed by anthropologist Clifford Geertz in the Moroccan sections of his book *Islam Observed: Religious Development in Morocco and Indonesia* (1968), and there are obvious parallels in our approaches. Like Geertz, I argue that the political role of a religion cannot be understood unless its religious one is. Like Geertz, I leap back and forth between the specific and the general, between stories about individuals and the structures they are meant to exemplify. Like Geertz, I try to mesh the methods of history and anthropology. But one of my main goals is to demonstrate the need for a less ethereal version of Geertz's conception of the "social history of the imagination" (1968, 19).

In chapter 1, "Al-Yusi as Exemplar: Two Interpretations," I present an alternative to Geertz's interpretation of the seventeenth-century scholar-cum-saint al-Hasan al-Yusi. Although we both use al-Yusi as an exemplar of the distinctive features of "the classical style" of Moroccan Islam, I argue that Geertz tends to interpret little stories without adequate attention to their symbolic and historical contexts. He also tends to reduce the semantic substance of religion to personality writ large.

I attempt to substantiate these criticisms of Geertz by focusing primarily on his interpretation of a folktale concerning al-Yusi's clash with the sultan Mulay Isma'il. I use this story to introduce the myth of the righteous man of God and to demonstrate that if anthropologists wish to trespass onto the historian's domain, as they should, they have to be willing to study real texts as well as metaphorical, behavioral ones.

In chapter 2, "Scholars and Sultans," I present an overview of the evolution of the religious and political roles of scholars and sultans in precolonial (pre–1912) Morocco. I stress the docility of most religious scholars (ulama) as opposed to the few who embodied the myth of the righteous man of God. I also discuss the disparity between the ulama's contractual conception of the caliphate and the more absolutist notion of sacred kingship favored by most Moroccan sultans.

In chapter 3, "Al-Kattani and the Ulama (1904–1909)," I examine the myth of the righteous man of God as embodied by Sidi Muhammad bin ʿAbd al-Kabir al-Kattani, who was flogged to death by order of the sultan Mulay ʿAbd al-Hafidh in 1909. I attempt to demonstrate that, unlike al-Kattani, most ulama played a thoroughly passive role in the Hafidhiyya revolt of 1907–08 and the anticolonial movements of the early twentieth century generally.

In chapter 4, "Popular Religion, Orthodoxy, and Salafi Scripturalism," I argue that Geertz's discussion of the ideological nature of reformist scripturalist Islam constitutes the most important contribution he makes in *Islam Observed*—even though the specific assertions he makes about Moroccan reformism are inaccurate. I also argue that the radical gap between popular and orthodox Islam imagined by Ernest Gellner did not exist before the rise of Salafi reformism in the twentieth century. Salafi reformism grew out of orthodox Islam, but it also transformed it.

Also in this chapter, I take the scholars Abu Shuʿayb al-Dukkali and Muhammad bin al-ʿArbi al-ʿAlawi as exemplars of two very different kinds of Salafi reformists. Al-Dukkali exemplified the scholar who gains wealth and high rank by submitting to the powers that be. Al-ʿAlawi, at least in his old age, embodied the myth of the righteous man of God both in his defiance of French colonialism in the 1940s and 1950s and in his defiance of King Hassan II in the early 1960s.

In chapter 5, "Holy and Unholy Kingship in Twentieth-Century Morocco," I argue that Geertz, like Elaine Combs-Schilling, fails to see the religious insignificance of the monarchy in late twentieth-century Moroccan Islam and ignores the political role of force and fear. Geertz's view of the Moroccan monarchy demonstrates how the relation between religion and power can be distorted by the neglect of both the strictly religious aspects of religion and the strictly political aspects of power.

In chapter 6, "Fundamentalism in Late Twentieth-Century Morocco," I examine the principal movements that have challenged the regime of Hassan II in the name of Islam. I discuss the similarities between these movements and twentieth-century revivalism in other religions and suggest that the controversial term *fundamentalism* reflects these similarities in ways that some of the alternative terms suggested by other scholars do not. I focus primarily on two men who came to represent, in the minds of many late twentieth-century Moroccans, the myth of the righteous man of God: al-Fqih al-Zamzami and ʿAbd as-Slam Yasin. These two men personify two distinct kinds of fundamentalism—one relatively traditional, the other more radical and ideological. I attempt to explain the appeal of such men and why they have been relatively unsuccessful when compared with their counterparts in Iran and Algeria.

In the final chapter, "Conclusion: Rethinking Geertz," I summarize the differences between my attempt to fuse history and anthropology in this book and what Geertz tries to do in *Islam Observed* and his later, more explicitly interpretive works.

Religion and Power in Morocco is based primarily on the analysis of Arabic texts from the seventeenth through the twentieth century and on ethnographic fieldwork undertaken for a year and a half in 1976–77 and during the summers of 1987, 1988, and 1990. Because of the political sensitivity of chapters 5 and 6, which deal with the reign of the current king of Morocco, Hassan II, I cannot say much about my Moroccan "informants." They are in no way responsible for any of the views expressed in this book, nor is any other individual or institution mentioned in this preface.

In 1976–77, my wife, children, and I lived for fifteen months in a popular quarter of a city in northern Morocco and for three months in a northern mountain village. During the summers of 1987, 1988, and 1990, I interviewed dozens of religious scholars, fundamentalists, and human rights activists, mostly in Morocco's capital, Rabat. All these interviews were conducted in Arabic. I also discussed Moroccan politics more casually with a number of Moroccan colleagues, sometimes in Arabic, sometimes in French, and sometimes in English. I have also benefited from over two decades of conversations with Moroccans in the United States and Europe from the early 1970s through the early 1990s. Although most of these people were scholars and students, they came from all social strata and ranged from a former minister in the Moroccan government to an illiterate old woman born in a mountain village.

The following institutions made my research in Morocco possible in 1976–77 and in the summers of 1987, 1988, and 1990: the Social Science Research Council; the Fulbright-Hays Program of the Department of Education; the Summer Faculty Fellowship Program of the University of Maine; and the John D. and Catherine T. MacArthur Foundation's Program on Peace and International Cooperation. The MacArthur Foundation grant enabled me to spend the summer of 1990 in Morocco and the 1990–91 year writing.

I thank Harvard University's Center for Middle Eastern Studies for allowing me to include a revised version of my paper "The Political Role of the Moroccan 'Ulama (1860–1912)" (Munson, in press) and the editors of Government and Opposition for permitting me to include a revised version of my paper "Morocco's Fundamentalists" (Munson 1991a). I also thank the editors of Religion for allowing me to include several passages from my paper "Geertz on Religion: The Theory and the Practice" (Munson 1986a).

I am grateful to the following people for their comments on all or parts of earlier versions of this book: Edmund Burke III, Ernest Gellner, George Joffé, Cynthia Mahmood, Susan Miller, Wilfrid Rollman, and Paul Roscoe. (I cannot mention the names of Moroccans.) Fawzi Abdulrazak and Muhsin Mahdi commented on an abbreviated oral version of chapter 1 presented as a lecture at Harvard's Center for Middle Eastern Studies in December 1990. Dr. Abdulrazaq, who is in charge of the Arabic holdings at Harvard's Widener Library, also helped me find and understand a number of important Moroccan sources. Bahman Bakhtiari and Alex Grab have made a number of helpful suggestions concerning the comparison of fundamentalist movements in different religions. Jean-François Clément helped me obtain some unpublished documents. Steve Bicknell drew the map of Morocco.

I thank Ellen Graham, who retired as senior editor at Yale University Press in June 1991, for her encouragement over the years, and Charles Grench and Lorraine Alexson for all they have done to make this a better book.

I thank my wife and children for the canoe and all the good times in it.

Note on Transliteration

I have used a simplified form of the standard transliteration of Arabic used by the *International Journal of Middle East Studies*. No diacritics are used, except for the 'ayn ('), made by pressing the root of the tongue against the back of the throat, and the hamza ('), or glottal stop—a quick closure of the vocal cords, as heard at the beginning and middle of *uh oh*. Q represents a k-like sound produced farther back in the mouth, *kh* the voiceless vibration of the uvula, similar to the final sound in the German pronunciation of *Bach*, and *gh* the voiced equivalent of this sound, similar to the French pronunciation of the initial r in *rouge*. *Dh* can represent either the initial sound of *the* (a voiced interdental fricative) or its emphatic counterpart.

The l in the Arabic definite article *al* (*the*) is pronounced like the first consonant of the following word if this is t, th, d, dh, s, z, sh, r, l, n, or any of their emphatic variants. Thus the name written 'Abd al-Rahman, (the slave of the merciful one) is pronounced 'Abd ar-Rahman. I have indicated this assimilation in my transliteration of common names and words to give the reader a better sense of how they are actually pronounced.

I have followed conventional English usage in writing well-known names. Thus I write Hassan II rather than al-Hasan al-thani and 'Allal al-Fassi rather than 'Allal al-Fasi. In citing Moroccans who write in Western languages as well as in Arabic, I use the transliteration they use in citing their writings in French or English and the standard scholarly transliteration (minus diacritics) in citing their writings in Arabic, with cross-references in the two bibliographies to avoid confusion. (Bibliography A includes Arabic sources and Bibliography B sources in Western languages.)

Chronology

1956 Morocco regains its independence

1958–1959 Crown Prince Hassan II directs the suppression of the Rif revolt

1961 Hassan II assumes the throne after Muhammad V's death

1962 Sidi Muhammad bin al-'Arbi al-'Alawi (d. 1964) opposes Hassan II's proposed constitution

1963 Socialists are accused of trying to kill the king. Moumen Diouri undresses at his trial to show where he was tortured.

1965 Riots in Casablanca. Mehdi Ben Barka is kidnapped and assassinated. Parliament is suspended.

1971 Attempted coup at Hassan II's forty-second birthday party at the royal villa of Skhirat

1972 Attempted coup. General Oufkir is killed and his wife and children are imprisoned.

1973 Attempted Marxist insurrection

1974 'Abd as-Slam Yasin sends the king his epistle entitled *al-Islam aw al-Tufan* (Islam or the Deluge)

1975 "The Green March" into the Western Sahara starts prolonged war against the Polisario guerrillas

1978–1979 The Iranian revolution encourages Morocco's fundamentalists

1981 Riots sparked by price increases

1983 Ahmed Dlimi is killed after an attempted coup

1984 Riots sparked by price increases and an increase in student fees become an abortive insurrection in northern Morocco

1990 The publication of Gilles Perrault's *Notre ami le roi* increases international criticism of human rights abuses in Morocco. The fundamentalist Islamic Salvation Front wins communal and provincial elections in Algeria. Riots in many Moroccan cities in December.

1991 Hundreds of thousands of Moroccans protest the Gulf War and Morocco's role in it. The Oufkir family and other political prisoners are released. In Algeria, the Islamic Salvation Front wins the first round of parliamentary elections.

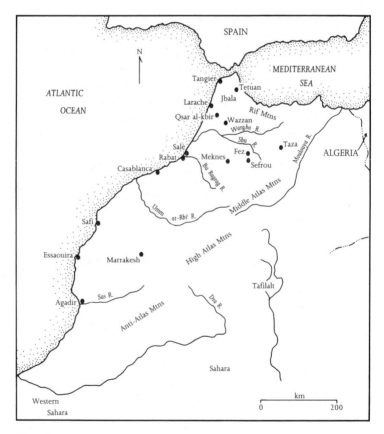

Morocco

One Al-Yusi as Exemplar: Two Interpretations

What has been the political role of Islam in Moroccan history? Geertz has written that when anthropologists try to answer such questions, they are always inclined to focus on the concrete and the specific in order to understand the abstract and the general. "We hope to find in the little what eludes us in the large, to stumble upon general truths while sorting through special cases" (1968, 4). Whether or not this is an accurate characterization of all anthropology, it does reflect what I have tried to do in *Religion and Power in Morocco*, as well as what Geertz tried to do in *Islam Observed*. We tend, however, to stumble upon very different general truths while sorting through the same special cases. These differences raise some basic questions about how one goes about linking the specific and the general, the little and the large.

Geertz sees the seventeenth-century scholar and saint al-Hasan al-Yusi as an exemplar of "the classical style" of Moroccan "spirituality."[1] He uses two folktales to paint a miniature portrait of al-Yusi, especially one concerning a clash between the saint and the sultan Mulay Isma'il, who reigned from 1672 to 1727. This story is important insofar as it illustrates some basic aspects of the relation between religion and power in Morocco. Geertz's interpretation of it is important insofar as it illustrates what happens when stories are interpreted without adequate attention to the symbolic and historical soil out of which they grow.

AL-YUSI: FRAGMENTS OF A BIOGRAPHY

Al-Yusi was born into a Berber-speaking transhumant tribe of the Middle Atlas Mountains in 1631. (Most of the inhabitants of Morocco's mountains are Berbers.) He lived at the time of "the maraboutic crisis"—*maraboutism* being a Western term referring to the fusion of the veneration of saints and descendants of the Prophet Muhammad with the mystical doctrines of Sufism. Geertz sees this crisis as having lasted from the fifteenth through the seventeenth century. He contends that during this period Morocco was fragmented into "a proliferation of zealous, insular, intensely competitive hagiocracies, sometimes called maraboutic states, though most of them were more like utopian communities, aggressive utopian communities, than proper states" (pp. 29–31). (I shall cite *Islam Observed* by page numbers only throughout the rest of this chapter.) The political situation Geertz refers to actually existed only from 1603 to 1668—from the death of the last powerful sultan of the Sa'adian dynasty to the consolidation of power by the first powerful sultan of the 'Alawi dynasty (Berque 1982, 22, 45, 81). It is true, however, that maraboutism began to flourish on a large scale in Morocco in the late fifteenth century (Laroui 1977a, 246–47).

"Somewhere around his twentieth year," says Geertz, al-Yusi descended from the mountains "to become, in legend anyway, first a pilgrim, then a rebel, and finally a saint." Geertz contends that al-Yusi wandered around Morocco "for the whole of his adult life," and he interprets this wandering as a reflection of the "restlessness" of the Moroccan "mode of being" (pp. 31–32). The historical al-Yusi actually wandered less than Geertz suggests. From his late teens to his late thirties, al-Yusi spent almost twenty years at the Sufi *zawiya* (lodge) of al-Dila' in the western foothills of the Middle Atlas Mountains (al-Yusi 1982, 1:81, 249; al-Qabli 1981, 46). After this zawiya was destroyed in 1668, al-Yusi often wandered not because of the restlessness of the Moroccan ethos, but because the sultans of Morocco feared his tremendous popularity and often ordered him to move from one place to another to prevent his becoming a political threat (al-Qadiri, 3:26; al-Jirari 1981, 24–27).

SEVENTEENTH-CENTURY HISTORY AND TWENTIETH-CENTURY FOLKTALES

Geertz contends that two incidents in al-Yusi's life "stand out, at least in the popular mind, as defining the nature of his saintliness and thus of saintliness in general" (p. 32). The first concerns the transmission of *baraka*, or "blessedness," to al-Yusi by his Sufi *shaykh*, or "master." (In the Sufi context, a shaykh, literally "elderly man," is a mystical teacher.) The second incident concerns al-Yusi's confrontation with the sultan Mulay Isma'il.

Geertz tells us that his two stories about al-Yusi derive mainly from the accounts of his informants, "for what they lack in historical accuracy they more than make up for in cultural penetration" (ibid.). Folk stories can, of course, be extremely useful in penetrating the "popular mind" of the period when they were told, but Geertz tends to assume that they also reflect the popular beliefs that prevailed three centuries earlier. He uses folktales recorded in the 1960s to substantiate his interpretation of al-Yusi as an exemplar of the classical style of Moroccan spirituality that prevailed from 1500 to 1800.

There are many texts that could be used to reconstruct the popular mind of al-Yusi's era. Al-Yusi's own *Rasa'il* (Epistles), for example, are brilliant portraits of religion, society, and politics in seventeenth-century Morocco. These epistles are generally not abstruse theological texts. Most were sent to al-Yusi's fellow Sufis (mystics), who read them to their students (al-Qabli 1981, 84, 112, 121). (This was a time when most Moroccan men belonged to Sufi orders.) Al-Yusi deliberately wrote most of them in simple Arabic prose in order to be understood by fledgling mystics (ibid., 84,

115). These epistles demonstrate that al-Yusi was indeed an exemplar, and an exemplary observer, of the collective imagination of seventeenth-century Morocco. But trying to reconstruct this imagination without recourse to the texts in which it is inscribed is like trying to interpret a poem in a language one does not read. This is what Geertz does in *Islam Observed*.[2]

Another problem with Geertz's use of his folktales is that he combines them with facts from Jacques Berque's excellent biography *Al-Yousi: Problèmes de la culture marocaine au dix-septième siècle* (1958) without carefully distinguishing between al-Yusi the saint in twentieth-century folktales and al-Yusi the seventeenth-century man. The two are by no means unrelated. Tracing the relation between them can be a valuable way of tracing the evolution of the Moroccan collective imagination, but the relation between twentieth-century folktales and seventeenth-century history cannot be understood unless the two are distinguished.

There are other, more specifically ethnographic problems with Geertz's two stories about al-Yusi (historians face comparable ones). He tells us nothing about his informants' social and educational backgrounds. He does not tell us in what context he recorded his stories. How easy was it to obtain these stories? How common are they? Although such questions are always important, they come immediately to mind in the present context because Paul Rabinow, who spent 1968–69 in the village near Sefrou where al-Yusi is buried, presents two very different images of the popular legend of al-Yusi. In *Symbolic Domination*, in which he relies primarily on *Islam Observed* and Berque's biography in discussing the historical al-Yusi, he writes: "I found that within the village of Sidi Lahcen there existed a fairly uniform and succinct set of stories about the saint. Almost everyone in the village could repeat the main episodes of the legend, and almost no one from the outside seemed to know them. Further, within the village itself, there was little variation from rendering to rendering" (1975, 17). In his later book *Reflections on Fieldwork in Morocco*, however, Rabinow writes that "even the saint's descendants themselves did not know very much about their progenitor," and there was "a general ignorance of his legend" (1977,

132).[3] When I spent a few hours in this same village in the summer of 1990, I too found that no one seemed to know anything about al-Yusi other than the fact that he was a great saint. This is typical. Few Moroccans know much about the saints they venerate (Reysoo 1991, 62, 113, 116). Yet Rabinow did apparently come across basically the same two stories about al-Yusi that Geertz tells in *Islam Observed* (Rabinow 1975, 18–19). More important, both are by and large typical of Moroccan folk stories about saints (see Brunel 1926; Cornell 1989; Crapanzano 1973; Dermenghem 194; Elboudrari 1985; Marcus 1985).

GEERTZ ON BARAKA

Geertz's first folktale begins as follows: "When, the story goes, Lyusi arrived at Tamgrut, the desert-edge oasis where ben Nasir was teaching, he found the old man critically ill with a loathsome disease, perhaps, from the sound of it, smallpox. The sheikh called his students to him, one by one, and asked them to wash his nightshirt. But each was so repelled by the sickness, so disgusted by his and the nightshirt's appearance, as well as afraid for his own health, that he refused to do it, or indeed to come any more into the sheikh's presence" (p. 32). Al-Yusi washed the nightshirt and "drank the foul water thus produced." He then returned to the shaykh, his eyes aflame "as though he had drunk a powerful wine." Then everyone knew that al-Yusi had imbibed the Sufi teacher's baraka.

Geertz declares that the significance of this story is that it shows that Moroccan spirituality has "for the most part" meant "extraordinary physical courage, absolute personal loyalty, ecstatic moral intensity, and the almost physical transmission of sanctity from one man to another" (p. 33). It is true that Moroccan folk stories often describe the transmission of baraka by spit or some other bodily fluid (Crapanzano 1973, 36–37, 48-50), but most of the qualities that Geertz sees as being distinctive of the meaning of baraka are personality traits that tell us nothing about the religious concepts that shape the way Moroccan Muslims interpret their lives.

Extraordinary physical courage, absolute personal loyalty, and ecstatic moral intensity can be found among kamikaze pilots, revolutionaries, and religious zealots all over the world. Listing such traits does not shed much light on how baraka was or is understood by Moroccans. Geertz ignores the religious significance of baraka and reduces it to personality traits. He severs it from the religious system from which it derives its significance and relies on analogies to "personal presence, force of character," and "moral vividness" (p. 44). This illustrates a recurrent problem in Geertz's work—the reduction of the semantic substance of belief to "personality writ large" (Benedict 1932; Munson 1986a). Geertz goes on to say of baraka: "It is a mode of construing—emotionally, morally, intellectually—human experience, a cultural gloss on life. And though this is a vast and intricate problem, what this construction, this gloss, comes down to, so at least it seems to me, is the proposition (again, of course, wholly tacit) that the sacred appears most directly in the world as an endowment—a talent and a capacity, a special ability—of particular individuals" (p. 44). Here Geertz reduces the religious significance of baraka to one of its social (and political) correlates, the fact that specific individuals are believed to possess it. Because of his neglect of the religious framework in which the notion of baraka is rooted, Geertz is unable to understand this social fact and its political implications.

The Quran is believed to be full of baraka, as is the phrase "in the name of God the merciful, the compassionate," which is supposed to be said when beginning prayer or any other virtuous act. All the amulets worn by both men and women to ward off the jnun (spirits) are imbued with the baraka derived from the verses of the Quran they contain. Anyone who performs the five pillars of worship (the attestation of faith, prayer, fasting, almsgiving, and the pilgrimage to Mecca) thereby obtains baraka (Westermarck 1926, 1:134). Cereals and the bread and couscous made from them are full of baraka, as are brides and bridegrooms, little children, and mothers of twins (ibid., 1:45–47, 106). None of this conforms to Geertz's assertion that "what most defines baraka . . . is that it is radically individualistic, a property of persons in the way strength, courage, energy, or ferocity are" (1983, 136).

The word *baraka*, both as a noun and a verb, occurs frequently in both everyday prayer and everyday speech. In prayer, the Muslim says to the Prophet Muhammad, "peace be upon you O Prophet and the mercy of God and his blessings" (*wa barakatuhu*). Also in prayer, the worshiper asks God to "bless" (*barik 'ala*) Muhammad and his descendants as he blessed Abraham and his descendants. In ordinary speech, the conventional way to say "thank you" in Moroccan Arabic is *baraka Allahu fik*, meaning "God bless you," to which one responds by inverting verb and subject: *Allah ibarik fik*, "God bless you [too]." When Moroccan Muslims refuse a beggar, they often say "may God bring the baraka" (*Allah ijib al-baraka*). When a limited supply of food turns out to feed many people, it is said to be full of baraka.

None of this is intelligible if, as Geertz claims, baraka boils down to the notion that "the sacred appears most directly in the world as an endowment—a talent and a capacity, a special ability—of particular individuals," or if it is true that "the best (but still not very good) analogue for baraka is personal presence, force of character, moral vividness" (p. 44).

THE SAINT AND THE SULTAN

We find this same neglect of the religious significance of baraka in Geertz's second story about al-Yusi, which concerns the latter's confrontation with the sultan Mulay Isma'il:

> When Lyusi, by then one of the country's most illustrious scholars, arrived in Meknes, Mulay Ismail received him as an honored guest, fed him and housed him, and brought him into his court as spiritual advisor. The Sultan was at that time building a large wall around the city, and the people working on it, slaves and others, were being treated cruelly. One day a man fell ill while working and was sealed into the wall where he fell. Some of the workers came secretly to Lyusi to tell him of this and to complain of their treatment generally. Lyusi said nothing to Mulay Ismail, but when his supper was brought to his chambers he proceeded to break all the dishes, one by one, and he continued to do this, night after night, until all the dishes

in the palace had been destroyed. When the Sultan then asked what had happened to all his dishes, the palace slave said, "That man who is our guest breaks them when we bring his food." (pp. 33–34)

The sultan asked al-Yusi to come to him and asked him why he was breaking the palace dishes. Al-Yusi answered, "Which is better —the pottery of Allah or the pottery of clay?" (p. 34), that is, he was rebuking Mulay Ismail for breaking men, the creations of God. Mulay Ismail ordered al-Yusi to leave the city. He did so but pitched his tent in the graveyard just outside the city limits. The sultan was furious and rode out to the cemetery, where he found the holy man praying. He asked al-Yusi why he had not left the city as ordered.

> Lyusi replied, "I went out of your city and am in the city of God, the Great and the Holy." Now wild with fury, the Sultan advanced to attack the saint and kill him. But Lyusi took his lance and drew a line on the ground, and when the Sultan rode across it the legs of his horse began to sink slowly into the earth. Frightened, Mulay Ismail began to plead to God, and he said to Lyusi, "God has reformed me! Give me pardon!" The saint then said, "I don't ask for wealth or office, I only ask that you give me a royal decree acknowledging the fact that I am a sherif, that I am a descendant of the Prophet and entitled to the appropriate honors, privileges, and respect." The Sultan did this and Lyusi left, still in fear for his safety, fleeing to the Middle Atlas forests, where he preached to the Berbers (and against the king) and ultimately died, was buried, and transformed into a *siyyid*, a man around whose tomb an elaborate devotional cult has developed. (pp. 34–35)

Geertz's informants would not have said that a *siyyid* (saint) is "a man around whose tomb an elaborate devotional cult has developed." Geertz is paraphrasing and adding his own interpretations to his informants' accounts. We have no way of knowing precisely what his informants actually said.

This is nonetheless a good story—as are most of those that Geertz tells. It is good in the sense of being graphic and dramatic, and good in the sense of providing valuable insight into the political role of Islam in Morocco. But Geertz ignores the conceptual universe and social-historical context in which the story is embedded, and his interpretation thus obscures its significance in the context of Morocco's religious-cum-political history.

THE MIRACULOUS AND GENEALOGICAL FORMS OF BARAKA

Geertz interprets the clash between al-Yusi and Mulay Isma'il in terms of the tension between "the miraculous and the genealogical" forms of baraka, which he contends "reflected much of the dynamic of Moroccan cultural history" (p. 45). He sees al-Yusi's request that the sultan grant him a decree attesting to his descent from Muhammad (in Geertz's version of the story) as representing the fusion of the miraculous and genealogical forms of baraka and the resolution of the tension between them (pp. 45, 47). Geertz also refers to his folktale about the sultan and the saints as a "commentary on the delicate relationship between strong-man politics and holy-man piety" (p. 33). Yet he fails to pursue this insight. *Religion and Power in Morocco* is an extended commentary on precisely this relationship and its significance in terms of the more general relationship between religion and power.

Leaping from his twentieth-century folktale to the seventeenth-century events it seemingly describes, Geertz declares that the advent of the 'Alawi dynasty, which came to power during al-Yusi's life-time, "represented the assertion of the supremacy of the genealogical view of the basis of baraka over the miraculous," or "the elevation of what Max Weber called hereditary charisma over what he called personal charisma" (p. 45).

> The triumph of the Alawites, prefaced, actually, by the brief emer-gence of another sherifian dynasty, the Saadian, which failed to stabi-lize, faced the religious populism of men like Lyusi—men for whom baraka gravitated naturally to those, regardless of station, righteous enough to deserve it—with the contrasting notion of an hereditary spiritual patriciate. But no more than the Indic tradition dissolved in the face of Islamization in Indonesia did the wonder-working view of sainthood dissolve in the face of the genealogical in Morocco. In fact, surprising as it may seem, the two principles—that charisma was an

individual talent and that it was a family patrimony—actually fused. (p. 47)

This then, according to Geertz, is what the conflict between al-Yusi and Mulay Isma'il meant. In interpreting stories, however, one needs to specify for whom a story allegedly means what the interpreter alleges it to mean. Does Geertz think seventeenth-century Moroccans in general saw the conflict this way? Or twentieth-century Moroccans? Or is this interpretation intended to represent the underlying historical significance of the conflict, whether Moroccans realized it or not? Geertz is never entirely clear about these matters. The fact is that no matter what Geertz himself means in speaking of the meaning of the clash between al-Yusi and Mulay Isma'il, his interpretation illustrates the dangers of trying to interpret specific events without adequate attention to the conceptual structures and historical contexts in which they are enmeshed.

BARAKA AND PURITY IN THE EVOLUTION OF MOROCCAN ISLAM

The role of baraka in the evolution of Moroccan Islam and the fusion of its saintly and sharifian forms can be understood only in the context of the interrelated concepts of the Islamic world view, notably Allah, the Prophet Muhammad, intercession on the day of judgment, and purity (tahara), all of which figure prominently in the basic rituals of Islam, in al-Yusi's writings, and in the everyday speech of twentieth-century Moroccans (Munson 1984; al-Yusi 1981, 1982). None of these concepts is discussed in Islam Observed.

Muslims believe that Muhammad was the last of the prophets sent by God (Allah) to guide "the sons of Adam" (humanity) after Adam and Eve were banished from the primordial garden (Quran, 2:36–38). Some Quranic verses depict Muhammad as merely a man, a "slave of God" like any other (6:50, 41:6). But most Muslims have considered him as having been ma'sum, that is, pure in the sense of being infallible and thus sinless. This belief in the Prophet's purity and sinlessness was taken for granted by seventeenth-century Moroccan Muslims, as it still is by many Muslims today (al-Yusi 1981, 2:341, 419, 456, 470, 498, 500, 504, 517).

The idea that Muhammad himself was pure and sinless was extended to include his descendants. The Quran attributes purity to "the people of the house" of Muhammad in the famous verse: "And God only wishes to remove all abomination from you people of the house and to purify you completely" (33:33). Since the Prophet's sons died in infancy, the notion of "the people of the house" has usually been understood to refer to the Prophet's patrilineal descendants by way of his daughter Fatima and her husband 'Ali, who was also the son of the Prophet's father's brother.[4]

These descendants came to be known in North Africa as the "honored ones," *shurafa* (shurafa'), one such descendant being a *sharif* in the case of a man and a *sharifa* in the case of a woman. There has been, since the very earliest period of Islam, a tension between the veneration of these honored descendants of the Prophet and the belief in the equality of all Muslims as articulated in the famous Quranic verse: "The most righteous among you is the most honored before God" (*Inna akramakum 'inda Allah atqakum*) (49:13). This verse is often cited to show that honor (*sharaf*) can be derived from conduct as well as from sharifian descent (al-Yusi 1982, 1:55). But even in the late twentieth century, only a minority of Moroccan intellectuals would go so far as to deny that the descendants of the Prophet are entitled to a special reverence.

The baraka, or blessedness, of the shurafa is inseparable from their purity or *tahara*. This term is normally used in Islamic texts to refer to "ritual purity" and the rules governing it (Reinhart 1990). One cannot pray or touch the Quran unless one is in this state, which is achieved by ablutions preferably performed with running water. One Iraqi-born scholar, commenting on an earlier version of this chapter, noted that "*tahara* is the difference between the Muslim and the unbeliever." Although many well-educated Muslims would disapprove of such a statement, most peasants, peddlers, and laborers would regard it as mere "common sense" (Munson 1984, 43–44). The idea that "unbelievers" are in some sense impure is found in many religions (see, e.g., Chaudhuri 1979, 189).

The Muslim concept of purity is closely linked to that of baraka. Muslims who return from the pilgrimage to Mecca are believed to be imbued with baraka. They are said to have been cleansed (purified) of their sins so that they will go to heaven when they die (Westermarck 1926, 1:136). A boy possesses much baraka when he is circumcised, and the act of circumcision is popularly referred to (in twentieth-century Morocco) as al-tahara, "the purity" or "the purification." This idea that purity and holiness are closely linked is, once again, found in many religions (Douglas 1966; Preston 1987)

The Finnish anthropologist Edward Westermarck, who spent a total of seven years in Morocco from 1898 to 1926 (1926, 1:v), says of baraka:

> It is polluted by contact with infidels. One reason why the Sultan Mulai 'Abdl'aziz ['Abd al-'Aziz] lost his baraka was the presence of Christians at court. The barbers of Andjra say that there is no baraka in the razors used by their colleagues in Tangier, because they are sharpened by Christians. . . . A scribe from the Rif told me that if a hajj, or person who has made the pilgrimage to Mecca, wants to retain his baraka, he must never go to the market and expose himself to the looks of the Jews who are gathered there. Nor are the latter allowed to come near the place at the market where the Muslims sell their grain, so as not to spoil its baraka. (ibid., 1:229)

At this point, some historians might object that like Geertz, I assume that twentieth-century ethnographic data reflect the beliefs of earlier centuries. But there is abundant historical evidence of the link between purity and baraka. Among the most common terms for sharifian descent in Moroccan texts, in al-Yusi's era as well as in the twentieth century, is al-nasab al-tahir, "the pure descent" (al-Ifrani 1888, 26–27; al-Wazzani 1942, 32). The eighteenth-century historian Muhammad bin al-Tayyib al-Qadiri refers to the Prophet's descendants as "the pure people of the house" (ahl al-bayt al-tahirin) (3:321).

This conception of the purity of the shurafa implies the idea of 'isma, or "sinlessness."[5] One well-known manifestation of this purity in Moroccan folktales concerns the popular belief in the ability of the shurafa to drink wine (which is forbidden in Islam) without sinning. Westermarck notes that Moroccans said of Sidi al-Hajj 'Abd as-Slam, the Sharif of Wazzan (d. 1892), that when wine "touched his saintly lips it was transformed into honey" (1926, 1:151). Rabinow tells a similar story that he heard near Sefrou in the late 1960s (1975, 22–23), but like Geertz, he does not mention the belief that the shurafa are pure and incapable of sin.

The idea that the shurafa's purity-cum-sinlessness would enable them to avoid the torments of hell in the hereafter was common in al-Yusi's day. The Wazzani sharif Sidi Muhammad bin 'Abd Allah (who died in 1708, seventeen years after al-Yusi) said that all those who became followers of his family would be protected on the last day: "Our place is like the place of Abraham, whoever enters it will be safe from the fire" (al-Mansur 1989, 19). The eighteenth-century Moroccan historian al-Qadiri, like many other orthodox religious scholars, criticized such ideas, but conceded that they were widely held (2:352).

INTERCESSION

The Muslim veneration of the Prophet's descendants is linked to the idea of intercession (shafa'a) on the day of judgment. Early in Islamic history, Muhammad came to be seen as the paradigmatic intercessor of the Muslims on this day. Although the Quran does not explicitly legitimate this idea, many of the hadiths (reports) concerning the customary practice of the Prophet do (Schimmel 1985, 84–85). Prayers asking for the Prophet's intercession became commonplace in Morocco as in the rest of the Islamic world (ibid.). In one of his many epistles, al-Yusi declared that Muslims had to believe in the Prophet's intercession just as they had to believe in the questioning in the grave by two angels, the day of resurrection, the bridge over hell, and all the other central elements of Islamic eschatology (al-Yusi 1981, 2:419; see also 2:331). In another epistle, al-Yusi stressed that the Muslim had to believe not only that the Prophet was and is pure and sinless, but also that he is "the gate of God" (bab Allah). "He who does not enter through him does not enter at all" (man lam yadkhul minhu la yadkhulu) (ibid., 2:401).

References to the Prophet's intercessory role occur in the litanies of all the Moroccan Sufi orders, even the most popular ones like the 'Isawa and the Hamadsha (Brunel 1926, 96, 123; Crapanzano

1973, 191). Orthodox religious scholars have often rejected this emphasis on the Prophet's intercession (Smith and Haddad 1981, 141), but like al-Yusi, most Moroccan Muslims have never questioned it. In the words of Annemarie Schimmel, "In the hearts of the masses, Muhammad is primarily the intercessor at Doomsday. . . . It is this trust in his help that has largely colored the popular veneration of Muhammad" (1975, 217).[6]

Just as the shurafa were traditionally believed to have inherited the Prophet's baraka, so too were they believed (some of them anyway) to have inherited the Prophet's role as intercessor on the day of reckoning. This belief was already common at the time of the Almohad dynasty in the twelfth and thirteenth centuries and probably long before that (al-Qabli 1978, 27). It was also common during al-Yusi's lifetime (al-Mansur 1989, 19).

SUFISM

The intercessory role of the shurafa was enhanced whenever they were also Sufi shaykhs. Geertz contends that as "an historical reality," Sufism in Morocco "meant fusing the genealogical conception of sanctity with the miraculous" (p. 48). This view of Sufism, which is also Geertz's interpretation of the end of the conflict between al-Yusi and Mulay Isma'il, reduces religious belief to the overt appearance of a specific social phenomenon associated with it. (One is reminded of Geertz's view that the concept of baraka boiled down to the idea that the sacred was an endowment of individuals.) Sufism did play an important role in the fusion of sharifian and saintly baraka, but it involved much more than this, as we can see from al-Yusi's own writings, for al-Yusi was one of the most influential Sufi mystics of seventeenth-century Morocco (see al-Qabli 1981).

Consider the following poem (as translated by Geertz from Berque's French):

My heart is scattered through my country.
One part is in Marrakech, in doubt;

Another in Khalfun; another in Meknes with my books;
Another in the Fazaz; another in Mulwiya among my tribesmen;
Another in the Gharb, among my friends of the town and of the
     countryside.
O God, reunite them. No one can do it but You.
O God, put them back in place.[7]

Geertz interprets this poem as yet another symptom of Moroc-can "restlessness" (pp. 31–32). However, in these verses, al-Yusi links his regret at having been forced to move so often to the Sufi theme of achieving the real unity that transcends the ostensible multiplicity of things. In his epistles, al-Yusi repeatedly discusses the "extinction" (fana') of the self (1981, 2:450–51). He says this state can be attained only after one has ceased to desire it (ibid., 2:452). He cites in this respect the words of the famous Sufi shaykh al-Bistami who, when asked, "What do you want," answered, "I want to not want" (uridu an la urida) (ibid., 2:332). Such themes pervade al-Yusi's writings (ibid., 2:316–470; 1982, 1:97–98, 149–151, 270–77, 2:416–433). Nothing in *Islam Observed* would give the reader the slightest clue that al-Yusi, whom Geertz describes as "a puritan and something of a zealot" (p. 35), ever thought or spoke this way.

Al-Yusi's mystical ideas were typical of Moroccan Sufism (and of Sufism generally). The quest for the effacement of the self and the mystical knowledge of God were the basic goals to which Sufis of all but the most popular Sufi orders have always striven (Abun-Nasr 1965; Cornell 1989; Ibn 'Ajiba 1982; Michon 1969, 1973; al-Sughayyir 1988). Some awareness of this is necessary if one wishes to under-stand the role of Sufism with respect to the fusion of "the miracu-lous and genealogical conceptions of sanctity"—which from Geertz's perspective is what Moroccan Sufism is all about (p. 48).

The Shadhili Sufi tradition that came to prevail in Morocco stressed the veneration of the Prophet and his descendants (al-Qabli 1978, 16–17). It was through them that the Sufi was able to attain the presence of God both mystically in this world and concretely in the hereafter. The fifteenth-century shaykh Muhammad bin Sulayman al-Jazuli declared: "The glorious one is he who is glorified by nobil-ity [sharaf] and lineage. I am a sharif in lineage. My ancestor is the

Messenger of God (may God bless and preserve him) and I am nearer to him than all of God's creatures. . . . Follow us, for he who follows us dwells in the highest of the highest places both in this world and in the hereafter" (Cornell 1989, 520).

The Sufi shaykh, especially the leading shaykh of a particular period (qutb al-zaman), was said to be a spiritual successor of the Prophet (ibid., 592, 623). Like the sharif, he was believed to have inherited the Prophet's role as intercessor on the day of judgment (Brunel 1926, 37). Even al-Yusi, who was critical of some aspects of popular Islam in his day, acknowledged the intercessory role of the Sufi shaykh, although he stressed that it was entirely dependent on God's will: "The shaykh does not have heaven or hell in his hands, nor this world nor the hereafter. For he is a slave [of God] like the rest of the slaves. But in his hands there is guidance towards God, and instruction, and high-mindedness" (1981, 2:348). This passage demonstrates that many seventeenth-century Moroccans did in fact believe that Sufi shaykhs had heaven and hell in their hands. This was directly related to the idea that they possessed baraka.

Given the role of the shaykh as spiritual heir of the pure and sinless Prophet as intercessor, it became common for Sufis to think of this inheritance in genealogical terms. Thus we find sharifian descent commonly (but not invariably) attributed to prominent Sufi shaykhs, especially after the sixteenth century (Cornell 1989, 32). Most of the Sufi orders (turuq) involved the veneration of a founding shaykh-cum-saint and his descendants, who were typically believed to be shurafa. The shrine of the founding and often eponymic shaykh-cum-saint was normally found at the order's principal zawiya (Harrak 1989, 118, 125–32).

SAINTS

Moroccan saints' tombs are found in every village and in all the popular quarters of every city. As in many other religions, they are also often found on mountaintops. The word *saint* is best used to translate the Arabic words *wali* and colloquial *siyyid* (*sayyid* in written Arabic). The first of these terms derives from the expression *wali*

Allah, "one who is close to God." The second term means "lord" and "possessor." A male saint, like a male sharif, is generally addressed and referred to as Sidi (Sayyidi in written Arabic), "my Lord" or "my Master," or Mulay (written Mawlay), which has the same meaning. A female saint is addressed and referred to as Lalla, "my Lady."

Like many Western writers, Geertz uses the French word marabout interchangeably with saint (1968, 33). But the Arabic word murabit from which marabout is derived refers specifically to saints and the patrilineal descendants of saints who are not shurafa (Westermarck 1926, 1:40). Moroccan texts always speak of shurafa and murabitun as mutually exclusive categories, the latter being of lower status (al-Qadiri 3:355; al-Manuni 1985, 1:459–60). The root verb of the Arabic noun murabit is rabata, meaning to bind, tie, or fasten (Wehr 1976, 321). So it would seem plausible to speak of a murabit as "a man tied, bound, fastened to God" as does Geertz (1968, 43). Murabit, however, is more specifically derived from rabata, with a long a in the first syllable, which can mean "to line up" and "take a fighting position" (Wehr 1976, 322). The word was first used in Morocco in conjunction with the word ribat, which refers to a quasi-monastic garrison in which men prayed and prepared for holy war against anyone considered an enemy of Islam (Brett 1980, 6; Hajji 1988, 21–23). This is how the Almoravid, or al-Murabit dynasty that ruled Morocco from the mid-eleventh to the mid-twelfth century, received its name. In later centuries, when the veneration of saints became widespread, the term murabit came to be used to refer to saints and their patrilineal descendants who were not shurafa and lacked the high status of the latter (Gibb and Kramers 1953, 473–75).

It should be stressed, however, that the murabit-sharif distinction one finds in texts (past and present) is either absent or ambiguous in twentieth-century Moroccan popular belief. The very notion that there is a conflict between what Geertz calls the "wonder-working" and "genealogical" forms of baraka would strike most twentieth-century Moroccans as bizarre. Scholars and the well-educated are, of course, perfectly aware of the distinction between descent from a saint and descent from the Prophet, but most Moroccans assume that the descendants of a saint (especially a prominent saint whose tomb is visited by pilgrims) are ipso facto descendants of Muhammad. The claims of the patrilineal descendants of such saints to be shurafa are often questioned by scholars but not by ordinary Moroccans (see al-Bu 'Ayyashi 1975, 1:237–39; al-Bu Zidi 1988, 201).

The veneration of saints, like that of the shurafa, was and remains an important aspect of Sufism. Sufis believe in a complex hierarchy of saints, culminating in a pure and sinless *qutb* (axis of the universe), who is said to be the greatest shaykh of his generation. Such a shaykh-cum-saint is said to have attained direct mystical knowledge of God (Michon 1973, 264). For most Muslims and even for most Sufis, however, saints have always been primarily a source of baraka and intercession.

Al-Yusi tells the story of a Sufi shaykh from the relatively orthodox zawiya of al-Dila' who visited the saint Sidi 'Abd Allah bin Hassun of Salé. The shaykh was sitting near the saint and was shocked by the way the visiting Arabs were kissing the holy man's hands and feet. He thought to himself, "how can this man give himself so freely to these people this way?" Even before he had finished this thought, the saint said, "O people, if it was said of a man that anyone who touched his flesh would not be touched by the fire, or would not be eaten by the fire, or something along these lines, should he withhold his flesh from the Muslims?" When the shaykh heard this, he knew the saint was speaking of him and repented and kissed the holy man's hand himself (al-Yusi 1982, 1:191). This story demonstrates that the idea of intercession by saints on the day of judgment evolved into the idea that one could gain entrance to heaven simply by touching saints and thereby absorbing their baraka-cum-sinlessness. These ideas are implicit in Geertz's story about the transmission of baraka to al-Yusi (pp. 32–33).

INTERPRETING THE CLASH BETWEEN AL-YUSI
AND MULAY ISMA'IL

We can now see why the categories of Sufi shaykh, saint, and sharif have often tended to coalesce. The Prophet was the paradigmatic source of baraka and purity as well as the paradigmatic intercessor. People thus attributed sharifian ancestry to the saints and shaykhs who possessed his attributes on a lesser scale. This is the logic underlying the fusion of what Geertz calls the wonder-working and genealogical forms of baraka.

It will be recalled that Geertz sees al-Yusi's clash with Mulay Isma'il as representing a conflict between the traditional, miraculous form of saintly baraka and its newer, genealogical form, represented by the sharifian 'Alawi dynasty, with al-Yusi's request for a decree attesting to his sharifian ancestry (in the story as told by Geertz) representing the resolution of the conflict (pp. 47–48).

Actually, most of the Muslim dynasties that have ruled Morocco have claimed sharifian ancestry at one point or another (al-Qabli 1978, 9; Agnouche 1987, 123–24, 161). Except in the case of the Idrissis (late eighth to early tenth century), the Sa'adians (mid-sixteenth to early seventeenth century), and the 'Alawis (who have ruled since the 1660s), these claims were not taken all that seriously.[8] That they were made at all, however, indicates that the special right of descendants of the Prophet to be the imams (leaders) of the umma (the Islamic community in general) was widely accepted centuries before Mulay Isma'il and al-Yusi were born.

A fourteenth-century scholar at the court of the Marinid sultan Abi 'Inan (1348–58) refused to stand in the presence of a prominent sharif, although the sultan had just done so. He justified this violation of protocol to the outraged sharif by declaring: "I carry in myself my sharaf [honor]: it is the knowledge that I dispense around me and that no one can doubt. As for yours, it is subject to doubt. Who can guarantee its authenticity after over seven hundred years? Anyway, if we were really convinced of it, we would have removed this one [pointing to the non-sharifian Marinid sultan] and put you in his place" (al-Qabli 1978, 36–37; Kably 1986, 322). These words were spoken more than three centuries before al-Yusi's encounter with Mulay Isma'il. Moreover, the sharifian Sa'adian dynasty that preceded the 'Alawis ruled most of Morocco during the latter half of the sixteenth century and much of the south long before and after that (Brignon et al., 1967). So it seems unlikely that al-Yusi would have been opposed to "the sherifian principle of religious legitimacy" in the late seventeenth century, when he clashed with Mulay Isma'il. The idea that a sultan had to be a sharif was, admittedly, less solidly entrenched in al-Yusi's day than it was to become in following centuries, but it was by no means new, as Geertz himself concedes (pp. 46-47).

These facts refer, of course, to history as opposed to folktales. Yet nothing in Geertz's version of his informants' version of the clash between al-Yusi and the sultan suggests that they interpreted the story as revolving around "the two principles—that charisma was an individual talent and that it was a family patrimony" (p. 47). Geertz observes that "in popular legend," al-Yusi was portrayed as a descendant of the Prophet (p. 30). So the Moroccans who told Geertz the popular legend about al-Yusi's conflict with Mulay Isma'il must have viewed him as a sharif. Rabinow's study of the village where al-Yusi is buried confirms this (1975), as do my own observations in 1990, when I found that everyone I spoke to in the Sefrou region where Geertz worked took it for granted that al-Yusi had been a sharif. (As has already been noted, most twentieth-century Moroccans assume that venerated saints and their descendants are shurafa.) So Geertz's informants could not have interpreted the conflict between al-Yusi and Mulay Isma'il as a conflict between miraculous and genealogical baraka, given that, in their eyes, al-Yusi had both.

The only reference to sharifian descent in Geertz's story comes when (according to Geertz's account of what his informants said) al-Yusi asked the sultan for a decree attesting to his descent from the Prophet. We shall see that most of Geertz's story belongs to a well-established genre of hagiography, but this particular point is anomalous. Saints do not usually make such requests in folk stories, nor does such a request occur in Rabinow's version of the clash between al-Yusi and Mulay Isma'il (1975, 19). But even if Geertz's informants did attribute such a request to al-Yusi, we have already seen that they would not have interpreted it as resolving a conflict between "miraculous and genealogical baraka," since they believed al-Yusi possessed both.

Shifting back from folktale to history, we should note that there does not appear to be any evidence that the historical al-Yusi ever requested a royal decree confirming his descent from Muhammad. Rabinow claims that he did (ibid., 16), but he gives no source for this claim, which appears to be based on *Islam Observed*. (Like Geertz, Rabinow does not use Moroccan texts.)

If we turn to al-Yusi's own writings, we find that he lists his ancestors without making any claim to descent from the Prophet (1982, 1:30). In a long epistle he wrote to Mulay Isma'il in 1685, al-Yusi says that he is a Berber, but as for his ultimate origin, only God knows (ya'lamuhu Allah) (1981, 1:213). Although this statement was clearly meant to leave open the possibility of descent from the Prophet or perhaps some other prominent Arab, it would be wrong to interpret it as an explicit claim of sharifian ancestry, as does the Moroccan religious scholar 'Abd al-Hayy al-Kattani (1982, 2:1155). Al-Yusi's twentieth-century descendants, however, definitely do claim to be shurafa, as do most patrilineal descendants of prominent Moroccan saints (al-'Alawi al-Madghari 1989, 111).

DECREES ATTESTING TO DESCENT FROM THE PROPHET

Royal decrees attesting to descent from the Prophet have played an important role in Moroccan history. Such decrees were already common by the late fourteenth century, three hundred centuries before the conflict between Mulay Isma'il and al-Yusi (al-Qabli 1978, 30). (The specific encounter depicted in Geertz's folktale never occurred, but we shall see that it corresponds in significant ways to one that did.) Sultans would often grant patrilineal descendants of saints such decrees in return for their political support (El Mansour 1990, 157–58). Since power and wealth were sometimes seen as reflections of baraka, ordinary Moroccans tended to accept the sharifian pretensions of the powerful and the rich more readily than those of the weak and the poor—even though shurafa have always been found in all social strata (al-Qabli 1978, 40). The powerful and the wealthy, especially descendants of saints venerated by ordinary Moroccans, were also the most likely to be useful to sultans; they were also able to afford the sums of money that often had to be paid to obtain royal decrees (Michaux-Bellaire 1917). Just as nineteenth-century European businessmen were able to buy titles of nobility, so too have many prominent Moroccan descendants of saints been able to purchase titles attesting to their descent from the Prophet. Such descent was much more than a source of political legitimacy, it was the paradigmatic source of status (or "symbolic capital") in Morocco from the eighth century to the colonial period (1912–56) (Bourdieu 1987, 160–63; Sebti 1986). It remains important today.

The sharifian families whose genealogies had been unquestioned for centuries naturally challenged the sharifian pretensions of upstarts (Laroui 1977b, 95). But if a certain family descended from a saint was generally viewed as also being descended from the Prophet, this had to be taken into account by the religious scholars appointed by sultans to investigate such matters (ibid., 93). Given that every village and town in Morocco has one or more saints, and given that, since the fifteenth century at least, most Moroccans outside the educated elite have tended to equate descent from a saint and descent from the Prophet, it is easy to see how the number of putative shurafa has multiplied over time.

Royal decrees attesting to sharifian ancestry, and in many cases even just to descent from a prominent saint, could enhance people's wealth as well as their status since they typically exempted families from taxes (Michaux-Bellaire 1917). Thus the proliferation of such decrees cut the state's tax base. This is one reason that sultans, including Mulay Isma'il, sometimes had surveys and genealogical studies undertaken to reduce the number of "true" shurafa (El Mansour 1990, 157–58). Thus, belief in the sanctity of sharifian ancestry was as relevant to the economic structure of the precolonial Moroccan state as it was to its religious, political, and social hierarchies.

AL-YUSI ON THE SHURAFA: THE EVIDENCE FROM HIS OWN WRITINGS

Geertz interprets the clash between al-Yusi and Mulay Isma'il in terms of al-Yusi's alleged resentment of the idea that the shurafa constituted a "hereditary spiritual patriciate" (p. 47). We have already seen the irrelevance of this interpretation with respect to al-Yusi the saint-cum-sharif in Geertz's folktale. We can also demonstrate its irrelevance with respect to the historical al-Yusi. In his 1685 epistle to Mulay Isma'il, al-Yusi writes, "I love the sultan," in part because "we have been ordered [by God] to love the people of the Prophet's house" (ahl al-bayt al-nabawi) (1981, 1:233). In another epistle to Mulay Isma'il that we shall examine in greater detail shortly, al-Yusi reminds the sultan that he is required to give some tax revenues to the shurafa (ibid., 1:238).

One could argue that al-Yusi felt obliged to stress his respect for the shurafa in writing to a sharifian sultan. But we find al-Yusi stressing the importance of venerating the shurafa even in his epistles to his fellow mystics. Thus in a letter to some Sufis of the eastern Rif, he writes: "you must glorify the people of the house" ('alaykum ta'dhim ahl al-bayt) (ibid., 2:405). There is no trace of enmity to the shurafa as a "hereditary spiritual patriciate" in any of al-Yusi's epistles.

It is true that in his book al-Muhadarat, al-Yusi does stress that honor (al-sharaf) is an achieved as well as an ascribed status, that is, individuals can attain it by their knowledge and piety as well as by descent from the Prophet (1982, 1:46–59). He cites in this respect the famous Quranic verse, "The most pious among you is the most honored before God" (ibid., 1:55). This expression of Islamic egalitarianism, however, is routinely cited by Muslims who would never dare to suggest that it is in any way meant to deny that the Prophet's descendants are entitled to special veneration (Michon 1969, 38). Al-Yusi's frequent references to the idea that Muslims are obliged to love and glorify "the people of the house" make it clear that he was not troubled by the logical contradiction between the idea of the equality of all believers and the veneration of the descendants of the Prophet. Like his fellow Sufis and virtually all his fellow Muslims in seventeenth-century Morocco, al-Yusi took it for granted that the descendants of the Prophet had a special place in Islam.

THE HISTORICAL CONTEXT OF THE HISTORICAL CLASH

Although the precise events in Geertz's folktale never happened, al-Yusi and Mulay Isma'il did clash in the late seventeenth century in a specific context that made the former a threat to the latter. The eighteenth-century historian al-Qadiri informs us that Mulay Isma'il feared al-Yusi because he attracted many followers and could have lead or encouraged the periodic Berber revolts that the sultan spent years trying to suppress (3:26). Al-Yusi had spent close to twenty years at the zawiya of al-Dila', which Mulay Isma'il's brother Mulay Rashid destroyed in 1668 (al-Qabli 1981, 1:46). For the preceding three decades, the Dila'is had been the 'Alawis' principal competitor for control of Morocco as a whole (Hajji 1988, 141–253). Al-Yusi and many of the Berbers of the Moulouya Valley and the Middle Atlas Mountains remained loyal to the Dila'i zawiya long after its destruction (al-Qabli 1981, 1:43–44). This worried Mulay Isma'il, who had to quell countless revolts in these regions and elsewhere. Among the most serious of these was a Dila'i-led Berber revolt in 1677 (al-Qadiri 2:229–30). Given al-Yusi's charisma as an eloquent and venerated Sufi shaykh capable of articulating popular grievances, he could have become a leader of popular opposition to the sultan. Most of al-Yusi's Moroccan biographers have stressed that this is why Mulay Isma'il kept ordering the holy man to move from one place to another, in the hope of thereby preventing him from building a political base (al-Qadiri, 3:26; al-Qabli 1981, 1:35-37; al-'Alawi al-Madghari 1989, 9, 28, 43, 133, 148–53).

None of this is mentioned in Islam Observed. Of course, Geertz is interested in the significance of his folktale in terms of the evolution of Moroccan Islam rather than in the actual historical clash between al-Yusi and Mulay Isma'il. However, he uses his twentieth-century folktale to interpret seventeenth-century history and vice versa. It is for this reason that his neglect of the historical context of the historical clash is significant. (I should stress that I am myself interested in both the folktale and the historical clash between al-Yusi and Mulay Isma'il only insofar as they reflect basic themes in Moroccan religious and political history.)

One might argue that Geertz's interpretation of the folktale corresponds to the historical fact that al-Yusi bitterly resented the sharifian 'Alawi dynasty's destruction of the "maraboutic" zawiya of al-Dila'. But the historical clash (like the one in the folktale) was not a reflection of maraboutic opposition to the sharifian principle of legitimacy. The latter was intertwined with Sufism and the veneration of saints in al-Yusi's day. We have already seen that al-Yusi venerated the shurafa. He never denied that the shurafa had a special right to rule their fellow Muslims. As for Mulay Isma'il's attitude toward marabouts, he had himself buried near the tomb of a saint who, like most prominent Moroccan saints, had been a Sufi shaykh in his lifetime (al-Nasiri 7:100). Mulay Isma'il's brother and predecessor Mulay Rashid, the very man who had destroyed al-Yusi's cherished zawiya of al-Dila', also had himself buried near the tomb of a famous saint (ibid., 7:43). The sultans of the 'Alawi dynasty were no more hostile to the wonder-working baraka of saints than al-Yusi was to the genealogical kind.

AL-YUSI AS ARCHETYPAL RIGHTEOUS MAN OF GOD

Turning back from history to folktale, the story Geertz recorded in the 1960s clearly depicts al-Yusi as a virtuous saint who used miracles to overcome an unjust sultan. If Geertz had attempted to compare his story about al-Yusi and Mulay Isma'il with other folktales about saints, he would have found that accounts of virtuous saints overcoming unjust rulers (and lesser officials) by miracles are commonplace (see Brunel 1926, 38–41, 54–56, 91–92). The theme of miraculous versus genealogical baraka is never mentioned in these stories. The sultans are simply presented as despotic rulers, even though they often belong to the sharifian Sa'adian and 'Alawi dynasties. In many stories, the sultan is named Mulay Isma'il because this ruler became the archetypal despot in popular folklore (ibid., 16; Crapanzano 1973, 35–36).

The following folktale, recorded by a French ethnographer in the early twentieth century, is typical. It pits the saint Sidi Muhammad (sometimes written M'hammad) bin 'Isa against Mulay Isma'il, even though the historical Muhammad bin 'Isa died over a century and a half before the historical Mulay Isma'il came to power in 1672 (Brunel 1926, 15–16).

> The sultan wanted to eliminate Sidi M'hammad bin 'Isa. He gave orders to his vizier (wazir) to take a hundred cavalrymen and arrest the shaykh. The latter was in the city. The horsemen surrounded him and the vizier advanced to inform him of the monarch's wish. Then suddenly the earth split open beneath his horse and the horrified minister saw the flames of hell. "If I escape from death, he thought, I will no longer touch the perfect shaykh." The fissure in the earth instantly closed and the horse was back on solid ground. The miracle terrified the vizier and the men with him. The shaykh was allowed to remain free. (ibid., 56)

Another folk story told of Sidi Muhammad bin 'Isa is also reminiscent of Geertz's. (The following account is a summary of that given in Mercier 1906, 179–81). At the time when men from all over Morocco were working on Mulay Isma'il's grandiose construction projects in Meknes, many of them left their jobs to listen to the saint and join his Sufi order. The sultan was furious and ordered the saint to leave the region. Instead, Sidi Muhammad sought refuge at the home of another saint, who gave him a goatskin for carrying water (girba). Sidi Muhammad began to blow air into the empty goatskin, and each time he did so, Mulay Isma'il's body swelled.

Mulay Isma'il sent a messenger to tell the saint to stop his magic. So the holy man emptied the goatskin and the sultan's swelling subsided. But the sultan wanted to test the saint further. So he had him locked in a garden full of lions. The ferocious beasts simply rubbed their backs against the saint's legs like kittens. Mulay Isma'il then ordered the saint to drink a basin full of liquid tar. The saint had a little girl do so, and she found it sweeter than honey. The sultan was by now convinced of the saint's sanctity, but the latter was so angry that he swore that he would never again set foot in Meknes, thus depriving it of his baraka and punishing the sultan for his evil conduct.

There is no reference to a conflict between miraculous and genealogical baraka in these stories. They are rather about a saint who used his baraka to punish an unjust sultan. René Brunel notes that Sidi Muhammad bin 'Isa is presented in such tales as "a defender of the weak and the oppressed" and that "the theme of the struggle of a saint against temporal power has always been conducive to the proliferation of multiple legends" (1926, 40, 55). Over and over again, one finds saints using miracles to force sultans and other government officials to stop oppressing their subjects. Such stories are as common in the hagiographic texts of the past as they are in the folktales of the present.[9]

AL-YUSI'S MOST FAMOUS EPISTLE TO MULAY ISMA'IL

When we compare Geertz's story about al-Yusi and Mulay Isma'il with al-Yusi's own writings and what other Moroccans have written about him, we see that it is a popular reflection of a classic theme in the Moroccan moral imagination, the myth of the righteous man of God who dares to defy an unjust sultan. The demand that the sultan be just and conform to Islamic law pervades several of al-Yusi's epistles to Mulay Isma'il (1981, 1:130–244). I shall focus primarily on his best-known one, which was apparently written in the 1670s, not long after Mulay Isma'il succeeded his brother Mulay Rashid in 1672 (al-Qabli 1981, 67). This epistle quickly became famous all over Morocco (ibid.). It was widely quoted and discussed by scholars during Mulay Isma'il's reign (1672–1727) as well as by later Moroccan historians writing about this period (ibid.; al-Qadiri 3:31–37; al-Nasiri 7:82–86). In 1935, it was discussed in considerable detail by 'Allal al-Fassi, the most famous Islamic reformer and Moroccan nationalist of the twentieth century (al-Fasi [1935] 1979, 39–44). It has, in fact, become one of the most famous Moroccan texts on the authority of kings. Yet it is not mentioned by Geertz.

Berque, from whom Geertz obtained most of his historical information about al-Yusi, provides a detailed summary of this epistle in French (1958, 91–92). Moreover, the epistle in its entirety appears in the French version of the standard history of Morocco by al-Nasiri (*Archives Marocaines* 9 [1906]: 110–19). So the fact that Geertz apparently does not read Arabic does not explain his failure to allude to this document, the importance of which is stressed by Berque himself (1958, 91–93).

The epistle begins with the conventional references to God and the Prophet and praise of the sultan:

> Praise be to God, blessing and peace upon our Lord [Sayyidna] Muhammad and his family [the shurafa] and companions. O axis and center of glory, possessor and sanctuary of glory, base and source of eminent honor [sharaf], locus and concentration of the highest excellence, the greatest sultan, the most majestic, the most magnificent, our Lord [Sayyidna] Isma'il son of [bin] Mawlana al-Sharif, may his banners remain victorious and may his days pass in power and success. Peace be upon our Lord and the mercy of God the most high and his blessings [barakatuhu]. (al-Yusi 1981, 1:237)

Al-Yusi concludes this preamble by stressing the rights Mulay Isma'il has over his subjects "by virtue of his position as sultan and his descent from 'Ali and Fatima" (ibid.). No opposition to a hereditary spiritual patriciate here.

Al-Yusi abruptly changes his tone when he begins the epistle proper by saying: "We have written this letter for at the moment this is all we can do" (fa katabna hadhihi al-bitaqa wa hiya fi'l-waqti muntaha al-taqa). There is, as Berque has observed, an implicit threat in the phrase "for at the moment this is all we can do" (1958, 91). Al-Yusi then writes:

> Our Lord [Sayyidna]—may God help him—knows that the land and all that is in it belongs to God the highest whose power is shared by no other. People are the male and female slaves of God. My Lord is one of the slaves [al-'ibad] that God on high has made king over the others as a test. If he rules them with justice ['adl], mercy, fairness, and righteousness, then he is God's deputy in his land [khalifat Allah fi 'ardihi], and God's shadow over his slaves, and he will occupy a high rank with God on high. But if he rules unjustly, violently, arrogantly, oppressively, and corruptly, then he will have become insolent to his master [God] in his kingdom and dictatorial and arrogant in the land without right. Then he will be subject to the terrible punishment and wrath of God on high. (al-Yusi 1:237–38)

(The contractual view of political authority al-Yusi articulates here will be discussed at length in chap. 2.)

Al-Yusi lists the three basic obligations of a ruler: "the collection and expenditure of taxes according to what is right," "the waging of holy war (jihad) to raise high the word of God," and "the granting of justice to the oppressed" (p. 238). Al-Yusi then declares that all three of these obligations "remain unfulfilled in our Lord's government" (ibid.). Al-Yusi says it is his duty to bring this situation to the sultan's attention so that he will not be able to say he did not know.

Al-Yusi rebukes the sultan for the way his tax collectors oppress his subjects, literally "his flock" (al-ra'iyya). He speaks of these officials "eating the flesh, drinking the blood, and sucking the marrow of the bones and the brains" of the people (p. 239). Al-Yusi urges the sultan to stop this oppression (al-dhulm). He also warns the king to be wary of his advisers who seek to delude him into thinking that all is well. Many of these people "do not fear God on high and do not shrink from sycophancy, hypocrisy, and lying" (p. 239).

With respect to holy war, al-Yusi tells Mulay Isma'il that he should not deprive tribesmen of their horses or weapons, so that they can use them to defend Islam against the European infidels occupying Muslim ports (p. 240). (The sultan had disarmed some rebellious Berber tribes.) Al-Yusi tells the sultan that the governors in the coastal regions exposed to European attacks should be men who are full of zeal for Islam rather than men who only think of "filling their bellies and reclining on couches" (p. 240).

As for the sultan's third obligation of providing justice to the oppressed, al-Yusi declares: "Those appointed to render justice are the governors and their subordinates. Yet they are involved in the oppression [dhulm] of the people. How can oppression be eliminated by those who perpetrate it? ... Our Lord [Sayyidna] should fear God and the call of the oppressed [al-madhlum] for there is no boundary between them. And he should strive for justice ['adl] for it is the foundation of rule [mulk]" (p. 241). Al-Yusi reminds the sultan of the conditional nature of Islamic rule. God grants kingship to those who pray and give alms and "command good and forbid evil" (Quran 22:41). God guaranteed kings his help, says al-Yusi, but only on condition that they do these things (p. 241). "The Arab and foreign sages agree that rule [al-mulk] based on injustice is neither strong nor sound. But rule based on justice is sound—even among the infidels. Infidel kings have lived hundreds of years in well-ordered rule, their words obeyed, free from all disturbance, because they governed their subjects with justice and took good care of their worldly affairs. How could it not be thus for one who takes care of his subjects' religious affairs as well as their worldly ones?" (ibid.). Al-Yusi reinforces his argument by citing Aristotle's warning to Alexander the Great that justice was the basis of good government (pp. 241–42).

Being a just ruler, says al-Yusi, means implementing Islamic law as it is interpreted by the religious scholars, or ulama ('ulama'). The sultan must "ask the ulama what to take and what to give" (p. 243). He contends that among the ancient "Sons of Israel" (Bani Isra'il), the ruler had been obliged to conform to the edicts of the prophets. So, too, among the Muslims, rulers were obliged to follow the ulama (ibid.). More specifically, al-Yusi tells Mulay Isma'il to follow the counsel of those ulama who fear God rather than those who fear the sultan (pp. 243–44). "With respect to both what we have said and what we have not said, do what they order and shun what they forbid. This is the path to deliverance if God on high so wills" (p. 244).

Al-Yusi then concludes his epistle in the conventional manner: "I ask that God grant our Lord success, guidance, and support, and that through him he make the land [al-bilad] and the slaves of God [al-'ibad] prosper and by his sword put an end to the deviant and the corrupt. Praise be to God, Lord of the worlds. Written by the humble faqir al-Hasan bin Mas'ud al-Yusi, may God forgive him."[10]

Everything al-Yusi says in this text is rooted in a classical tradition of Islamic political thought and rhetoric (see Lambton 1981). For the moment, however, the important point is that the basic message of the epistle is that sultans must rule justly in accordance with the laws of God or face divine punishment. Geertz's folktale, like countless similar ones, says the same thing in a popular idiom.

Both the seventeenth-century text and the twentieth-century folk-tale revolve around the idea of just rule.

AL-YUSI AS EXEMPLAR IN MOROCCAN HISTORIOGRAPHY

To get a sense of al-Yusi's impact on the Moroccan moral imagination, we may consider what Moroccan historians have said of him. According to the eighteenth-century historian al-Qadiri, Mulay Isma'il himself cited al-Yusi as an example of the kind of religious scholar who "fears only God and not us" (3:37). This famous statement is usually quoted by al-Yusi's twentieth-century Moroccan biographers (al-Qabli 1981, 75; al-'Alawi al-Madghari 1989, 8). Al-Qadiri also says that al-Yusi "was distinguished from his contemporaries by daring to speak the truth to the caliph [khalifa] of the time" (3:25). In response to an earlier historian who suggested that al-Yusi did not understand that disarming unruly tribesmen was in the interest of the Islamic community, the nineteenth-century historian al-Nasiri stresses that al-Yusi's epistle discussed above was about the basic duties of a ruler, including the duty of providing justice to the oppressed vis-à-vis their oppressors (al-Nasiri 7:82).

In an early twentieth-century biographical dictionary, the Sufi scholar 'Abd al-Hayy al-Kattani observes that al-Yusi was known for his "willingness to speak freely about what he thought was right" (1982, 2:1155). In an article first published in 1935 (reprinted in 1979), 'Allal al-Fassi (d. 1974), the leader of Morocco's nationalist movement against French rule, describes with obvious admiration al-Yusi's "frankness" (al-saraha) in addressing the sultan (al-Fasi 1979, 39–40). In his classic study of the zawiya of al-Dila', first published in 1964, the historian Muhammad Hajji says of al-Yusi's epistles to Mulay Isma'il: "He addressed him in a frank manner that no one else dared to resort to in communicating with this sultan renowned for his strength, power, and violence" (Hajji 1988, 107). In an article published in 1979, the scholar 'Abd al-Hadi al-Tazi asks: "Has the history of France preserved, for example, the presence of an individual like al-Yusi, able to speak frankly to Louis XIV without being subjected to the various kinds of punishments known at that time?"

(al-Tazi 1979, 290). Similar statements praising al-Yusi's courage in demanding that Mulay Isma'il rule justly are to be found in virtually everything Moroccans have written about him in the late twentieth century (al-Jirari 1981, 88–89, 93, 98; al-Qabli 1981; Znibir 1979, 281). One also hears such statements from well-educated Moroccans whenever al-Yusi's name is mentioned. All this is especially impressive because Moroccans have always had to be careful in praising al-Yusi's defiance of Mulay Isma'il. To praise al-Yusi is, in effect, to endorse his view that a ruler's legitimacy is contingent on his being just. Saying such things in Morocco has often been dangerous.

It is true that most Moroccans in the late twentieth century are probably unfamiliar with the epistle to Mulay Isma'il discussed above. But *all* Moroccans are familiar with its message that a ruler must rule justly or face divine retribution. Regardless of how many people know of al-Yusi's clash with Mulay Isma'il—as depicted in either text or folktale—it embodied ideas that have always had, and continue to have, a direct impact on the way most Moroccans have viewed rulers and those who rebel against them.

Geertz says that his conception of the "social history of the imagination" includes the following dimensions:

> First, the mere story of what came after what and when must be at least generally outlined; without sequence, descriptions of the past are catalogs or fairy tales. Second, the major conceptual themes which were in this way produced must be isolated and related to one another, and their symbolic embodiments, the cultural vehicles of their expression, must be expressed with some specificity, so that ideas are not left floating in some shadow world of Platonic objects but have a local habitation and a name. Finally, and perhaps most important of all, the sort of social order in which such ideas could and did seem to almost everybody to be not merely appropriate but inevitable . . . must be depicted and analyzed. (1968, 19–20)

This sounds very much like the *histoire des mentalités* as practiced by Marc Bloch (Bloch [1924] 1983; Darnton 1984, 3). It also sounds very much like what I have tried to do in *Religion and Power in Morocco*.

But *Islam Observed* bears little resemblance to this theoretical manifesto. It includes no discussion of how the "conceptual themes" of Moroccan Islam are "related to one another." Baraka is not examined in relation to the other concepts of Moroccan Islam. Instead, Geertz likens it to "personal presence, force of character," and "moral vividness" (1968, 44). The semantic substance of religious belief is thus reduced to the overt appearance of behavior, to personality writ large.

Islam Observed was published in 1968, long before Geertz advocated the "thick description" of events as a way of understanding cultures "from the native's point of view" (1973, 3–30). But Geertz's writings revolved around the interpretation of vignettes even in his early writings. One sees this in the way he bases his discussion of "the classical style" of Moroccan Islam in *Islam Observed* on his folktales about al-Yusi. Geertz's interpretation of these stories illustrates a recurrent problem in his writings: his failure to situate his stories in the context of the structures that give them meaning.

The other obvious problem with Geertz's social history of the Moroccan Muslim imagination is that it is, in fact, ahistorical. He attempts to reconstruct the collective imagination of the past without using the texts in which it is inscribed. Geertz has likened ethnography to trying to read a manuscript that is "foreign, faded, full of ellipses, incoherencies, suspicious emendations, and tendentious commentaries" (1973, 10). Fair enough. But if anthropologists wish to transcend the boundary between history and anthropology, as they should, they have to learn to read real texts as well as metaphorical, behavioral ones—and indigenous ones as well as those written by Orientalists.

It would be absurd to expect anthropologists, or anyone else engaged in the comparative study of different cultures, to be able to read all the languages involved (assuming they are written). One can write an excellent ethnography of a village or tribe without ever reading a single indigenous text. But when one's goal is "the social history of the imagination," the inability to read the language in which that imagination is preserved becomes a crippling handicap. One is shut out of the very world one seeks to depict. A very important, and generally overlooked, advantage of such texts is that they are generally written by and for people of the same culture. In reading them, the foreign scholar is in effect eavesdropping on "the other" invisibly—without distorting the ethnographic situation by his or her presence. So the study of indigenous texts can be extremely useful, even in studying one's contemporaries. It becomes essential when one seeks to reconstruct how literate peoples saw the world centuries ago.

Two Scholars and
Sultans

The authority of the sultans of Morocco has been based
on two distinct and theoretically irreconcilable conceptions of monarchy. On the one hand, they are sacred kings,
representatives of God and the Prophet who must be
obeyed unconditionally. On the other hand, they are legitimate only by virtue of having been selected by the representatives of the Islamic community, especially the ulama,
and only so long as they implement God's laws and rule
justly. I refer to these two contrasting forms of legitimacy
as *hierocratic* and *contractual*. Although Geertz sees "the
fusion" of these two notions as a distinctively Moroccan
phenomenon (1968, 76–77), they have actually coexisted
in uneasy tension throughout most of the Islamic world
throughout most of Islamic history (see Sourdel 1978).
Similar tensions can be found in notions of kingship outside the Islamic world (Tambiah 1976, 483; Walzer 1974,
35–40, 47–64, 88).

In the decades after the Prophet died in 632, there
emerged three different views as to who should succeed

him. The position that came to be associated with the Shiʿite sects of Islam was that ʿAli and his patrilineal descendants should be the imams, or "leaders," of the Islamic community in part at least because they had inherited the Prophet's purity and infallibility. (The name Shiʿite is derived from the term shiʿat ʿAli, "the faction of ʿAli.") The position that prevailed among the people who came to be known as Sunni Muslims was that a khalifa (caliph) should be chosen by a council of the most influential men of the Islamic community. Although the Sunnis (named after the Sunna, or "customary practice" of the Prophet) rejected the Shiʿite view that only ʿAli and his descendants could rule the Islamic world, they did restrict the pool of potential caliphs to the men of the Prophet's tribe of Quraysh. The radically egalitarian Kharijites (those who go out), however, argued that any virtuous Muslim man, even a slave, could be elected to the caliphate-cum-imamate. Whereas the Shiʿites stressed the need for absolute obedience to their holy imams, the Kharijites stressed that Muslims were obliged to depose any imam who failed to uphold the laws of Islam (see Dabashi 1989). The Shiʿites and the Kharijites thus represented the hierocratic and contractual antipodes of early Islamic political thought. The Kharijites have also come to be seen as the archetypal fundamentalists of Sunni Islam in that they demanded strict conformity to the Quran and condemned those Muslims who rejected their views as infidels who deserved to die (Levi della Vida 1978).

Despite numerous Shiʿite and Kharijite revolts during the early centuries of Islam, the Sunni sect prevailed, as it still does today. At least 85 percent of all twentieth-century Muslims (including all those in Morocco) are Sunni, while only about 14 percent are Shiʿites and fewer than 1 percent belong to the Ibadi sect that grew out of the moderate wing of the early Kharijite movement. The only large country with an overwhelmingly Shiʿite population is Iran, although slightly over half of Iraq's population is also Shiʿite. Smaller pockets of Shiʿism also exist in most of the predominantly Sunni lands east of Egypt.[1]

Shiʿism and and Kharijism as organized sects were eradicated in what is now Morocco by the eleventh century, but the tension between quasi-Shi'ite and quasi-Kharijite conceptions of authority has persisted right up to the present. The conception of authority favored by Moroccan rulers has generally been closer to the hierocratic imamate of the Shi'ites. The more orthodox Sunni conception of authority favored by most Moroccan ulama (including al-Yusi) has generally been closer to the contractual imamate of the Kharijites (see Tozy 1984).

THE CALIPHATE

Sunnis believe that after the Prophet's death in 632, the Islamic world was briefly ruled by four "rightly guided caliphs" (al-khulafa' al-rashidun). Then the Umayyad dynasty transformed the elective caliphate into what amounted to a hereditary monarchy. The Umayyads (661–750) and the 'Abbasids (750–1258), however, were still called khalifas, (Ibn Khaldun 1958, 1:414–51).

The word sultan originally meant "authority" or "government." It became the usual title of Muslim rulers after the demise of the 'Abbasid caliphate and the emergence of many independent Muslim states (Lewis 1988, 51–53). Sultans of these independent states often also claimed the title of khalifa, although in principle there was supposed to be only one for the entire Islamic world. Even the Ottoman sultans eventually came to be known as caliphs—despite the fact that they were not descended from the Prophet's tribe of Quraysh (Sourdel 1978, 943–46). Because the Ottomans controlled most of what is now known as the Islamic "Middle East" from the fifteenth century until World War I, the Ottoman caliphate was eventually recognized by most of the Islamic world. Its abolition by Mustapha Kemal's secular Turkish republic in 1924 sparked widespread protests in many Muslim countries (Enayat 1982, 52–68). Yet Morocco was never part of the Ottoman empire, and its kings still called themselves caliphs at the end of the twentieth century (Tozy 1984, 83–87).

The word khalifa can be translated as "deputy," "successor" or "replacement." Sunni ulama have generally stressed that the term originally referred to the caliph's role as "successor of the Prophet," rather than to the idea that he was the "deputy of God" (*khalifat Allah*).[2] They often cite the famous hadith according to which the first caliph, Abu Bakr, said, "I am not the khalifa of God, I am rather the khalifa of the messenger of God" (al-Jirari 1986, 968). In other words, Abu Bakr is alleged to have rejected the hierocratic conception of authority implicit in the title *khalifat Allah*. This title nonetheless eventually prevailed in governmental usage. It came to be associated with the epithet "shadow of God" (*dhill Allah*), which was of pre-Islamic Persian origin (Arjomand 1984, 94; al-Yusi 1981, 1:237).

This conception of the caliph as God's deputy and shadow on earth undermined the authority of the ulama as the guardians and interpreters of God's law, and they generally rejected it—at least in principle (Crone and Hinds 1986, 21). The ulama saw themselves as "the heirs of the prophets," whom rulers had to consult to ensure that their actions were lawful. Al-Yusi went so far as to contend that rulers should obey the ulama inasmuch as they understood God's laws better than anyone else (1981, 1:243). This was a quixotic ideal but a perfectly logical one given the ulama's conception of their role (Harrak 1989, 73, 200).

One obvious difference between the hierocratic and contractual conceptions of the caliphate has to do with succession. In the former, hereditary succession is perfectly legitimate. In the latter, it is not. From the perspective of the ulama, the caliph was supposed to be selected by them and other leaders of the Islamic community (the *umma*). In practice, however, from the Umayyad period (661–750) up through the twentieth century, Sunni rulers who claimed the title of *khalifa* routinely designated their successors (usually their sons) before dying (Sourdel 1978, 938; al-Ifrani 1888, 18, 77, 174). The selection of these successors had to be ratified by "those who loosen and bind" (*ahl al-hall wa'l-'aqd*), that is, the ulama, the shurafa, and other notables (al-Ifrani 1988, 16, 79, 83–84, 99–10). Yet in practice, the ulama and the others were generally forced to ratify the wishes of the sultan in power. In many cases, successors thus chosen and legitimated were challenged by brothers or other kin after the reigning sultan died. The ulama and the others who loosen and bind would then have to swear allegiance to whichever pretender had the strongest, and closest, army (Agnouche 1987, 224–30).

The idea that the caliph was supposed to be chosen by the Islamic community remained embodied in the institution of the bay'a, or oath of allegiance. A caliph was not legally a caliph until he had received the bay'a of the ulama and the other notables, just as the Prophet Muhammad had received the bay'a of some his earliest followers (al-Jirari 1986, 971). For the ulama, the bay'a was, in principle, a contract obligating both the ruler and the ruled. The ruler committed himself to rule justly in conformity with Islamic law (al-Shari'a), whereas the ruled committed themselves to obedience only so long as the ruler fulfilled his part of the bargain (ibid., 976; al-Yusi 1981, 1:237).

This contractual conception of a sultan's authority was generally subordinated to the idea that the sultan-cum-caliph should be obeyed in all circumstances. Already in the fourteenth century, Ibn Khaldun acknowledged that the bay'a typically involved no more than the legitimation of the most powerful pretender (1958, 1:429). Some Sunni political theorists, themselves ulama, adapted to historical practice by stressing that even an unjust caliph was better than the anarchy that would prevail if no ruler were in power (Lewis 1988, 70, 99–102). This argument was inevitably buttressed by the famous Quranic verse "O you who believe, obey God, obey the messenger and those in authority" (4:59). In both theory and practice, however, the ideal of a just caliph selected by and answerable to the ulama and other leaders of the Muslim community was never eradicated—as al-Yusi's epistle to Mulay Isma'il makes clear.

THE HIEROCRATIC FACETS OF MOROCCO'S SUNNI SULTANS-CUM-CALIPHS

The notion of sacred kingship inherent in the belief that the caliph was the deputy and shadow of God often took a distinctly Shi'ite form. The Sunni caliphs were also called imams, although in principle the Sunni meaning of this word had nothing to do with the pure and sinless imams of Shi'ism. (The basic meaning of imam is "he who stands in front" and leads prayer.) The Sunni ulama have generally condemned the Shi'ite conception of infallible imams descended from the Prophet. This idea has nonetheless had a major impact on the Sunni conception of the caliphate.

The 'Abbasids who overthrew the Umayyads in 750 sought legitimacy (and Shi'ite support) by stressing that they too were "people of the house" of the Prophet through the Prophet's father's brother al-'Abbas. This did not satisfy the Shi'ites, who believed that only the patrilineal descendants of the Prophet by way of 'Ali and Fatima could be legitimate imams. 'Ali's great grandson Idris I brought this idea to Morocco in the late eighth century and founded the Idrissi dynasty, which ruled central Morocco from the late eighth to the early tenth century. The Idrissis, Morocco's first Muslim dynasty, were in turn driven from power by the Shi'ite Fatimids, who were initially based in what is now Algeria. The Fatimids attempted to disseminate the Shi'ite idea of the pure and sinless imams in North Africa in the tenth and eleventh centuries ((Laroui 1977a, 109–12; Sourdel 1978, 943–44).

The next major Moroccan dynasty, the Almoravids (al-Murabitun), which ruled from the mid-eleventh through the mid-twelfth century, was neither Shi'ite nor sharifian. It grew out of a puritanical Sunni revivalist movement that demanded strict conformity to Islamic law as interpreted by the Maliki school of Sunni Islam.[3] Yet even these staunchly orthodox Sunnis appear to have accepted the idea that the caliph should be not only from the Prophet's tribe of Quraysh, but from the Prophet's clan of the Bani Hashim. The most famous of the Almoravid rulers, Yusif bin Tashfin, is reported to have refused to accept the caliphal title of "commander of the faithful" (amir al-mu'minin) on the ground that it belonged only to the 'Abbasids by virtue of their genealogical link to the Prophet (Agnouche 1987, 106). (The fact that a sultan would have invoked this argument is significant, no matter what other motives he may have had.)

The Almoravids were succeeded by another puritanical movement advocating a return to the pristine Islam of the Prophet, the Almohads (or al-Muwahhidun), who ruled from the mid-twelfth to the mid-thirteenth century. Their movement was founded by a religious scholar who claimed to be the messianic *mahdi* and a descendant of Muhammad. Later Almohad sultans eventually repudiated these messianic claims, but they still claimed descent from the Prophet (Lévi-Provençal 1928, 21–23 [Arabic], 30–35 [French]).

Unlike the Almoravids and the Almohads, the Marinid dynasty, which ruled from the mid-thirteenth through the late fifteenth century, did not grow out of a revivalist movement demanding strict conformity to the Quran and the Sunna. The Marinids were simply the leaders of a Berber tribal confederation. They thus lacked the religious authority of the preceding dynasties. To remedy this, they curried the favor of the ulama and the shurafa, and some of them claimed sharifian ancestry and the title of caliph (Kably 1986, 261–62, 285–95).

The Marinids were followed briefly by the related Wattassid dynasty and then by the sharifian Sa'adians, who ruled from the mid-sixteenth to the early seventeenth century. The sharifian 'Alawi dynasty emerged out of the chaotic period following the death of the last powerful Sa'adian sultan in 1603. (Berque 1982). Mulay Isma'il's brother and predecessor Mulay Rashid (1664–72) was the first 'Alawi sultan to rule over Morocco as a whole after his destruction of the zawiya of al-Dila' in 1668. (This was the zawiya where al-Yusi lived for roughly twenty years.)

Before their conquests of the late seventeenth century, the 'Alawis did not have anything like the status of the Idrissi shurafa descended from Morocco's first Muslim sultans, Mulay Idris I and II (Kably 1986, 299–300). They were virtually unknown outside the Tafilalt region of southeastern Morocco. Whereas the tomb of Mulay Idris II in Fez was a nationally venerated shrine in the seventeenth century, as it has been ever since, the tomb of the 'Alawis' eponymic ancestor Mulay 'Ali al-Sharif in the Tafilalt was of minor significance (see Beck 1989, 5). Even today, after over three centuries of 'Alawi rule, the tomb of Mulay 'Ali al-Sharif is of minor significance compared with that of Mulay Idris II. Yet once the 'Alawis became sultans, their sharifian status was greatly enhanced, even though Idrissi shurafa still tend to view them as *nouveaux sacrés*.

The belief that the sharifian 'Alawi sultans were imbued with baraka became a major source of their legitimacy in the minds of ordinary Moroccans. In May 1819, sultan Mulay Sulayman was taken prisoner by some Berber tribesmen he had been fighting. The Berber women sought to touch him to obtain his baraka (al-Nasiri 8:136). His tent was torn into little pieces that were distributed among the tribesmen in the belief that they were imbued with the sultan's miraculous blessedness (El Mansour 1990, 189). Similarly, even after Sultan Mulay 'Abd al-'Aziz was overthrown by his brother in 1908, enthusiastic crowds of Moroccan Muslims continued to touch and kiss his hands and clothes in the hope of absorbing his baraka (Holt 1914, 50–51). It is true that when one contender for the throne defeated another, it was popularly assumed that the winner's baraka was greater than that of the loser. Even in defeat, however, the king remained sacred. Baraka was more than "a summary term" for those qualities that "enable some men to prevail over others" (Geertz 1983, 136).

In the late nineteenth and early twentieth centuries, several Europeans noted that when the sultan passed through the country-side, people would ask him to dip his fingers into jars of milk so as to transmit his baraka to the region and ensure its prosperity (Doutté 1909, 187; Weisgerber 1947, 93). Prominent shurafa were commonly asked to do the same thing (Brives 1909, 226). In the early twentieth century, Westermarck was told that the sultan's baraka was renewed every morning by forty saints passing over his head (1926, 1:38–39).

> It is on the Sultan's baraka that the welfare of the whole country depends. When it is strong and unpolluted the crops are abundant, the women give birth to good children, and the country is prosper-ous in every respect; in the summer of 1908 the natives of Tangier attributed the exceptionally good sardine fishery to Mulai al-Hafid's accession to the throne. On the other hand, in the reign of his prede-cessor the deterioration or loss of the Sultan's baraka showed itself in disturbances and troubles, in drought and famine, and in the fruit falling down from the trees before coming ripe. Nay, even in those parts of Morocco which are not subject to the Sultan's worldly rule

the people believe that their welfare, and the crops especially, are dependent on his *baraka*. (Ibid., 1:39)

When Westermarck speaks of "those parts of Morocco which are not subject to the Sultan's worldly rule," he is alluding to the much-discussed dichotomy between those regions effectively controlled by the state and the more peripheral and often Berber regions not so controlled. It should be stressed that even in the mountains not effectively governed by the Moroccan state, the sultan's religious *and* political legitimacy was nonetheless recognized. Moreover, revolts were common even in the lowland cities that were the centers of state power (see Burke 1972a, 179; Cigar 1978, 1981; Munson 1989, 1991b).

The idea that kings possessed great baraka was common even with respect to dynasties that were not generally seen as being descended from Muhammad. Thus we find sources claiming that pregnant women would place shirts belonging to the non-sharifian Almoravid sultan Yusif bin Tashfin (1060–1106) on their legs to facilitate delivery (Agnouche 1987, 122). Marinid historians described the founder of the Marinid dynasty in similar terms: "He had a baraka known to all, and his prayers were heard. His turban and his shirts were a source of baraka for the Zenata, and were given to pregnant women to ease their deliveries. The water with which he performed his ablutions were also a source of baraka, and was given to the sick to cure them" (ibid., 123; cf. Lévi-Provençal 1928, 406, 410). One is reminded of the kings of medieval France—and of the fact that kingship is always in some sense sacred (Bloch [1924] 1983; de Heusch 1987; Grottanelli 1987, 313).

THE ULAMA

Having sketched the evolution of the hierocratic aspect of Moroccan kingship in precolonial Morocco, we now turn to the ulama, in principle the advocates of the contractual caliphate and the guardians of the sacred law. The word ulama ('ulama') is derived from the verb 'alima, "to know." Thus the ulama are "those who know," specifically, those who know the laws of God. They are not priests. Any virtuous Muslim man can lead collective prayers in Islam; that is, any virtuous Muslim male can serve as imam in the basic sense of this term. The ulama, however, were traditionally the judges and educators of Islam. They were among those who were supposed to select kings and ensure that they ruled according to the laws of God. They were also supposed to offer kings frank advice (nasiha) to ensure that they implemented the laws of God.[4]

The ideal scholar, said al-Yusi, should "sit in his house, surrounded by books of knowledge" (1981, 1:155). Although he should let rulers know when their actions are contrary to the laws of God, he should avoid government positions. The ulama who accept such positions tend to forget their duty to serve God and become deluded by the things of this world (ibid., 1:152). Al-Yusi cites in this respect the famous hadith: "The best kings are those who visit the ulama and the worst ulama are those who visit the kings" (ibid., 1:155). The great philosopher and Sufi al-Ghazzali (d. 1111) said that all benefits derived from rulers were illicit because everything they owned was either stolen or suspected of being so (Goitein 1968, 207). The sixteenth-century Sufi al-Sha'rani said that when forced to attend a sultan's banquet, righteous scholars would munch on bread they had hidden in their cloaks rather than eat the prince's food (ibid., 207). The greatest Sufi shaykhs of Morocco, who were also ulama, are often described as having rejected the gifts and food of kings (Cornell 1989, 651–52; Ibn 'Askar 1913, 20, 88, 142). (The righteous men of God who defied unjust sultans were usually Sufi shaykhs.) Even twentieth-century ulama have endorsed the traditional idea that the scholar should spurn official positions to avoid compromising his principles (al-Susi 1963, 3:63–77).

Most ulama, however, never conformed to these ideals. Government positions (notably as teachers, judges, notaries, and administrators) meant, and still mean, a regular income. So while the scholar who refused such positions was respected, those who accepted them were well fed. It is true that some ulama were able to live on income from religious endowments (awqaf) or from offerings to their ancestral saint, if they had one. But sultans had long arms.

Serving them (which is how government employment was seen) could mean wealth and power, whereas incurring their wrath could be fatal (as we shall see). So scholars who refused to serve kings were venerated but not often emulated. This is even truer of scholars who dared to criticize kings. Yet no matter how rare such men have been, they have embodied fundamental conceptions of just rule, and they have achieved mythic status in both history and folklore.

'ABD ALLAH BIN YASIN (d. 1058) AND THE ALMORAVIDS

Among the most famous exemplars of the righteous scholar in early Moroccan history is 'Abd Allah bin Yasin. (The word bin means "son [of]" and is written ibn when not sandwiched between names.) A Sanhajan tribal leader hired Ibn Yasin to teach the true Islam of the Quran and the Sunna to his nomadic followers in the Sahara. But the scholar's insistence on strict conformity to the sacred texts led to his expulsion by the nomads. Ibn Yasin then established a ribat, or center for prayer and religious instruction, where he was joined by a growing number of converts to his puritanical revivalist Islam. His followers at the ribat came to be known as al-Murabitun (Almoravids). He taught them "to desire paradise and fear the eternal fire" and to fight those who refused to accept the true Islam of the Quran and the Sunna (Ibn Abi Zar' 1860, 171). These zealous holy warriors of the Sahara quickly conquered most of what is now southern Morocco.

After Ibn Yasin died in 1058, the sultans of the Almoravid dynasty continued to spread his fundamentalist version of Islam. The real founder of this dynasty was Yusif bin Tashfin, who ruled from 1060 to 1106. Ibn Tashfin is often described as the archetypal just ruler. He is said to have scorned the pleasures of this world. He wore only simple woolen garments and ate only barley and the meat and milk of camels. He is praised for imposing only taxes prescribed by the Quran and the Sunna and for consulting with the ulama to ensure that all his policies conformed to the laws of God. He is also venerated for having established the city of Marrakesh and for having conquered most of northwestern Africa and southern Spain (ibid., 190–92).

IBN TUMART: THE RIGHTEOUS SCHOLAR AS MAHDI

Moroccan historians contend that after Yusif bin Tashfin died in 1106, the piety of the early Almoravids gradually gave way to decadence. (Whenever Muslim dynasties become weak and are overthrown, Muslim historians portray them as morally decadent.) The Almoravids were soon challenged by a righteous man of God reminiscent of Ibn Yasin—Muhammad bin Tumart (d. 1130). Like Ibn Yasin, and indeed like the Prophet Muhammad, Ibn Tumart demanded that Muslims return to the true Islam of God. (The Quran is full of stories about righteous prophets urging people to return to "the straight path.") Ibn Tumart stressed the idea of *tawhid*, or the "oneness" of God, thus his followers became known as *al-Muwahhidun* (*Almohads*) or "those who unify." (Calling them "Unitarians" conjures up wrong images.) Ibn Tumart, like most comparable revivalists, condemned those Muslims who disagreed with him as infidels. He specifically referred to the Almoravids as infidels because they took the Quranic verses describing God (*Allah*) in human terms literally, whereas such descriptions had to be understood allegorically. He insisted on strict conformity to the literal text of the Quran and the Sunna in virtually all other respects. He condemned the Almoravid ulama for neglecting these basic texts and for relying instead on later legal treatises (Bourouiba 1973; Hopkins 1971; Lévi-Provençal 1928).

Ibn Tumart preached his doctrine in many of the cities of North Africa after returning from Mecca. He was famous for his defiance of sultans and government officials in general. After causing a furor in the streets of Marrakesh by overturning jars of wine and smashing musical instruments, he was brought to appear before the Almoravid ruler 'Ali bin Yusif (the son of Yusif bin Tashfin). The righteous scholar told the sultan:

> I am but a poor man who thinks of the hereafter and not at all of this world, where I have nothing to do but command good and forbid

evil; is that not what you should be doing? You who are, on the contrary, the cause of evil, whereas it is your duty to implement the precepts of the Sunna and you have the power to make others implement them as well. Crime and heresy appear everywhere in your domain, and this is contrary to the orders of God. . . . Do your duty, for if you neglect it, you will have to account to God for all the wrongs done in your empire. (Ibn Abi Zarʿ 1860, 245).

Ibn Tumart is also said to have written the following letter to the sultan (presumably from a safe distance):

From him who rises for the religion of God [al-qaʾim bi-din Allah], who acts according to the Sunna of the Prophet, Muhammad bin ʿAbd Allah—may God grant him success—to him who is deluded by the things of this world, ʿAli bin Yusif. . . . You do not fear the punishment of the Lord of the worlds, and you do not think of those around you who do evil [al-dhalimin], those who have strayed from the straight path and then regretted it. And all the people followed them. They are the most doomed of the doomed. God has commanded me to refute the arguments of those who do evil and to call the people to that which is certain. And we ask God to reward those who do good. Do not delude yourself for the Muslims are upon you. . . . We must fight and defeat . . . those who deviate from the straight path and deny that which God has given. The revealed word teaches us that you are not among the believers. . . . He who ignores one order of the Sunna is like one who ignores it in its entirety. Thus it is permitted to shed your blood. (Lévi-Provençal 1928, 11 [Arabic], 17–18 [French]).

This letter obviously goes beyond frank advice and declares a holy war against the sultan. It thus represents the realization of the revolutionary potential inherent in the mainstream nasiha tradition exemplified by al-Yusi's epistle.

In 1120, the sultan ʿAli bin Yusif ordered the ulama of his court to debate Ibn Tumart (who was not yet the leader of a revolutionary army). The fiery reformer humiliated them by his superior intellect —as righteous men of God always do in such stories. So some of the ulama said that Ibn Tumart was a dangerous heretic, and the sultan ordered him to leave Marrakesh. According to some accounts, he initially sought refuge in a cemetery (ibid., 111; Ibn Abi Zarʿ 1860, 247).

According to Ibn Tumart's friend and follower al-Baidaq, the sultan heard about the scholar's hiding place: "So he sent a messenger who said to him, 'Did the king not expel you from his domain?' The sinless one [al-maʿsum] answered, 'It is not his domain, I am with the dead.' The messenger returned to inform the king of his refusal and his words, 'It is not his domain, I am with the dead.' So ʿAli bin Yusif said, 'Let us go to him,' and they went. ʿAli bin Yusif said to him, 'Did I not forbid to remain in my domain?' 'I am not in your domain, I am with the dead.' The prince went away" (Lévi-Provençal 1928, 69 [Arabic], 111 [French]). We find a slight variant of this twelfth-century account in an early fourteenth-century history (Rawd al-Qirtas), which says that Ibn Tumart pitched his tent in the cemetery (Ibn Abi Zarʿ 1860, 248). These two accounts are strikingly similar to the folk story Geertz recorded about al-Yusi in the 1960s (1968, 34). Both the medieval "historical" accounts and the modern "folk" one appear to tap the same mythic vein.[5]

To return to Ibn Tumart, he fled from the cemetery to the mountains (as did al-Yusi in Geertz's folktale). In the High Atlas village of Tinmal, far from the sultan's soldiers, he founded a ribat. Like Ibn Yasin before him, he preached his puritanical version of Islam to Berber tribesmen and soon gathered an army of zealous believers —who would eventually conquer much of northwestern Africa and Spain. Like many men who demanded a return to the Islam of the Quran and the Sunna, Ibn Tumart consciously modeled his actions on those of the Prophet. He called his flight from Marrakesh to the High Atlas a hijra, or "flight," this being the name of the Prophet's flight from Mecca to Madina in 622. He had his followers swear their bayʿa of allegiance under a tree, as Muhammad's followers had done (Hopkins 1971, 959; Lévi-Provençal 1928, 73 [Arabic] and 118 [French]).

Also like many other "righteous rebels" of Islam, Ibn Tumart embraced the hierocratic conception of authority favored by sultans as soon as he began to attract many followers. It will be recalled that in the twelfth-century account of the cemetery scene quoted above, Ibn Tumart is described as "the sinless one" (al-ma'sum). This relates to Ibn Tumart's claim to be "the pure and sinless imam" (al-imam al-ma'sum) in essentially the Shi'ite sense of the term: "Belief in the imamate is an obligation for all. It is one of the bases of the religion, one of the pillars of the law. . . . The imam is infallible, for he who errs cannot correct error, just as he who is corrupt cannot destroy corruption. . . . Unity is possible only when the destiny of the people is left to the one who has authority, that is, the infallible imam exempt from injustice and tyranny. . . . He who does not believe in the imamate can only be an infidel [kafir], a hypocrite, a deviant, a heretic, an atheist" (Agnouche 1987, 152–53).

Thus we find Ibn Tumart, the righteous man of God who exhorted Muslims to worship only God, also telling them to venerate him as the pure and sinless imam, a Shi'ite concept that most Sunni ulama have condemned as a travesty of Islam. This illustrates a more general point: the righteous men of God who have been able to mobilize great numbers of people in Moroccan history have typically been regarded as sacred as well as righteous, saints as well as scholars. They have invariably been said to possess great baraka and have usually claimed to be descendants of the Prophet—as did Ibn Tumart. Such men always urge their fellow Muslims to return to the pristine Islam of the Prophet. Yet their political efficacy is always due, at least in part, to notions that are difficult to reconcile with this pristine Islam. In other words, the most effective Muslim advocates of a return to orthodoxy have been themselves of questionable orthodoxy.

Ibn Tumart illustrates this not only with respect to his claim to be the infallible imam, but also with respect to his claim to be the mahdi, who will come at the end of time to usher in an age of justice. (He will be a descendant of the Prophet.) Ibn Tumart proclaimed himself the mahdi in the following terms: "May God bless our Lord Muhammad, the messenger of God, who predicted the coming of the mahdi to make fairness and justice prevail on earth after it had been full of tyranny and injustice. . . . The tyranny of the princes exists, corruption reigns on earth, the consummation of the centuries is for today" (ibid., 154).

This messianic theme has always been more of more central importance in Shi'ism than in Sunni Islam. Yet Moroccan rebels have periodically claimed to be the mahdi (Hammoudi 1981; al-Yusi 1982, 1:257–69). Ibn Tumart represents, in this as in other respects, an important aspect of the evolution of the Moroccan moral imagination, the righteous scholar transformed into messianic revolutionary.

THE NASIHA TRADITION AND THE LIMITS OF THE ULAMA'S AUTHORITY

Few of the scholars who dared to defy sultans ever went as far as Ibn Tumart. They were more like al-Yusi. They condemned sultans in harsh terms and warned them of their fate on the day of judgment, but they did not usually make revolutions. The following passages of a letter from the famous fourteenth-century Sufi scholar Ibn 'Abbad (d. 1390) to the Marinid sultan 'Abd al-'Aziz (1367–72) are typical:

> You must supervise your governors and consider that among your virtuous acts and what is required of you with respect to your subjects [ra'iyyatkum]. For there has appeared among them corruption, and a lack of frank counsel [nasiha] to you and to your subjects. The result has been that they have absolute control over the subjects and have introduced unlawful practices ... which have earned them wealth and high status. ... The worst of calamities will occur when God will ask you to account for this. The curse of the oppressed will be upon you [du'a' al-madhlumin 'alaykum]. And it is said in a hadith, "The call for revenge of the oppressed is answered even if it is from an unbeliever."
>
> Know O Commander of the Faithful, that justice is among the conditions of authority. (al-Manuni 1979, 228)

The similarity of this fourteenth-century rhetoric to that of al-Yusi's seventeenth-century epistle to Mulay Isma'il is obvious. Al-Yusi was echoing words written by many scholars before him. While such men were more common than messianic revolutionaries like Ibn Tumart, they were always greatly outnumbered by the ulama who endorsed whatever a particular sultan wanted endorsed.

Indeed, the theme of the righteous man of God being persecuted by hypocritical ulama seeking a sultan's favor is a leitmotif of the myth. In some cases, this persecution is related to the hostility of some strictly orthodox ulama to Sufism—the righteous man of God typically being a Sufi shaykh. (See Cornell 1989, 284–85, 368–72, 522–23, 677; Touati 1989, 1219–21).

Men like al-Yusi embodied an ideal rather than common practice. The case of one of al-Yusi's students, 'Abd as-Slam Guessous (d. 1709), demonstrates one reason why this was the case. In the late seventeenth and early eighteenth centuries, Mulay Isma'il repeatedly clashed with the religious scholars of Fez, the most influential in Morocco, over the enslavement of free Muslims. He had created an army of black slaves ('abid) to avoid having to rely on unreliable tribal forces. Some ulama objected that the sultan's agents were forcibly recruiting free dark-skinned Muslims into this army. The sultan tried to persuade the ulama that only men who were unquestionably slaves were being drafted. The protests continued nevertheless (Meyers 1974).

The sultan's governor eventually coerced some ulama to, in effect, endorse the enslavement of free men. One scholar, however, continued to defy the sultan: the Sufi al-Hajj 'Abd as-Slam Guessous (al-Qadiri 3:205–8). (The title al-Hajj means one has made the pilgrimage to Mecca.) All of Guessous's property was confiscated. He was put in chains and displayed in markets while a government official cried, "Who will ransom this captive?" People would then throw coins and jewelry at the venerated scholar. On 5 July 1709, after performing his ablutions and praying, Guessous was strangled to death and buried secretly at night (al-Du'ayyif 1986, 85).

Shortly before his death, Guessous managed to smuggle out the following message: "Praise be to God, the undersigned attests, and may God, his angels and all his creation be my witnesses, that I have only refused to accept the enslavement [of free Muslims] because I have found nothing in the law that would authorize it. I am convinced that if I had accepted it, of my own free will or under duress, I would have betrayed God, his messenger, and his law. And I would have feared eternity in hell because of it" (al-Qadiri 3:208). The emphasis here is on conformity to the law of God rather than on the theme of justice stressed in al-Yusi's epistle. However, for men like al-Yusi and Guessous, the two were intertwined. Guessous clearly believed that the enslavement of free men was unjust.

The case of Guessous illustrates the limits of the ulama's authority. In principle, they were the guardians of the laws of God to whom sultans were supposed to defer. In practice, they tended to defer to sultans. Guessous's death illustrates what could happen to ulama who took the duty of frank counsel too seriously.

FATWAS AND THE ROLE OF THE ULAMA

The issuance of fatwas (legal decrees) was one of the two most conspicuous political tasks of the religious scholars, along with that of writing and signing the bay'as of new sultans. Fatwas were usually issued by the ulama in response to requests from sultans seeking to legitimate decisions of questionable Islamic legality. Sultans were supposed to conform to the decrees of the ulama, but they did not always do so. For example, after the French occupied Algiers in 1830, the people of the western Algerian city of Tlemcen asked the Moroccan sultan to accept them as his subjects. The commander of the faithful asked the ulama of Fez to issue a fatwa on the issue. Almost all of the ulama ruled that he should not accept the bay'a of the people of Tlemcen because they had sworn allegiance to the Ottoman emperor. The sultan did so anyway (Burke 1972b, 101–2, 117; al-Nasiri 9:27-29).

Sultans did not usually overtly defy the ulama, just as the ulama did not usually overtly defy sultans. A good example of this is the issue of exports to Europe in the 1880s. The representatives of the European nations in Morocco had asked that Sultan Mulay Hassan I (al-Hasan I) permit the previously forbidden exportation of Moroccan grain, livestock, and pack animals and that he reduce the export duties on them (al-Manuni 1985, 1:458, 463). Given the power of "the Christians," who had defeated Moroccan armies in 1844 and 1860, the sultan was inclined to comply with these demands. Other Moroccans were not.

In a decree dated 10 April 1886 (6 Rajab 1303), Mulay Hassan noted that he had already consulted with "those known for their goodness, merit, piety, reason, intelligence, and subtlety," and that these people, most of whom were ulama, had opposed the idea of complying with the European demands (ibid., 1:464). So the sultan came up with a compromise. He proposed to allow Europeans to export the hitherto prohibited goods for a trial period of three years. During this period, the government would determine if this policy were in the country's interest or not. Further restrictions would be that the standard customs tariffs would be paid and that these things could be exported only for a period of three months out of the year and only in years when the harvest was good. The sultan submitted this compromise not just to the ulama of Fez, but to the shurafa, murabitun, merchants, artisans, "the ordinary people of Fez" ('ammat ahl Fas), and various prominent individuals (ibid., 1:459). The guardians of God's law disapproved of this extension of the principle of consultation (mushawara) but did not openly challenge the sultan on this point (al-Nasiri 9:192).

The ulama of Fez issued a fatwa reluctantly accepting the sultan's compromise with respect to grain but not to animals. They also warned of the dangers inherent in exporting anything at all to Europe, but they concluded their fatwa by saying: "The perspective of our master [Sayyidna]—may God grant him success—is broader with respect to these matters, and may our Lord—may He be praised—make eternal the greatness of our master [Mawlana] who is aided by God, and preserve through him the Sunna of his ancestor [the Prophet Muhammad], blessings and peace be upon him" (al-Manuni 1985 1:473). This last passage (and the fatwa contained other similar "ritual" praise of the sultan) drained the fatwa of any overt challenge to the sultan's authority—despite the manifest aversion of the ulama to the sultan's compromise. By saying that the sultan's perspective was "broader," they were in effect saying he could ignore their reservations. Such deference to the sultan's authority, which we saw even in al-Yusi's fiery epistle to Mulay Isma'il, was customary (see Miller 1992, 75–76). One could even say that it was mandatory. Thus, after echoing the reservations of the ulama from Fez with respect to exports, one prominent scholar wrote (in 1886):

> If we examine how God the exalted treats his slave ['abduhu], the commander of the faithful, our master [Mawlana] al-Hasan, may God help him, we find, praise be to God, that he is well-treated, accompanied by divine solicitude and watched over by the eye of the Lord. Success accompanies him wherever he goes. . . . He is so full of the utmost zeal in his commitment to the religion and to the country [al-watan] that he has greatly surpassed in this and other virtuous qualities the kings of his dynasty that preceded him. Therefore the best decision is to entrust him with this matter and to place our trust in his good judgment and successful selection and to answer him that the authority in this case rests with him and him alone [al-amr fi dhalika ilayhi wa la ila ghayrihi] since he is the one to whom God gave authority over us and the task of watching over us and counseling us. . . . Whatever the commander of the faithful has chosen will be our choice [fa ma akhtarahu amir al-mu'minin akhtarnahu]. Whatever gladdens his heart and is endorsed by him will be endorsed by us. (al-Nasiri 9:191–92)

The attitude of scholars to sultans in precolonial Morocco was usually one of servile submission. This was owing in part to the sultan's Islamic legitimacy as imam and commander of the faithful. More important, however, it was owing to the ulama's awareness of the sultan's power. They knew that Mulay Isma'il had had 'Abd as-Slam Guessous strangled in 1709. Sultans were not supposed to treat the guardians of God's laws this way, and they did not often do so. But they could, and the ulama realized this. Moreover, sultans could reward as well as punish. They could, for example, grant the ulama property and money, and pay for their pilgrimages to Mecca. Such practical considerations encouraged deference and discouraged defiance (see Burke 1972b; al-Fasi 1931, 1:47; Laroui 1977b, 99–101; al-Susi 1983, 47–48, 64).

Yet virtually every era had its al-Yusis. In the nineteenth century, there was Muhammad bin al-Madani Gannun (d. 1885), a religious scholar of Fez renowned for his asceticism, his understanding of

Islamic law, his condemnation of heretical innovations (al-bida*),
and his acerbic criticism of the powerful officials and princes who
attended his lectures at the mosque-cum-university of al-Qarawiyyin
in Fez (al-Fasi 1931, 2:169; Gannun 1:308). Abdallah Laroui has said
of Gannun that he epitomized the authority of the ulama that sultans could circumvent but never definitively break (1977b, 102).
Gannun's case, however, illustrates just how fragile this authority
could be when confronted by the power of a sultan. Gannun's
failure to conform to the docile deference usually shown by the
ulama to the sultan and other powerful officials resulted in his
imprisonment. Although he was freed after protests by tulba (students studying to be ulama), Gannun became far more circumspect
in his speech as a result of his experience in prison. "That sharp-
ness vanished and that biting tongue was silenced" (dhahabat tilka
al-hidda wa inqata*a dhalika al-lisan al-murr) (al-Fasi 1931, 2:169). The
sultan had broken the man of God.

Abdallah Laroui is correct in saying that the precolonial ulama
were the only group to whom the sultan felt obliged to justify his
actions (1977b, 100). They were the guardians of God's law and as
such were of tremendous symbolic significance in a political order
ostensibly based on this law. In the final analysis, however, the sultans were usually able to force most ulama to legitimate whatever
they wanted legitimated. Only a few scholars ever conformed to the
ideal of the righteous man of God, just as few sultans ever conformed to the ideal of the just ruler.

Three Al-Kattani and
the Ulama
(1904–1909)

In his excellent book *Prelude to Protectorate in Morocco*,
Edmund Burke concedes that most ulama had traditionally been relatively docile but suggests that they
became more active during the final years of the reign of
Mulay 'Abd al-'Aziz (1894–1908), when Morocco was
desperately struggling to escape from the clutches of
French colonialism (1976, 80, 217). Many Moroccan
scholars also attribute an active political role to the ulama
at this time and see the Hafidhiyya revolt of 1907–08 as
having revived the classical contractual bay'a between
the commander of the faithful on the one hand and the
ulama and other notables on the other (al-Manuni 1985,
2:191–395). But, in fact, only Sidi Muhammad bin 'Abd
al-Kabir al-Kattani (1873–1909) and a handful of other
ulama were politically assertive during this period.
Al-Kattani's dazzling persona has tended to obscure this
fact.

During the first decade of the twentieth century,
Morocco's "Sharifian Empire," like most of the other

surviving monarchies of Africa and Asia, gradually succumbed to European power. French troops inched forward from Algeria and a series of treaties and loans reduced Moroccan sovereignty to a diplomatic illusion (Burke 1976; Dunn 1977). The sultan's failure to oppose the French encroachments and the fact that he spent much of his time surrounded by Europeans led many Moroccans to believe that Mulay 'Abd al-'Aziz was "selling the country to the Christians" (Saint-Aulaire 1953, 120).

'Abd al-'Aziz's predicament is illustrated by the controversy surrounding his execution of a Muslim who killed a British missionary on 17 October 1902. The missionary, a man named Cooper, had entered an alley next to the zawiya of Mulay Idris II, the patron saint of Fez and the ancestor of the Idrissi shurafa. The unsuspecting Englishman had thus defiled the sacred space around the zawiya, which unbelievers were not allowed to enter. After an enraged crowd had surrounded Cooper, one Muslim shot him and then sought sanctuary at the saint's tomb. The sultan had this man brought to his palace (Arnaud 1952, 154; Burke 1976, 61; Pinon 1904, 154).

The murderer of the missionary came to the palace accompanied by the caretakers and shurafa of the Idrissi zawiya, holding the sacred wooden tablet on which Mulay Idris II was said to have written verses of the Quran (Arnaud 1952, 155). The sultan kissed the sacred tablet. Then, after interrogating the man himself and giving the Idrissi shurafa a donation to their zawiya, the commander of the faithful had the man shot in the presence of several representatives of the British vice-consul (ibid., 155–56; Burke 1976, 61).

In terms of the international balance of power, 'Abd al-'Aziz had acted rationally. He had avoided alienating the British, who had preserved Morocco's independence for most of the nineteenth century (al-Manuni 1985, 2:161). The Muslims of Morocco, however, did not see the incident as the British did. They felt that the Christian who had violated the sanctuary of Mulay Idris had deserved to die and that the sultan had himself violated this sanctuary by killing a man who had been under the protection of Mulay Idris and the Idrissi shurafa (Burke 1976, 61). This incident served to crystallize growing concern about the sultan's failure to oppose the European subjugation of Morocco. Alluding to the sultan's close relationship to his British adviser, Harry MacLean, some Moroccans said "it is not a son of Mulay al-Hassan that we have at our head, but a son of MacLean" (Arnaud 1952, 157). People commonly referred to 'Abd al-'Aziz as a "Christian" (Nisrani) (Ashmead-Bartlett 1910, 149).

The execution of the murderer of the British missionary sparked the revolt of Bu Hmara, who claimed to be the sultan's long-imprisoned brother and who was sometimes also depicted as the mahdi (Dunn 1981; 1991). Bu Hmara, "the man with the she-ass," was but one of a number of rural holy men who emerged, as in the fifteenth and early sixteenth centuries, to fill the vacuum left by the shadow of God's inability to wage a holy war against the unbelievers. Most of these marabouts were popularly venerated as shurafa and were affiliated with Sufi orders (Burke 1976). Yet there were many other prominent shurafa-cum-Sufi shaykhs who actively supported the French, the most famous example being that of the Wazzanis (Joffé 1991a, 1991b).

What was the political role of the ulama of Fez, the religious and political capital, in the face of the European threat and the commander of the faithful's failure to oppose it? By and large, it was a passive one. Burke notes that some ulama condemned the French occupation of the Touat oasis in 1900 (1976, 217). Such condemnation, however, did not translate into action of any kind, let alone a revolt against 'Abd al-'Aziz. Some ulama also criticized 'Abd al-'Aziz's implementation of a non-Quranic tax in 1901 that eliminated the traditional tax exemptions of the shurafa (ibid., 51–53). Once again, this did not prompt the guardians of God's law to revolt against the shadow of God.

Burke contends that the ulama's discontent "played an important role in the origin and early successes of" the revolt of Bu Hmara (ibid., 217). It is certainly true that many ulama initially sympathized with Bu Hmara (al-Susi 1966, 303). Some even saw him as a harbinger of the mahdi if not the mahdi himself (al-Kattani 1962, 182). Still, 'Abd al-'Aziz had no trouble in getting the ulama of Fez to issue a fatwa condemning Bu Hmara's revolt and declaring that obedience to the imam was obligatory according to the Quran and the Sunna (ibid., 179–81).

THE ULAMA AND THE FRENCH DEMANDS OF 1904–1905

Although Burke stresses (correctly) that the ulama rarely acted as a cohesive group, he contends that in 1904–05, it was "the strong collective action of the ulama of Fez that enabled the government to boldly challenge the proposed French reforms and set the stage for German intervention" (1976, 217). He is alluding here to a number of important events beginning with the Anglo-French accord of 8 April 1904. According to this treaty, France renounced its claims to Egypt in return for British acceptance of its right to colonize Morocco (Martin 1923, 414). The French took advantage of their new entente cordiale with Great Britain to force the sultan to accept a new loan agreement and a series of other "reforms" that would have given the French control of the Moroccan economy and of the army and police. The reforms were portents of outright French rule and caused great anxiety among Moroccans (Saint-Aulaire 1953, 95).

In early October 1904, the sultan created a majlis al-a'yan, or "council of notables," to discuss the French demands. Burke tends to see this council as having symbolized the determination of the ulama to oppose French imperialism. He himself notes, however, that "most of the appointees were merchants and secular notables" (1976, 82). Other sources confirm that the ulama represented only a small minority of the members of the council of notables (al-Manuni 1985, 2:192, 203).

Most of the notables, including the ulama, appointed to the council tended to follow the recommendations of the sultan. The historian Ibn Zaydan notes that when Mulay 'Abd al-'Aziz asked for their advice, they would answer "that which our Lord the Sultan decides is good" (Ibn Zaydan 1929–33, 1:396). It will be recalled that such servile deference was common in the fatwas of the ulama. Ibn Zaydan goes on to say of the members of the council that "their presence and absence amounted to the same thing" (ibid.). Another religious scholar who observed the majlis's activities observed that "the viziers of 'Abd al-'Aziz had no respect for the representatives that the latter had gathered from all over the country" (Laroui 1977b, 381).

The majlis was never directly involved in the negotiations of 1905. The French refused to discuss their demands with the majlis as a whole as suggested by 'Abd al-'Aziz, after he had received assurances of German support (Burke 1976, 81). Instead, they agreed to allow fifteen notables to listen silently to the reform proposals (ibid., 82). The French diplomats who were trying to induce 'Abd al-'Aziz to accept their reforms believed that the sultan never intended for the majlis to have any real authority. They saw it as a ploy designed to enable the sultan to resist French pressure without having to bear the responsibility for this resistance himself (Saint-René Taillandier 1930, 238, 247–50; Saint-Aulaire 1953, 138). The plausibility of this view is demonstrated by the fact that after the sultan induced the council to demand an international conference to discuss the French plans for Morocco (believing that Germany would reject them), he never consulted it again (al-Manuni 1985, 2:194–95, 202). The 1906 Act of Algesiras produced by the very conference demanded by the council diluted Moroccan sovereignty at least as much as the French demands of 1904–05, and yet the sultan never submitted it to the council for its approval.

In short, despite the Moroccan nationalist view of the 1905 council of notables as an important step toward democracy and constitutional monarchy (al-Fasi 1948, 94), it appears to have been an illusion designed to shore up the sultan's position vis-à-vis the French and vis-à-vis his increasingly disgruntled subjects. When the majlis no longer served the ruler's purposes, he forgot about it. It was not pressure from the council of notables or from the ulama of Fez that induced Mulay 'Abd al-'Aziz to oppose the French reform proposals of 1904–05. It was rather German pressure, culminating in the Kaiser's celebrated visit to Tangier in March 1905 (Saint-Aulaire 1953, 125–48). In the words of Morocco's grand vizier at the time, "While France was in the process of raping Morocco, the Emperor Wilhelm gave it a tremendous kick in the butt" (ibid., 139).

Burke notes that the German foreign minister had assured the sultan that Germany would support Moroccan resistance to the French demands on 2 January 1905 (1976, 81). Burke also acknowledges that the Kaiser's visit to Tangier in March 1905 "virtually assured the rejection of the French reform proposals" (ibid., 85). Abdallah Laroui, too, notes that the majlis's rejection of the French proposals was due to the vagaries of German diplomacy rather than to the courage of the notables—most of whom were not ulama (1977b, 378). It may well be true that the Germans would not have blocked the French reforms if Mulay 'Abd al-'Aziz had not manifested his desire to resist them in the fall of 1904 (Guillen 1967, 826–27). But the ulama did not force, and could not have forced, the sultan to reject the French demands on their own.

SIDI MUHAMMAD BIN 'ABD AL-KABIR AL-KATTANI (1873–1909)

During the crisis produced by the French reform proposals of 1904–05, most Moroccan ulama were as servile as usual, saying whatever the sultan wanted them to say. The sultan's majlis, however, included at least one scholar who was definitely more than a palace puppet—Sidi Muhammad bin 'Abd al-Kabir al-Kattani. Since al-Kattani's role in the events of 1904–09 is often construed as reflecting the activism of the ulama in general, it should be noted that he was not a typical religious scholar. The ulama of Fez had tried to have him executed for heresy in 1896–97, much as the Almoravid ulama had tried to have Ibn Tumart executed in the twelfth century (al-Kattani 1962, 77-88; al-Mu'aqqit 1932, 165–72). Among the charges made against him, insofar as doctrinal deviance was concerned, was that he had claimed to be "the seal of the saints" (khatm al-awliya'), in direct contact with the Prophet Muhammad himself.[1] The ulama of Fez had also accused him of aspiring to replace 'Abd al-'Aziz as sultan, although this charge was eventually dismissed (al-Fasi 1931, 1:47; al-Kattani 1962, 78, 84).

Al-Kattani's son and hagiographer contends that the ulama who sought to have him executed were envious because he was venerated by people of all social strata and because the new Kattaniyya order was attracting people away from the older Sufi orders (al-Kattani 1962, 77). Another motive may have been that, like most scholars who have exemplified the myth of the righteous man of God, al-Kattani frequently criticized the ulama for thinking of their own interests rather than of their duties as guardians of Islam (ibid., 79, 81; al-Yusi 1981, 1:152–55, 196). Thus the ulama had a number of possible reasons for trying to convince the sultan to have al-Kattani executed. For present purposes, the crucial point is that the relationship between al-Kattani and the majority of the ulama (especially in Fez) was, to say the least, strained. Some ulama did eventually become al-Kattani's followers. Yet many remained hostile toward him for the rest of his life (Cagne 1988, 428; Laroui 1977b, 413).

Al-Kattani embodied the ideal of the righteous scholar to a greater degree than any of his peers. He was also more of a populist political figure than any of his fellow ulama. His son claims that he once refused to ride a mule until some braided silk was removed from the animal—even though he liked to wear elegant clothes himself (al-Kattani 1962, 39, 81). He reportedly declined to drink coffee out of cups of silver and gold in the palace of the Khedive of Egypt because they were prohibited by Islam (ibid., 97). He traveled extensively among Berber tribes exhorting them to join his Sufi order and to conform to the laws of God in all aspects of life (ibid., 17). (Few people saw these exhortations as mutually exclusive in early twentieth-century Morocco.) He preached to poor artisans and visited prisoners in jails (ibid., 117). He complained that the mosques were empty "except for the tradesmen and artisans, even though it is not proper for the people of knowledge [ahl al-'ilm] to neglect the attendance of collective prayer" (ibid., 38). His strongest supporters were always tribesmen, artisans, and the urban poor—not his fellow ulama (Maitrot de la Motte Capron and Trenga 1936, 24, 60, 143, 187; Cagne 1988, 428).

Al-Kattani argued that the Christians were in the process of subjugating Morocco because the ulama no longer taught mathematics or the basic rituals of Islam to the people (al-Kattani 1962, 38). The ulama were neglecting their role as exemplars to be emulated by ordinary believers. The Muslims in general were neglecting their faith and imitating the Christians. "How could they not defeat us when we have forsaken the practices of our Prophet and filled our time with their practices, their machines, their goods, their trinkets, and their novelties?" (ibid., 37). This was to become a leitmotif of twentieth-century fundamentalism (see chap. 6).

Al-Kattani forbade the drinking of tea by the members of the Kattaniyya Sufi order because its production and importation were controlled by Europeans, and its consumption by Moroccans was "a prelude to the occupation of Morocco" (ibid., 93). At the same time, he blamed Morocco's Jews for bringing about European involvement in Morocco's internal affairs. He and his followers would harrass and threaten Jewish merchants in markets, forcing them to flee to the Jewish quarter (ibid., 202).

Al-Kattani seems to have been influenced by pan-Islamist ideas while in Egypt and Mecca in 1903–04 (Laroui 1977b, 373). Despite his being a Sufi shaykh, much of what he said was reminiscent of the nascent Salafi reformist theme of returning to the true Islam of the Prophet to overcome the onslaught of European imperialism (al-Kattani 1962, 34–37). The appeal of al-Kattani's populist, protonationalist and reformist ideas was enhanced by the widespread belief in his baraka (ibid., 17; al-Wazzani 1942, 34–35). He was not an ordinary scholar immersed in medieval texts. He was a holy man venerated by illiterate artisans and tribesmen as well as by learned Sufis. Unlike most ulama of his day, he usually veiled his face, as had the Almoravids in the eleventh and twelfth centuries (al-Kattani 1962, 114–15). This added to the aura of sanctity and mystery that surrounded him.

Jacob Niddam, a Moroccan Jew of Fez who had good reason to worry about this charismatic holy man, wrote in 1908 that:

> as of last night, our good riflemen of Bab Ftuh have had to cease functioning. The sharif al-Kattani, leader of these wild ones, was considered, among these ignorant people, a divine being. Before any of them would fire his weapon, he would submit it respectfully to this famous saint. The latter had only to place his hand on the trigger, at least according to what they say, for the gun's owner to hit his target. Thus the influence of this saint grew day by day. Our gover-

nors, fearing that he would be proclaimed king, have stopped these exercises. (Maitrot de la Motte Capron and Trenga 1936, 37–38)

Everywhere he went, people sought to absorb al-Kattani's baraka, in some cases even kissing the hooves of his mule to do so (al-Kattani 1962, 91). On the German steamship that took him and his entourage to Egypt on the way to Mecca, his students said they did not fear the terrors of the sea so long as they were near him (ibid., 93). Al-Kattani's son contends that "no one met with him without seeing a miracle" (ibid., 114). He cites the case of "a ray of light emerging from his chest" (ibid., 116). Above and beyond these distinctive features of his public persona, al-Kattani eventually differed from most of his fellow scholars by his willingness to defy the reigning sultan. This defiance, however, followed years of docility.

Al-Kattani was acquitted of the charges leveled against him in 1897 thanks to the intervention of the renowned Sufi shaykh Ma' al-'Aynayn, who declared that "he who does not understand his words should not oppose him" (ibid., 1962, 86). For the next seven years, al-Kattani enjoyed Mulay 'Abd al-'Aziz's favor. The sultan often sought his advice and assistance in pacifying rebellious tribes (ibid., 179–85). In 1903, Mulay 'Abd al-'Aziz paid for his pilgrimage to Mecca (al-Fasi 1931, 1:47). Huge and enthusiastic crowds greeted him in all the towns and villages where he stopped (al-Kattani 1962, 88–93). (Al-Yusi, too, had attracted large and enthusiastic crowds.)

Al-Kattani returned to Morocco in the summer of 1904. By the fall of that year, if not sooner, he was generally recognized as the leader of the opposition to the French demands for reforms that would have given France effective control of Morocco's military and economy (Burke 1976, 77). He repeatedly urged 'Abd al-'Aziz to reject the French proposals (al-Kattani 1962, 185). He opposed allowing more Christians (as Europeans were generally referred to) to live in Morocco's ports, noting that once they had settled in Casablanca, "it had become like part of their land in all things and it was stripped of the dignity of Islam" (al-Manuni 1985, 2:231). The great caliphs of the past had never sought the help of unbelievers, claimed al-Kattani, and Mulay ʿAbd al-ʿAziz should not do so now. The French proposals were contrary to the Quran and the Sunna and should be rejected (ibid., 2:230–31). In February 1905, al-Kattani recommended waging a holy war against the French. He told the council of notables that "our Lord [the sultan] should not forget that there are among his subjects men capable of defending themselves." To which the elderly and pragmatic grand vizier responded, "If the French resort to force, will your baraka stop them?" (Saint-René Taillandier 1930, 247). Many Moroccans were convinced it could.

As has already been observed, it was Kaiser Wilhelm II, not al-Kattani, who ultimately induced Mulay ʿAbd al-ʿAziz to reject the French demands until they had been approved by an international conference. Al-Kattani was undoubtedly expressing the views of most Moroccan Muslims in rejecting the French demands. But the sultan's insistence that he could not accept the demands until they had been discussed by the countries that had signed the 1880 Treaty of Madrid was not the sort of response to French imperialism that the Sufi mystic of Fez would have conceived of on his own. This ploy was suggested by the Germans (Martin 1923, 417–18). Even in the streets of Fez, Moroccans spoke of "the sultan of the Prussians" (sultan al-Bruz) saving Morocco from the French (Saint-Aulaire 1953, 137). As for al-Kattani, he only heard of the plan after it had been advocated by Mulay ʿAbd al-ʿAziz (al-Kattani 1962, 187). Al-Kattani's fiery denunciations of the French demands stiffened ʿAbd al-ʿAziz's resolve in late 1904 and thereby encouraged the Germans to assume the old British role of guarantors of Moroccan independence (Guillen 1967, 826–31). Yet if al-Kattani's goals had not temporarily meshed with those of the sultan and German imperialism, he would not have achieved them. This is demonstrated by the sharif's utterly fruitless opposition to the Act of Algesiras of 1906.

When al-Kattani first learned that ʿAbd al-ʿAziz favored an international conference, he urged that it be held in Fez (al-Kattani 1962, 187). The sultan rejected this idea, as he did al-Kattani's suggestions as to which men should represent Morocco, and the conference was held in the little Spanish town of Algesiras. When it ended up producing a document that reinforced European influence in Morocco, al-Kattani urged Mulay ʿAbd al-ʿAziz not to sign it. The Germans, however, had been unable to win significant international support in Algesiras and were no longer able to block the French diplomatically. So on 18 June 1906, the commander of the faithful signed the document that in effect gave infidel France the right to subjugate Muslim Morocco (Burke 1976, 88). Al-Kattani, like most Moroccans who understood what was happening, was, of course, furious.

THE HAFIDHIYYA REVOLT OF 1907–1908

The outrage provoked by the Act of Algesiras in 1906 was compounded the following year when French troops occupied the Moroccan cities of Oujda and Casablanca. The occupation of the latter city in particular, in the summer of 1907, precipitated the Hafidhiyya revolt of 1907–08 (named after the sultan's brother Mulay ʿAbd al-Hafidh). The ulama are often said to have led this revolt, which is also often depicted as exemplifying the proper political role of the religious scholars of Islam vis-à-vis sultans (al-Jirari 1986, 979). In fact, the ulama did not initiate the revolt, and most of them supported it only when forced to do so. The Hafidhiyya revolt thus illustrates not the activism but the passivity of most of the guardians of God's law even as their country was gradually being colonized by unbelievers from Europe.

After the French occupied Casablanca, less than six months after having occupied the northeastern city of Oujda, the sultan Mulay ʿAbd al-ʿAziz had his *Wazir al-Bahr* (Minister of the Sea or foreign minister) meet with the ulama and other notables of Fez to justify the French action and the government's failure to oppose it. When the minister had finished speaking, only al-Kattani dared to challenge his (and thus the sultan's) defense of the occupation and only one other scholar, *al-fqih* al-Sanhaji, endorsed al-Kattani's challenge publicly. The other ulama did not say a word (al-Kattani 1962, 188–89).

On the morning of 16 August 1907, the sultan's brother Mulay ʿAbd al-Hafidh convened a meeting of the elite of Marrakesh, including the ulama, the shurafa, the merchants, and the qaids (powerful tribal leaders).[2] ʿAbd al-Hafidh said to the crowd: "The Christians have taken Oujda and Casablanca, and no one in Morocco has risen to defend our Muslim brothers. God cannot permit that the law of the Quran be thus ignored. Descendant of the Prophet, I am touched to the bottom of my heart by this state of affairs and I come asking you to gather and choose another candidate from among the shurafa who will take in hand the cause of my brother" (René-LeClerc 1908, 43).

One of the assembled men then endorsed this suggestion and proposed that ʿAbd al-Hafidh himself be chosen as "sultan of the holy war" (ibid.). A document incorporating the deposition of ʿAbd al-ʿAziz and the bayʿa of ʿAbd al-Hafidh as the new imam was then circulated. The text of the bayʿa stressed the classical theme of the conditional and contractual nature of the caliphate:

> The validity of the imamate is based on the [following] conditions, without which it ceases to exist: justice, knowledge, soundness of the senses and the limbs, sound judgment conducive to the administration of subjects and the regulation of affairs; courage resulting in the protection of the land of Islam and holy war against the enemy; and Qurayshi ancestry. . . . When these conditions are not fulfilled, a man cannot be contracted to rule. And if he is already the ruler, he must be removed. The texts concerning this in the book [the Quran] and the hadiths of the messenger of God are known to everyone. There is no room for disagreement or doubt in this. (al-Manuni 1985, 2:355)

Although the rhetoric of this bayʿa reflects the contractual conception of the caliphate, the ulama's role in its promulgation does not. It was initiated not by the guardians of God's law, but by al-Madani al-Glawi and other powerful southern qaids—who were in turn supported by the Germans (Martin 1923, 416, 545; al-Susi 1983, 52, 57, 60, 73). The first scholar to sign the bayʿa was Mulay Mustafa al-ʿAlawi, the chief judge of Marrakesh and a member of the royal family. At first he refused. Then, according to one account, al-Madani al-Glawi pulled out a pistol and threatened to shoot him. So the venerable scholar signed and the other terrified notables, including the ulama, followed suit (René-LeClerc 1908, 43). According to Mulay Mustafa's own account, as recorded by two French writers, al-Glawi called him a Christian when he refused to sign, and several of al-Glawi's henchmen grabbed the hood of Mulay Mustafa's burnous and raised their daggers above his head. At this point, Mulay Mustafa ran and embraced Mulay 'Abd al-Hafidh to save himself (Tharaud and Tharaud 1920, 197–98). Another scholar tried to avoid endorsing the revolutionary bay'a by sneaking out of the city to a farm he owned. He was discovered and forced to sign like his peers (MAE 1907, 341). Even 'Abd al-Hafidh's close associate, Idris Minnu, concedes that al-Madani al-Glawi's zeal (hamasa) played an important role in inducing the ulama and other notables of Marrakesh to sign the bay'a of August 1907 (al-Susi 1983, 52).

It is thus clear that the ulama did not initiate the deposition of Mulay 'Abd al-'Aziz. This is not to deny that some ulama in Marrakesh sympathized with 'Abd al-Hafidh's revolt. Still, their role in it was a passive one. Some were clearly horrified by the idea of overthrowing the shadow of God, no matter what he had done or failed to do. The contractual ideal of the caliphate notwithstanding, the principle of absolute submission to the shadow of God continued to prevail in the minds of many ulama (Gharrit 1928, 103). More important, in practical terms, the behavior of the ulama in 1907 was primarily dictated by fear rather than principle.

The pliancy of Morocco's ulama during the Hafidhiyya revolt of 1907–08 is further illustrated by the fact that a few days after the bay'a of 'Abd al-Hafidh in Marrakesh, 'Abd al-'Aziz was able to force twenty-seven prominent ulama of Fez to issue a fatwa reaffirming the legitimacy of his rule and the illegitimacy of 'Abd al-Hafidh's revolt (Afrique Française, Jan. 1908, 34–35). 'Abd al-'Aziz had these venerable scholars of sacred law abruptly brought to his palace—at night—to write and sign this decree. When some of them suggested postponing its writing until they had a chance to study the relevant legal texts, the sultan's men refused to let them leave until they had finished the task right then and there (al-Kattani

1908, 15–16). So despite the fact that many of the ulama of Fez sympathized with the revolt against ʿAbd al-ʿAziz, they wrote and signed a fatwa denying its legitimacy—as they had done a few years earlier with respect to the revolt of Bu Hmara.

Locked in the sultan's palace and bullied by his soldiers, the ulama of Fez (including al-Kattani) echoed the official position of the French and Moroccan governments that the French had not really invaded Muslim territory at all:

> If they occupy, at this moment, certain points on the borders, it is, according to their own declarations, only to exercise their right to obtain reparations for the massacre of their nationals and to protect the other foreigners living in the country. . . .
>
> Thus, since it has just been established that Muslim soil has not been invaded, there should be no change in the present state of affairs and it is not permissible to revolt against our lord, may God perpetuate his greatness.
>
> The fallacious arguments of the rebel [ʿAbd al-Hafidh] by means of which he has captivated the hearts of the ignorant masses are not admitted by the law. (*Afrique Française*, Jan. 1908, 34–35)

The ulama forced to write this fatwa also noted that only the commander of the faithful had the right to declare a jihad, which he would do when necessary if he thought the Muslims were strong enough to win. Although the ulama did not explicitly repudiate the contractual conception of the caliphate in this fatwa, they did stress that Muslims had to obey their imam, citing the famous Quranic verse, "O you who believe, obey God, obey the messenger and those in authority" (ibid.). It was only after the sultan's army left Fez in September 1907 that Sidi Muhammad bin ʿAbd al-Kabir al-Kattani and *some* other ulama of the city dared challenge his rule (Cagne 1988, 423–25; al-Kattani 1962, 194).

As for the eventual deposition of ʿAbd al-ʿAziz and the bayʿa of ʿAbd al-Hafidh by the ulama of Fez in January 1908, the guardians of the sacred law once again acted under pressure rather than of their own free will. This time, the pressure came from angry mobs of peasants, artisans, and the urban poor. On 15 December 1907, peasants swarmed into Fez refusing to pay a market tax imposed by

Mulay ʿAbd al-ʿAziz.[3] Joined by the city's poor, the peasants broke open the strongboxes where the tax revenues were kept and attacked a number of shops, the French post office, and the offices of the government's tobacco monopoly. The crowds also tried to pillage the Jewish quarter, but its gates were shut before they could (*Afrique Française*, Jan. 1908, 31). After two days of this rioting, merchants succeeded in restoring order by means of a makeshift militia composed largely of porters and slaves. The sultan's army was absent, having left Fez in September when Mulay ʿAbd al-ʿAziz had decided he would be safer in Rabat, near French troops and ships (Burke 1976, 108).

It was in this tense context that the ulama of Fez agreed to depose Mulay ʿAbd al-ʿAziz formally and sign a bayʿa swearing allegiance to Mulay ʿAbd al-Hafidh. According to one contemporary French source, an agitated crowd of twenty thousand people escorted some of Fez's most prominent ulama to the mosque-cum-university of al-Qarawiyyin. Here they were asked to endorse a petition declaring that Mulay ʿAbd al-ʿAziz was no longer fit to rule because of his subservience to the French and his failure to implement the laws of Islam. The ulama wrote a little note at the bottom of the petition asking if they could answer the following day. The crowd was infuriated by this response, and one of their leaders told the ulama, with a pistol in his hand, that the people could not wait a day. The ulama then requested, and were granted, half an hour in which to respond. The huge crowd, now estimated at about forty thousand people, waited silently outside. After the half hour had elapsed, the ulama endorsed and signed the decree deposing ʿAbd al-ʿAziz as commander of the faithful (*Afrique Française*, Jan. 1908, 36).

There are slightly different accounts of the events that led the ulama of Fez to sign the bayʿa of ʿAbd al-Hafidh in January 1908 (see Burke 1976, 115–16; Cagne 1988, 410–29; Laroui 1977b, 393–99). Contemporary French sources all insist that the ulama of Fez were coerced into signing the bayʿa by angry mobs mobilized by al-Kattani (*Afrique Française*, Feb. 1908, 66; MAE 1908, 91–92; Michaux-Bellaire 1908, 402). Mulay ʿAbd al-ʿAziz himself stressed that the revolt in Fez had involved tanners, shoemakers, weavers, and other artisans and tradesmen who had overpowered the ulama (al-Manuni 1985, 2:339–40). It is, of course, true that 'Abd al-'Aziz, like the French, sought to discredit the bay'a of 'Abd al-Hafidh, whose support was due largely to the belief that he was going to drive the French from Morocco. A number of Moroccan ulama who lived through the Hafidhiyya revolt, however, paint a similar picture.

The scholar Muhammad Gharrit writes that the bay'a of January 1908 took place in the sanctuary of Mulay Idris I "after guidance and threats" (1928, 104). Gharrit likens the angry crowds to a raging sea and cites the case of a scholar who was almost killed when he said he did not want to sign. He contends that "the most renowned of scholars were under the control of insolent fools" (ibid.). The scholar Ibn Zaydan notes discretely that the Fez bay'a took place "after turmoil and disorder the details of which I leave to others to describe" (1929–33, 1:448). Even 'Abd al-Hafidh al-Fasi, who was al-Kattani's cousin, student, and supporter, says that while some ulama signed the Fez bay'a of January 1908 sincerely, others did so "out of fear of the masses" (khawfan min al-'amma) (1931, 1:48). Al-Fasi, who studied with al-Kattani for over ten years, notes that many of the ulama and notables who signed the bay'a of Mulay 'Abd al-Hafidh did so because they were afraid that "the masses" would demand that al-Kattani himself be proclaimed sultan if they did not (ibid., 47). In short, then, the authority of the guardians of God's law was once again subordinated to brute force. This time, however, the brute force was that of angry mobs rather than that of a sultan or a qaid.

THE CONDITIONS OF THE FEZ BAY'A

The distinctive feature of the Fez bay'a of January 1908 was that it made allegiance to the new sultan 'Abd al-Hafidh contingent on his acceptance of a number of specific conditions, notably the liberation of the territories occupied by France, the elimination of all European interference in Moroccan affairs, the duty to consult the people (al-umma) with respect to negotiations with foreign powers, the elimination of non-Quranic taxes, the protection of the traditional prerogatives of the ulama and the shurafa, and a general revival of the principles of Islam. (See Burke 1976, 115–16; Cagne 1988, 411–15, 455–56; Ibn Zaydan 1929-33, 1:452–53; al-Kattani 1962, 199–200; Laroui 1977b, 396).

There was nothing new about the *principle* that all bay'as were conditional. Ulama like al-Yusi had often stressed this. Moreover, even explicit conditions had sometimes been included in earlier bay'as (al-Manuni 1985, 1:379, 381; 2:346). Yet never had so many explicit conditions curtailing the authority of a ruler been included in a bay'a. Some of the ulama and other notables of Fez objected to the bay'a of January 1908 noting that "conditions cannot be imposed on kings" (ibid., 2:345). These people recognized that the Fez bay'a was a radical innovation in the context of Moroccan history. It translated the abstract ideal of a contractual caliphate into a concrete reality. It was thus a major step toward a truly constitutional monarchy. Or at any rate, it would have been if it had ever been implemented.

Although the original version of the Fez bay'a had been drafted by the scholar Ahmad bin 'Abd al-Wahid bin al-Muwaz in relatively traditional terms, al-Kattani declared: "there is no benefit to be expected from this revolution if the bay'a of the commander of the faithful is not tied to conditions that implement the goals of the umma" (al-Kattani 1962, 198, 206). (Although the word umma refers to the Islamic community in general, in practice it is often used to refer to the Muslim people of a particular country.) This statement is in the spirit of the classical contractual ideal. It probably also reflected al-Kattani's awareness of the idea of constitutionalism that was exciting many Middle Eastern intellectuals at this time (ibid., 206; Laroui 1977b, 374–82).

Some time after the bay'a was approved, a group of the leading ulama of Fez went to Meknes to congratulate Mulay 'Abd al-Hafidh. He was so outraged by the conditional character of the bay'a that for several days, he would not even meet with them. When he did, he scolded them angrily, saying that the conditions diluted his power and hindered his ability to govern. The frightened ulama then disavowed the conditions, blaming them entirely on al-Kattani. They insisted that he had forced them to accept them (al-Kattani 1962, 211–12). Such was the pusillanimity of most Moroccan ulama when confronted by the power of kings. Of course, such behavior was perfectly rational since those guardians of God's law who kowtowed to sultans prospered, whereas those who did not usually suffered. Yet it did illustrate the disparity between historical reality and the contractual relationship that was supposed to exist between rulers and "the heirs of the Prophet."

AL-KATTANI DEFIES ʿABD AL-HAFIDH

During the winter and spring of 1908, al-Kattani appears to have been the most powerful man in Fez. In the absence of the former sultan ʿAbd al-ʿAziz and the new one ʿAbd al-Hafidh, he is said to have headed a revolutionary committee composed of supportive ulama and representatives of the city's various neighborhoods. This group extorted large sums of money from the families of officials who had served ʿAbd al-ʿAziz and had some of the latter's supporters arrested. Al-Kattani's council is also reported to have shut down the city's foreign post offices and brothels (Weisgerber 1947, 182). It seems, however, to have dissolved after Mulay ʿAbd al-Hafidh arrived in Fez in June 1908.

During the rest of 1908 and early 1909, the relationship between al-Kattani and ʿAbd al-Hafidh became increasingly strained. It is sometimes said that the cause of this strain was that al-Kattani was a Sufi and the sultan a Salafi reformist (al-Fasi 1948, 133). It is true that al-Kattani disagreed with ʿAbd al-Hafidh about some Sufi practices. Al-Kattani's son claims he responded as follows to the sultan's criticism of the Sufis' chanting of God's name and rhythmic dancing:

"It is not enough to condemn Sufi dancing alone. We must also condemn golden watches, golden snuff boxes, and silk clothes and remove them." The sultan had in his hand a golden snuff box and was wearing a golden watch and a silk waistband. "Then we must go out and whenever we come across a place of lust or a wine shop, we must shut it down. And each time we come across a merchant who does not know how to buy and sell [honestly], we must set him straight. And if we come across a zawiya and find heretical innovations and forbidden things, we must set them straight too. But it is not right to overlook all that is forbidden and reprehensible except when it comes to Sufism." This is to discriminate for no reason. The sultan rose and left in anger. (al-Kattani 1962, 215)

Whatever the accuracy of this account, there clearly was some tension between al-Kattani and Mulay 'Abd al-Hafidh owing to the latter's criticism of *certain aspects of Sufism*. Yet we shall see in the next chapter that the sultan himself was a Sufi. So the Sufi versus Salafi interpretation of the conflict between al-Kattani and 'Abd al-Hafidh is inadequate.

French sources sometimes portray the clash between the two men in terms of competition for the throne and the tension that has often existed between Idrissi and 'Alawi shurafa (Michaux-Bellaire (1908, 393–95). There is, however, no evidence that al-Kattani's hostility to 'Abd al-Hafidh was *primarily* due to a desire to be sultan or to the idea that the Idrissis had a greater right to rule than the 'Alawis. It was due rather to the sultan's manifest inability and unwillingness to implement the conditions of the bay'a of Fez, especially with respect to opposing France's increasingly obvious intention to colonize Morocco (Cagne 1988, 410–56; Burke 1976, 129–30; Laroui 1977b, 400–6).

Like Mulay 'Abd al-'Aziz before him, Mulay 'Abd al-Hafidh, the "sultan of the jihad" was turning out to be incapable of stopping the onslaught of French imperialism. His coffers were too empty, his armies too weak. Al-Kattani could not accept such excuses. So in the spring of 1909, he fled from Fez to the Middle Atlas mountains, from where he hoped to start a revolt against 'Abd al-Hafidh and a holy war against the French. Soldiers captured al-Kattani and his family and brought them back to Fez in chains. The sultan then had the venerated religious scholar flogged to death and buried in the middle of the night (al-Susi 1983, 65–66; al-Kattani 1962, 218). Like Mulay Isma'il two centuries earlier after the death of 'Abd as-Slam Guessous, 'Abd al-Hafidh did not relish the thought of a public funeral for the man of God he had killed.

The Hafidhiyya revolt of 1907–08 was not comparable to the constitutionalist revolution of 1906–11 in Iran, which really was led by ulama (Martin 1989). It is true that the weakened state of the sultanate in 1907–08 enabled the Moroccan ulama to play a more conspicuous political role than they usually did. Still, even in these years, most scholars remained pawns manipulated by those who held real power, be it the reigning sultan, or al-Madani al-Glawi, or Sidi Muhammad bin ʿAbd al-Kabir al-Kattani when he was able to mobilize huge crowds of artisans, shopkeepers, and peasants. In this period, as in previous centuries, no one denied that approval by the ulama was a prerequisite of legitimate rule. But nor did those with power have any difficulty in forcing the ulama to legitimate whatever it was they wanted legitimated.

Al-Kattani was not a typical religious scholar. His relations with most of the ulama of Fez had been strained ever since they had tried to have him executed in 1896–97. Like most men who embodied the myth of the righteous man of God who dares to defy an unjust sultan, he criticized his fellow ulama for thinking of their own self-interest rather than the well-being of the Muslim community (the umma). Not surprisingly, they did nothing to prevent or protest his murder. Many of them had always viewed him as an iconoclastic and fanatical rabble-rouser. He was only about thirty-five years old when he died, far younger than most prominent ulama, and yet he was the most influential Moroccan scholar of his time (Cagne 1988, 422–28; al-Muʾaqqit 1932, 165–72; al-Kattani 1962, 77–88; Laroui 1977b, 388, 406, 413).

Al-Kattani's power obviously did not derive from his being a religious scholar alone. It was due in part to the popular belief in his baraka, both as a sharif and as a Sufi shaykh (al-Wazzani 1942, 34–35, 47–48). It was also due to his ability to articulate the grievances of most Moroccans in the face of France's manifest determination to subjugate Morocco (Michaux-Bellaire 1908, 395, 402). Al-Kattani thus illustrates an important point already alluded to with respect to Ibn Tumart. Righteous scholars posed a real threat to sultans only when they were seen to be sacred as well as righteous, when they were believed to possess great baraka as well as knowledge. They also only posed a threat to sultans when they articulated widespread grievances, typically grievances that were not essentially religious. In the case of al-Kattani, he articulated the despair of a people on the verge of being colonized, a despair he could only articulate and explain in terms of Islam.

Four Popular Religion,
Orthodoxy, and
Salafi Scripturalism

The central theme of Clifford Geertz's book *Islam Observed* is that the dilution of the authority of the classical religious symbols of Islam in the nineteenth and twentieth centuries led to its "ideologization" in both Morocco and Indonesia:

> Victims, in this dimension, anyway, of an altered social situation, a steadily increasing number of Indonesians and Moroccans are discovering that though the religious traditions of Kalidjaga and Lyusi are accessible, and indeed attractive, to them, the certitude those traditions produced is not. The transformation of religious symbols from imagistic revelations of the divine, evidences of God, to ideological assertions of the divine's importance, badges of piety, has been in each country, though in different ways, the common reaction to this disheartening discovery. (1968, 61–62)

Geertz is making an important point, along the lines of Karl Mannheim's distinction between the largely unconscious acceptance of tradition and the conscious defense

77

of it when "other ways of life and thought appear on the scene" (Mannheim 1953, 115). "Traditional" believers simply take their religious beliefs for granted. They do not see them as being in need of defense. They do not even see them as beliefs; they are simply the way the world is. But when tradition is challenged by alternative conceptions of the world, some people leap to its defense—inevitably transforming it in the process. Tradition defended is never entirely traditional.

We see this in the Salafiyya reformist movement that emerged in Morocco and most of the rest of the Islamic world in the late nineteenth and early twentieth centuries (Brown 1966; Merad 1978). The Salafis advocated a return to the pristine Islam of al-salaf al-salih, "the virtuous forefathers" as a means of overcoming European dom- ination (al-Fasi 1948, 133–36). They sought to purify Islam of what they considered heretical innovations, notably Sufism and the ven- eration of saints, and to revive the "true" Islam of the Quran and the Sunna. They also sought to purify Islam of Western cultural influences, although they, in fact, often reinterpreted Islam in terms of Western concepts. Thus the idea of "consultation" (shura), which had traditionally referred to the idea that a sultan should consult with the ulama to be sure that his policies confirmed to Islamic law, was now interpreted to mean that the head of state should implement the will of the people as represented by a democratically elected legis- lature (al-Fasi 1967, 61–69).

The ideological dimension of Salafi scripturalism is especially obvi- ous in the writings of ʿAllal al-Fassi (1910–74), who became the movement's most famous spokesman by the late 1930s. In a book published after years of futile efforts to create a constitutional mon- archy in independent Morocco, al-Fasi writes that the prophets of Islam tried to eliminate "tyrants who put themselves in the place of gods and enslave and oppress the people" (al-Fasi 1963, 205). This is not how the traditional Moroccan peasant saw prophets or sultans. Al-Fassi contends that Islam does not accept the idea of divine kingship or the idea that kings are in any way the representatives of God (ibid., 206). Islam "considers the ruler and the ruled equal in terms of rights and duties" (taj·alu al-hakim wa'l-mahkum fi'l-huquq wa'l-wajibat sawa') (ibid.). This is clearly a critique of the traditional conception of Moroccan sacred kingship rooted in the contractual conception of the caliphate. But al-Fassi goes on to condemn "the bishops and monks who first established feudalism, created slavery in its broader sense, paved the way for oppressive kings and leaders, and advocated the class system" (ibid.). Elsewhere he contends that "the first to think of the political equality of men and women in the modern age were the democratic Islamic republics established at the end of the Czarist period in the Russian empire" (al-Fasi [1952] 1979, 158). Such language reflects the apologetic ideologization and westernization of Islam that resulted from the subjugation of the Islamic world by Europe.

Revivalist-cum-nativistic movements like the Salafiyya have often emerged in response to European domination. These movements always borrow from the Western cultures they ostensibly seek to reject. Their basic message is: return to the ways of the virtuous ancestors and God (or the gods) will restore the bountiful golden age that existed before foreign domination. In some cases, especially among tribesmen and peasants, there are explicitly miraculous and messianic dimensions to such movements (Linton 1943; Wallace 1956). Among the educated elites of complex societies with ancient "great" traditions, the emphasis tends to be on the revival (actually reinterpretation) of those aspects of sacred scripture apparently most compatible with European "modernity" (Gombrich and Obeyesekere 1988; Tambiah 1976, 428). Salafi scripturalism is of the latter variety.

Geertz deserves credit not only for recognizing that Salafi reformism is, to some extent anyway, an ideologized form of Islam, but also for his awareness of the role of European colonialism in stimulating its diffusion: "In a curiously ironical way, intense involvement with the West moved religious faith closer to the center of our peoples' self-definition than it had been before. Before, men had been Muslims as a matter of circumstance; now they were, increasingly, Muslims as a matter of policy. They were *oppositional* Muslims. Not only oppositional, of course; but into what had been a fine medieval contempt for infidels crept a tense modern note of anxious envy and defensive pride" (1968, 65). One sees this syndrome whenever a people of one religion are dominated by people of another. Beliefs that were once taken for granted suddenly become emblems of identity, usually "national" identity. (One thinks of Catholicism in Ireland and Poland.)

Although some of Geertz's comments on Moroccan Salafi reformism are insightful, his discussion of this topic reflects, once again, his neglect of indigenous texts as well as his tendency to generalize on the basis of little or no evidence. The pivotal theme of *Islam Observed* is that the classical religious symbols of Islam in Morocco lost their authority but not their appeal for a small but significant minority of Moroccans and Indonesians—apparently in the late nineteenth and twentieth centuries (pp. 17, 61). This is an interesting assertion, but Geertz provides no evidence to substantiate it. The same holds true for his assertion that the growth of "positive science" was a major cause of the weakened authority of the classical symbols of Islam (pp. 102–3). He contends that "even the humblest peasant or shepherd" knew, by the mid-twentieth century, that "general laws inductively established" were challenging the revelations of God (p. 103). One would like to know what any peasant or shepherd ever said or did to give Geertz this impression.

Geertz contends that the Moroccan reformists sought to segregate religion and secular life (pp. 17, 105–6). Once again, he provides no evidence to support this contention. The Salafis actually tended to stress that Islam should govern *all* aspects of life—precisely the opposite of the argument Geertz attributes to them (al-Fasi 1948, 135; al-Fasi, 1952, 115). When told by a French officer to avoid political matters in his lectures on Islam, the famous Moroccan Salafi Muhammad bin al-'Arbi al-'Alawi answered: "Anyone who claims to give lectures on the religion of Islam without discussing politics is either a liar, a hypocrite, or an ignoramus. For Islam demands the liberation of the human being and calls for both justice and freedom and the quest for knowledge. The message of Islam came to liberate the human being from his shackles, the shackles of this world and the torments of the hereafter" (al-Asfi 1986, 77). Such statements, which pervade the Salafi literature

(Ghallab 1991; Merad 1978), are somewhat difficult to reconcile with Geertz's assertion that Moroccan scripturalists sought to separate religion from secular life (1968, 106).

Another problem with Geertz's view of Moroccan scripturalism is his failure to situate it in the context of the relation between popular and orthodox Islam as it has evolved over time. This is a crucial point. While it is true that twentieth-century scripturalism was to some extent an ideologized response to European domination, it was also deeply rooted in the Muslim imagination. Throughout Islamic history, revivalists have urged Muslims to return to the pristine Islam of the Quran and the Sunna. Rebellion was almost always legitimated in these terms, with rulers condemned for having deviated from this scriptural Islam—as in the case of Ibn Tumart's revolt against the Almoravids in the twelfth century. (In the final analysis, revolt had to be justified this way.) Like similar revivalist movements elsewhere, Salafi reformism was to some extent an invented tradition (Hobsbawm and Ranger 1983), but it was also firmly rooted in a real one.

GELLNER'S PENDULUM SWING MODEL OF POPULAR AND ORTHODOX ISLAM

The best-known model of the relation between the folk and great traditions of Moroccan Islam is that of Ernest Gellner, who draws heavily on Hume's contention that "men have a natural tendency to rise from idolatry to theism, and to sink again from theism into idolatry" (Hume [1757] 1976, 57). Gellner sees Moroccan Islam as having oscillated throughout history between the puritanical scripturalist religion of the literate urban bourgeoisie and the ritualistic anthropolatrous religion of the illiterate rural tribes (1969, 7–8). He characterizes urban orthodox Islam as "Protestant" and the rural popular religion as "Catholic" (ibid., 11).

Orthodoxy, says Gellner, revolved around holy scripture and thus entailed literacy. It was strictly monotheistic and egalitarian (among believers). It emphasized moderation and sobriety and abstention from ritual excesses (1969, 7). In this form of Islam, there were no

intermediaries between the believer and God. The more anthropolatrous, popular Islam stressed hierarchy and mediation between
the believer and God. The mediators were Sufi shaykhs, saints, and
shurafa. This form of Islam was characterized by ritual indulgence
in contrast to the puritanism of urban orthodoxy (ibid.).

Gellner concedes that the popular religion was not solely a rural
phenomenon. It also existed among the urban poor. But whereas
among the tribes it served as a kind of social lubricant, making
possible the resolution of conflicts, in the cities it provided "ecstatic
consolation" for the poor (1981, 54). Orthodox Islam, however,
served to ratify the "style of life" of the urban bourgeoisie (1969, 8).
This aspect of Gellner's model appears to have been inspired by
Max Weber (see Weber 1963, 94–108).

Gellner contends that the tribes of Morocco's mountains and
deserts would periodically revolt against the reigning dynasty in the
name of the puritanical Islam normally associated with the towns
(1969, 4). This was possible because the ideals of urban orthodoxy
were always present among the rural tribes, although they were
subordinate to the norms of popular belief (ibid., 9-10). Once successful, the puritanical revivalist movements would eventually revert
back to the anthropolatrous popular religion, thus rendering them
vulnerable to future puritanical revolts. Gellner sees this pendulum
swing as having been unhinged by "modernity" (1984, 56). The
modern state monopolized violence, whereas the precolonial one
did not. So the tribes atrophied, as did the saints who formerly
served to mediate their conflicts (ibid.).

Gellner is right to point out that puritanical reformist movements
did periodically emerge to advocate a return to the pristine Islam of
the Quran and the Sunna—Ibn Yasin's Almoravids and Ibn Tumart's
Almohads being the most obvious examples. But Gellner overlooks
the fact that no puritanical reformist movements have managed to
seize and retain control of the Moroccan state since the Almohads
did so in the middle of the twelfth century. Many have tried, but
none has succeeded.

More important, Gellner attempts to impose the relation between
popular and orthodox Islam that he observed in the 1950s and

1960s on the whole of Moroccan history. On the basis of his fieldwork among the High Atlas Berbers, he sees Sufism as a distinctive component of popular religion (1981, 54), whereas it actually pervaded both popular and orthodox Islam at least from the fifteenth century through the first decades of the twentieth. Most of the ulama Gellner sees as embodying orthodoxy were themselves Sufi mystics (al-Jabiri 1988, 51–52; Laroui 1977b, 132, 224). Al-Yusi, 'Abd al-Slam Guessous, and al-Kattani were all Sufis as well as ulama, as were most of the men who have exemplified the myth of the righteous man of God in Moroccan history. Such men generally belonged to relatively orthodox Sufi orders in which knowledge of God's laws and mystical knowledge were considered complementary rather than antithetical (al-Yusi 1981, 2:355). There were, of course, more popular and less orthodox orders that most ulama condemned (Crapanzano 1973).

It is true that some ulama did periodically criticize Sufism in general (al-Wazzani 1942, 111–14). The theme of the righteous saint-cum-Sufi being persecuted by sycophantic "court ulama" who do not understand the mystical truths of Islam is in fact a leitmotif of the myth of the righteous man of God. So the tension between orthodoxy and Sufism that Gellner describes did exist. But the Sufis persecuted by ulama were typically renowned ulama themselves —and often from the same urban elite as their persecutors (see Cornell 1989). Gellner's model works as an ideal-type conception of a recurrent tension in Islamic theology but not as a model of its social manifestations.[1]

Anthropologists, because of their neglect of Moroccan historiography, often believe that the late twentieth-century distinction between popular and orthodox Islam existed throughout Moroccan history. That is not the case. In the seventeenth century, al-Yusi, who studied at the Nasiri zawiya in Tamgrut, condemned the veneration of ostensibly sacred objects and charlatans posing as saints (1981, 1:100, 102, 105). Yet he himself regularly visited saints' tombs all his life (al-'Alawi al-Madghari 1989, 137). He stressed that seeking to obtain baraka from the tombs of true saints, so long as one understood their role in Islam, was perfectly all right (1981, 1:102).

That al-Yusi felt obliged to defend the legitimacy of the visitation of saints demonstrates that he was aware that this practice had been criticized ever since the ninth century by some ulama, notably those associated with the Hanbali school (Gibb and Kramers 1953, 20–21, 151–52, 618–21). Outright condemnation of the veneration of saints, however, was extremely rare in Morocco until the 1920s. In the late nineteenth and early twentieth century, the overwhelming majority of Morocco's ulama continued to assume that the veneration of saints was an integral part of Islam (al-Fasi 1931, 2:84; al-Nasiri 8:122).

There has indeed always been a distinction between popular and orthodox Islam in Morocco—as there inevitably is in all world religions encompassing people of various social strata. Yet learned scholars as well as illiterate peasants have always prayed the same prayers every day of their lives. While there is much that is different in the ways they have interpreted their religion, there is also much that is the same. Anthropologists have often overlooked this point because of their neglect of Islam's basic rituals (Tapper and Tapper 1987). Moreover, Islam's great and folk traditions were even more intertwined in the past than they are in the late twentieth century. This becomes obvious when one examines the principal attempts at Islamic reform from the late eighteenth through the early twentieth century.

FORERUNNERS OF TWENTIETH-CENTURY REFORMISM

In sketching the history of Islamic reformism in Morocco, one could begin with the revivalism of the Almoravids in the eleventh century and that of the Almohads in the twelfth. But modern reformism is usually thought of as beginning with the Sultan Sidi Muhammad bin 'Abd Allah, who reigned from 1757 to 1790. Sidi Muhammad insisted on the strict application of Islamic law and the elimination of heretical innovations in both town and country. He endorsed the Hanbali school's insistence on the need for belief in the literal text of the Quran and the Sunna (al-Nasiri 8:68).

Like al-Yusi, Sidi Muhammad condemned charlatans who used

Sufism to exploit the gullible masses and extremist Sufis (*ghulat al-sufiyya*) who did not conform to Islamic law. He was especially critical of the philosophical mysticism favored by some ulama, but he was himself a member of the Nasiriyya Sufi order and regularly visited saints' tombs and sent gifts to them. His attempts at reform did not constitute a full-fledged critique of Sufism or the veneration of saints in general (Harrak 1989).

Sidi Muhammad bin 'Abd Allah's son Mulay Sulayman, who reigned from 1792 to 1822, is also often cited as a forerunner of twentieth-century reformism. He, too, condemned heretical innovations (*bida'*) and stressed the need to conform to the Quran and the Sunna. He criticized the popular Sufi orders and banned their festivals in honor of saints on the ground that the rhythmic dancing, clapping, and mixing of men and women at such gatherings were all contrary to the Quran and the Sunna (Abun-Nasr 1963, 94–95; Brignon et al. 1967, 269; al-Nasiri 8:123).

Mulay Sulayman was influenced by the puritanical revivalism of the Wahhabis, who controlled Mecca and much of Arabia in the early nineteenth century. Although more sympathetic to the Wahhabis than most of the ulama of his time, Mulay Sulayman insisted that visiting the shrines of saints to ask for their intercession was not only permitted but recommended by Islamic law—so long as people remembered that saints could not grant requests themselves but could only ask God to do so. Since ordinary Muslims with little education did not understand these things, said the sultan, the Wahhabis were right to restrict access to saints' tombs. But Mulay Sulayman never banned the visitation of saints in Morocco. Rather, he specified the proper rules concerning such practices. Although he condemned many aspects of popular Sufism (including the use of musical instruments), he himself belonged to the relatively orthodox Sufi order of the Nasiriyya—as had his father. Thus, Mulay Sulayman's reformism was considerably less radical than that of the Wahhabis or of Morocco's twentieth-century Salafi reformists. Yet even his relatively moderate demands for a return to the Islam of the Prophet disturbed many Moroccan ulama (El Mansour 1990, 137–43, 161; al-Nasiri 8:123).

The *Salafiyya* reformist movement emerged in Egypt in the late nineteenth century and then spread to the rest of the Islamic world, including Morocco (Voll 1982). It was introduced to Morocco in the late nineteenth century, initially by the scholar 'Abd Allah bin Idris al-Sanusi (d. 1931). Al-Sanusi, who was apparently unrelated to the famous Sanusis of Cyrenaica, made the pilgrimage to Mecca in the 1870s (al-Fasi 1931, 2:81–82, 84). He may have absorbed some of the new reformist ideas emerging at this time in Egypt. Upon his return to Morocco, the sultan Hassan I gave al-Sanusi a house and appointed him to the council of ulama that met regularly in Fez to discuss the *Sahih* of al-Bukhari, a famous collection of hadiths (al-Fasi 1931, 2:84). Such were the benefits of being in a sultan's good graces. During the course of discussing the *Sahih* of al-Bukhari with his fellow ulama, al-Sanusi angered many of them by his insistence on conformity to the literal text of the Quran and the Sunna without recourse to later interpretations. Some ulama even accused al-Sanusi of denying sainthood and miracles (*al-wilaya wa'l-karamat*) (ibid.). This was a very serious accusation in the eyes of most late nineteenth-century Moroccan ulama, who bore little resemblance to the Wahhabi-like ulama imagined by Gellner.

Al-Sanusi's life illustrates once again the political docility of most ulama, including those with Salafi proclivities. After living many years in Damascus and Istanbul, al-Sanusi returned to Morocco after Mulay 'Abd al-'Aziz became sultan in 1894. The new sultan was as generous to him as his father Hassan I had been. He helped al-Sanusi move to Tangier and continued to support him financially after he abdicated in 1908. In 1910–11, al-Sanusi traveled with Mulay 'Abd al-'Aziz (at the latter's expense) to Egypt and Syria (al-Fasi 1931, 2:85). He does not seem to have had any qualms about accepting gifts from the sultan deposed for "selling the land of Islam to the infidels."

The guardians of Islamic law did not enjoy seeing unbelievers control the Islamic world—and their country in particular. Except for unusual men like Sidi Muhammad bin 'Abd al-Kabir al-Kattani, however, they generally did nothing to stop the European onslaught. This tendency, as well as the inadequacy of the maraboutic-scripturalist dichotomy with respect to early twentieth-century Morocco, is exemplified by the life and work of Sidi Muhammad bin Ja'far al-Kattani, the patrilateral cousin of Sidi Muhammad bin 'Abd al-Kabir.

THE MARABOUTIC SCRIPTURALISM OF SIDI MUHAMMAD BIN JA'FAR AL-KATTANI (D. 1927)

Unlike his famous cousin Sidi Muhammad bin 'Abd al-Kabir, Sidi Muhammad bin Ja'far al-Kattani is known mainly for his writings rather than for his actions. More specifically, he is best known for two of his books: *Salwat al-anfas* (Solace of the Souls), which was published in 1899, and *Nasihat ahl al-Islam* (Frank Counsel to the People of Islam), which was first published in 1908. The first of these works celebrates the saints, Sufis, shurafa, and ulama buried in Fez. The second calls for a return to the pristine Islam of the Prophet. Like most ulama of his day, Sidi Muhammad bin Ja'far al-Kattani saw no contradiction between the two.

The full title of *Salwat al-anfas* is *Salwat al-anfas wa muhadathat al-akyas bi-man uqbira min al-ulama wa'l-sulaha' bi-Fas*, or "The Solace of the souls and discourses of the fine ulama and saints buried in Fez."[2] Most of the saints al-Kattani writes about were also ulama in their lifetime, as is true of most Moroccan saints (Lévi-Provençal 1922, 383). Al-Yusi's case is typical in this respect. *Salwat al-anfas* is in effect an excellent ethnographic description of the elite's veneration of saints, Sufis, and shurafa in late nineteenth-century Fez (Laroui 1977b, 109–11). Speaking of the saints, al-Kattani declares: "without them, the sky would not give forth rain, the earth would not produce plants, and misfortune would pour down upon the people of the world" (1899, 1:25; Abun-Nasr 1965, 5–6). Such was the Protestantism of Morocco's precolonial urban elite.

Very few ulama of the late twentieth century would still speak of saints as Muhammad bin Ja'far al-Kattani did in 1899. Yet much of al-Kattani's *Nasihat ahl al-Islam*, has a decidedly modern ring to it—at least in the sense that much of its rhetoric and virtually all of its reasoning remain commonplace among some Salafi reformists and

most fundamentalists. This text is, in fact, a milestone in the evolution of the Islam of the precolonial ulama toward later, more ideological forms of reformism and fundamentalism. Its basic argument
is that God enabled the first Muslims, "the righteous ancestors"
(al-salaf al-salih), to thrive and conquer much of the world because
they conformed to his laws. Then the believers deviated from the
laws of God. That is why the unbelievers of Europe were able to
subjugate them. If they would return to the straight path, they would
once again thrive and God would liberate them from the domination of the infidels and eliminate all social injustice. This argument
has been the central theme of twentieth-century reformism and
fundamentalism. It remains as persuasive to some Moroccans in
the late twentieth century as it did when al-Kattani's Nasiha was first
published, which is undoubtedly why it was reprinted in an inexpen-
sive commercial edition in 1989. (Page references in the following
section refer to this 1989 reprint unless other sources are indicated.)

Al-Kattani writes at the beginning of his book that it is intended
to explain the reasons for the suffering of the Muslims at the hands
of "the enemies of God and his Prophet" (the Europeans) and
thereby guide the believers to deliverance (p. 83). He notes that the
idea of nasiha (frank counsel) is a classical one in Islam, citing the
hadith, "he who advises you frankly loves you and he who flatters
you deceives you" (p. 87). Al-Kattani stresses that the ulama are the
guardians of Islamic law, so rulers must consult them and listen to
them (pp. 85–87). He says his text is actually aimed primarily at the
rulers of the Islamic world. If they do not implement it, then "they
will be sinning against and cheating God on high as well as their
subjects" (p. 147). Al-Kattani's son Idris notes that the book was
actually originally intended primarily for Morocco's Mulay ʿAbd
al-ʿAziz, even though it was not printed until after he had been
overthrown by ʿAbd al-Hafidh in 1908 (I. al-Kattani 1989, 28–29).

Speaking of the Europeans' subjugation of the Islamic world,
al-Kattani writes: "They, may God destroy them, have gone to great
lengths to prepare themselves. They go to the Muslim lands in
every direction. They turn toward them from every side. They see
no opportunity in Islam without seizing it. . . . There are no limits

to all this, so that of the Islamic umma that numbers some 300 million people, only about a third now remains [in 1908] free and independent" (p. 88). Referring specifically to Morocco, al-Kattani notes that it was once great and powerful but has now fallen prey to the infidels who are "determined to extinguish the light of Islam" ('azimin 'ala itfa' nur al-Islam) (p. 89). Given the numerical strength of the Muslims in Morocco and elsewhere, and given the ready availability of money, horses, and weapons with which to fight, al-Kattani asks "how can we bear the humiliation and disgrace of submitting to the slaves of the cross" (ibid.)? (The phrase 'ibad al-salib could also be translated as "worshipers of the cross.")

Al-Kattani condemns the Muslims (and especially Muslim rulers) for failing to prepare for holy war against the infidels who are conquering the Islamic world: "Satan the accursed has deafened our ears and blinded our eyes. He has led us astray. He has enticed us and caused us to neglect our duty to prepare ourselves with the utmost zeal. So fear and respect have been erased from the hearts of the enemy" (p. 124). Like most of al-Kattani's text, this passage is full of Quranic imagery (see Quran 2:18). Al-Kattani points out that God could, of course, easily defeat the unbelievers if he wanted to, but he uses them to test the believers' faith (p. 126). This is as classic a theme in Islam as it is in the other monotheistic religions (Munson 1988a, 12–14).

Al-Kattani argues that the neglect of jihad (holy war) has led to the humiliation of the Muslims:

Because of this you see that the Muslims have become contemptible after having been mighty, poor after having been rich, fighting each other after having fought the infidels altogether, fragmented after having been united. The blessings [al-barakat] have dwindled and the good things of the earth have disappeared. Shame has vanished and hypocrisy is everywhere. The rulers oppress and the wicked prevail. Affliction has descended upon us. Disasters, calamities, and suffering are great. The enemies have become insolent and many are the Muslims who have become their captives. Verily, there is neither power nor strength but through God [la hawla wa la quwata ila billah]. We belong to God and to God shall we return. (p. 129)

Al-Kattani laments the fact that Muslims (and especially rulers) have become friendly with the infidels and dependent on their advice and aid (p. 165). In some countries, he says, unbelievers have even been appointed to rule over Muslim subjects (p. 180). All this is contrary to God's law and absolutely forbidden (pp. 165–81).

God has allowed the Christians to subjugate the Muslims, says al-Kattani, because the latter have embraced the customs, ideas, and laws of the former (p. 191). Al-Kattani sees this as apostasy and the repudiation of the law of Islam (ibid.). He considers the European concept of freedom to be among the most noxious of the infidel concepts to have penetrated the Islamic world:

> Among the totality of these destructive precepts and inane ideas is what they call freedom [al-hurriyya], by which they mean that people can embrace whatever religion or doctrine they want, and do whatever they please without any restrictions from anyone, male or female. There is thus nothing to stop a man from converting from Islam to Christianity, or from adopting the doctrines of the Mu'tazala or the Qadariyya, or from abandoning prayer, fasting, or the other duties of the religion of Muhammad, or from committing adultery or the act of Lot, or from earning interest and other forbidden things. It is obvious that this implies the abrogation of the law of Muhammad, indeed its absolute negation. (p. 191)

Al-Kattani pursues his criticism of the infidel conception of freedom with respect to the idea that Muslims, Jews, Christians, and believers in other religions are all equal. He contends that the Europeans' goal in disseminating such notions is "the rejection of the glory and power of Islam" (p. 192).

During the course of reviling Muslims who have adopted European customs and laws, al-Kattani alludes to the distinction between "the rule of God and the rule of ignorance" (hukm Allah wa hukm al-jahiliyya) (p. 198). This distinction, like much of what al-Kattani has to say in Nasihat ahl al-Islam, later became commonplace in the fundamentalist literature of the twentieth century (Sivan 1985, 22–27). The term jahiliyya can mean ignorance in general, but is usually understood to refer to the "heathen" period preceding the revelation of the Quran. Al-Kattani sees those Muslims who accept any form of government not based on the word of God as being like the heathen polytheists of pre-Islamic Mecca. More frequently, however, he simply stresses that such Muslims are apostates—except in cases where they have no choice (p. 198).

Al-Kattani's contends that another reason for the weakness of the Muslims is the prevalence of unjust and tyrannical governments in the Islamic world (pp. 205–13). He declares that "injustice brings ruin and justice brings prosperity" (p. 205). God punishes those who rule unjustly and tyrannically both in this world and in the hereafter (p. 206). The subjugation and humiliation of oppressive Muslim rulers by the infidels of Europe are simply reflections of God's wrath (p. 211).

Three categories of Muslims bear the primary responsibility for effecting the revival of Islam: the rulers, the ulama, and the shurafa (p. 260). Rulers must be just. This entails caring for the poor and defenseless, implementing God's laws, and consulting the ulama to ensure that all governmental policies conform to these laws (pp. 260–65). A ruler who does not consult the ulama does not deserve to remain in power (p. 263). The ulama are the heirs of the prophets and the guardians of the religion who must serve as guides for all Muslims (pp. 265–68). All of this, of course, is familiar.

Al-Kattani, from one of the most venerated sharifian families in Morocco, stresses that the shurafa are the natural leaders of the Islamic world. The Prophet ordered all Muslims "to follow, cling to, and emulate them" (p. 269). Al-Kattani also endorses the traditional hierocratic idea that obedience to a ruler is tantamount to obedience to God (p. 260). He does not mention the idea that rulers who violate the laws of God should be deposed, though he does say that rulers who do not consult the ulama do not deserve to rule (p. 63).

Al-Kattani notes that the end of time may be near, in which case nothing can save the Muslims. If that is not the case, he hopes that his advice will benefit those "whom God seeks to purify from impurity" (man arada Allah tathirahum min al-arjas) (p. 269). He concludes by praying for God's help and the Prophet's intercession (p. 270).

Nasihat ahl al-Islam is, in many respects, a classical example of the nasiha tradition, in which the righteous scholar reminds the ruler of his duty to implement the laws of God. The book is reminiscent of al-Yusi's epistle to Mulay Isma'il—although al-Kattani never attacks Mulay 'Abd al-'Aziz as directly as al-Yusi attacked Mulay Isma'il. Despite his emphasis on the need for conformity to the Quran and the Sunna, al-Kattani never criticizes Sufism or the veneration of saints. His references to the Prophet's intercession and the duty to obey rulers and follow, cling to, and emulate the shurafa (pp. 269–70) are a far cry from the Protestant and unmediated Islam depicted as orthodox by anthropologists and later Salafi reformists like 'Allal al-Fassi. For al-Kattani, as for al-Yusi, *maraboutism* and *scripturalism* were intertwined. He was in contact with Salafis like Shakib Arslan and Muhammad Rashid Rida (M. I. al-Kattani 1989, 12), yet he believed that without the saints there would be no rain.

Later Salafis like 'Allal al-Fassi would ideologize and westernize Islam to a much greater degree than did al-Kattani in the *Nasiha*. As mentioned, al-Fassi, who was the most influential Salafi reformist in Morocco from the late 1930s through the early 1970s, condemned sacred kingship, "feudalism," and "the class system" (1963, 206). He said Islam was the first religion to proclaim the equality of men and women (1979 [1952], 158), and he said Muslims had to liberate themselves from "the mentality of the hypocritical class of the bourgeoisie" (al-Kababi 1989, 57). Al-Kattani would have found most of this either unintelligible or heretical.

In many respects, al-Kattani, who like most ulama of early twentieth-century Morocco was a Sufi, resembled al-Yusi more than al-Fassi. But the world in which al-Kattani wrote the *Nasiha* was not that in which al-Yusi wrote his epistle to Mulay Isma'il. From beginning to end, the *Nasiha* is an Islamic response to European domination. Al-Yusi, too, had exhorted Mulay Isma'il to drive the unbelievers from Morocco's ports. Yet there was a relative parity in Morocco's relations with European powers in the seventeenth century that no longer existed in al-Kattani's day. By the late nineteenth century, Morocco and the rest of the Islamic world were at the mercy of industrialized Europe. The Muslims were weak and poor, the unbelievers rich and powerful. Al-Yusi could not have imagined Muslims imitating the customs of the infidels, whereas al-Kattani fulminates constantly against such imitation, because by 1908 it had become commonplace. His book represents a traditional response to this new situation, a response that echoed what some Moroccan ulama had been saying for decades (Brown 1972, 136–39; Laroui 1977b, 320–33).

The Nasiha resembles al-Yusi's epistle in that its language is relatively simple and concrete—despite the endless citations of Quranic verses and hadiths. Unlike much of what Moroccan ulama wrote (and write), the Nasiha was intended to reach a broad audience rather than a handful of scholars. Except for his cousin Muhammad bin ʿAbd al-Kabir, very few ulama of Muhammad bin Jaʿfar al-Kattani's time articulated the fears and dreams of Morocco's Muslims as clearly as he did in Nasihat ahl al-Islam. It is not surprising that it became the most influential of al-Kattani's many writings (Abdulrazak 1990, 233).

This brings up another distinctive feature of Muhammd bin Jaʿfar al-Kattani's work as opposed to earlier works like al-Yusi's epistle to Mulay Ismaʿil. The Nasiha was a printed book rather than a manuscript laboriously copied by hand. To be sure, it was printed lithographically rather than by movable type. But whereas no more than a few dozen copies of al-Yusi's text may have existed during its author's lifetime (though his epistles were often read aloud to groups of Sufis), some six hundred copies of the Nasiha were printed during al-Kattani's.[3] Although most Moroccans were illiterate and never read the book, it was unquestionably one of the most widely read and discussed texts of early twentieth-century Morocco. It was used, for example, along with copies of al-Afghani's newspaper al-ʿUrwa al-wuthqa, to teach the true spirit of Islam to the Rifis of northern Morocco during their war against Spain from 1921 to 1926. Muhammad bin ʿAbd al-Karim al-Khattabi, the leader of the Rifi resistance, had studied with Muhammad bin Jaʿfar al-Kattani at al-Qarawiyyin and continued to correspond with him throughout the Rifian war (M. I. al-Kattani 1989, 13; cf. Pennell 1986).

Despite his eloquent exhortations about the need to wage jihad against the infidel imperialists, Sidi Muhammad bin Jaʿfar al-Kattani never did so himself. He tended to flee rather than fight. In 1907, he fled to the Arabian city of Madina, where the Prophet is buried, because he feared that the French would soon occupy Morocco (M. I. al-Kattani 1989, 9). It was in Madina that he wrote the Nasiha (I. al-Kattani 1989, 28). He returned to Morocco after Mulay 'Abd al-'Aziz was overthrown by Mulay 'Abd al-Hafidh in 1908. 'Abd al-Hafidh sent two horsemen to invite him to the palace upon his arrival in Fez, but because of his desire to avoid contact with kings and other rulers, Muhammad bin Ja'far al-Kattani allegedly told the sultan's men that he would visit Mulay 'Abd al-Hafidh at another time "if God willed" (ibid., 33). We have already seen that the idea that one should keep one's distance from rulers was a classic motif of the literature on the righteous scholar-cum-Sufi shaykh (Cornell 1989, 651–52; al-Yusi 1981, 1:155).

In the spring of 1909, Mulay 'Abd al-Hafidh had Muhammad bin Ja'far al-Kattani's cousin Muhammad bin 'Abd al-Kabir flogged to death. This was apparently enough to overcome Sidi Muhammad bin Ja'far's aversion to kings. He went to the sultan's palace and convinced him to free his remaining relatives. 'Abd al-Hafidh asked the renowned scholar to participate in the daily scholarly discussions of hadiths that he sponsored at the palace. At first al-Kattani declined, but then agreed to attend once a week (I. al-Kattani 1989, 33–35).

In August 1909, the sultan asked Muhammad bin Ja'far to compile a comprehensive guide to the principal books of hadiths. Although 'Abd al-Hafidh had his cousin killed a few months earlier and had long ago given up trying to fight the French, the author of Nasihat ahl al-Islam complied with the sultan's request. He spent about fifteen days writing a textbook on the hadith literature that is reportedly still used by Islamic universities in India and Pakistan (I. al-Kattani 1989, 35–36).

Yet al-Kattani became increasingly disturbed by the growing French influence in Moroccan affairs and felt obliged to once again leave the country. He obtained the sultan's permission to return to Madina in 1910. 'Abd al-Hafidh provided him and his family with the supplies and letters they would need to make the trip (ibid., 37). Many other prominent and wealthy Moroccan families also fled to Arabia and other regions of the Ottoman Empire in the years immediately preceding and following the imposition of the French protectorate on Morocco in 1912. This reflected the belief that if Muslims could not prevent the occupation of their land by unbelievers, they should emigrate to an independent Muslim land where the laws of God were still in force (M. I. al-Kattani 1989, 10–12; Laroui 1977b, 320; al-Wazzani 1942, 61).

After abdicating in August 1912, Mulay ʿAbd al-Hafidh visited al-Kattani in Madina. At first, the shaykh greeted him coldly, but seeing that the former sultan "was like a drowning man seeking rescue," he took pity on him and told him to go to the tomb of the Prophet Muhammad and "repent before God for all that you have done" (I. al-Kattani 1989, 38). Mulay ʿAbd al-Hafidh did as he was told. On 23 October 1913, the former sultan of Morocco wrote a bayʿa to al-Kattani vowing to be his disciple in Sufism: "I call upon God and his Prophet, may God bless him and grant him peace, to witness that I have imposed upon myself the bayʿa of my shaykh and teacher, the exalted sharif, the exemplary scholar, Sidi Muhammad bin Jaʿfar, a bayʿa for which I thank God. I take him as intermediary [wasita] between me and my Lord, may he be exalted and may his gifts be glorified. I take upon myself the duty to obey him in all that he commands and all that he forbids" (ibid., 40). ʿAbd al-Hafidh thus used the idea of the bayʿa, normally thought of in terms of the oath of allegiance sworn to a new sultan, to represent the inversion of his relationship to Sidi Muhammad bin Jaʿfar. He was now the ruled rather than the ruler. (No trace of the contractual caliphate here.) Al-Kattani answered by saying that "the real bayʿa is to God and his Prophet, our Lord Muhammad, may God bless him and grant him peace" (ibid., 41). But he accepted ʿAbd al-Hafidh as his disciple.

The sultan who had signed the Treaty of Fez, which turned Morocco into a French protectorate in March 1912, was now, slightly more than a year later, the student and disciple (murid) of the shaykh who had equated acceptance of infidel rule with apostasy. As for the murder of Sidi Muhammad bin ʿAbd al-Kabir al-Kattani, Sidi Muhammad bin Jaʿfar carefully avoided the subject. But he and the former sultan often discussed the latter's role in handing Morocco over to the French. ʿAbd al-Hafidh insisted that it was not his fault (ibid., 44).

Mulay ʿAbd al-Hafidh's relationship with Sidi Muhammad bin Jaʿfar al-Kattani is significant in several respects. As noted in the last chapter, ʿAllal al-Fassi has depicted the conflict between the two men in terms of the tension between reformism versus maraboutism (al-Fasi 1948, 133). One also encounters this interpretation in Western sources (Julien 1978, 79–80). We have seen that ʿAbd al-Hafidh did indeed argue with Sidi Muhammad bin ʿAbd al-Kabir about some Sufi practices (al-Kattani 1962, 215). He even wrote a short book condemning the Tijaniyya Sufi order for its heretical innovations (al-Fasi 1948, 133). His relation to Sidi Muhammad bin Jaʿfar after his abdication, however, demonstrates that he was himself a devout Sufi in 1913. Given his close ties to Sidi Muhammad bin Jaʿfar al-Kattani even before his abdication, it would seem that ʿAbd al-Hafidh, like most ulama of his day, never opposed Sufism per se, only its less orthodox manifestations.

The relationship between Mulay ʿAbd al-Hafidh and Sidi Muhammad bin Jaʿfar al-Kattani is also significant in that it exemplifies the contradiction between the shaykh's fiery rhetoric and the passivity of his own political behavior. The closest he ever came to defying a sultan was when he declined ʿAbd al-Hafidh's invitation to visit the palace upon his return to Fez in 1908. His relatives take great pride in citing the French newspaper that called Muhammad bin Jaʿfar al-Kattani "France's greatest enemy in Morocco" when he died in 1927 (M. I. al-Kattani 1989, 13). But the fact is that this Kattani did nothing to resist the French conquest of Morocco other than put words on paper. Some Moroccans even told the French orientalist Evariste Lévi-Provençal that Sidi Muhammad bin Jaʿfar al-Kattani received a pension from the French High Commissioner in Syria, where he lived from 1919 to 1926 (ibid., 12,15; Lévi-Provençal 1922, 380; al-Wazzani 1942, 63). Whether or not this is true, al-Kattani's political behavior was as passive as that of most of his fellow ulama. He may have resembled his cousin Sidi Muhammad bin ʿAbd al-Kabir al-Kattani in some of what he said, but not in what he did.

AL-DUKKALI, THE DOCILE SALAFI (1878–1937)

The Kattani cousins are rarely called Salafis, despite their call for a return to the Islam of al-salaf al-salih (the righteous ancestors). They were Sufi shaykhs, whereas the term Salafi is usually applied to reformists hostile to Sufism. But even the two men commonly referred to as the most influential Moroccan Salafis of the early twentieth century, Abu Shu'ayb al-Dukkali (1878–1937) and his student Muhammad bin al-'Arbi al-'Alawi (1880–1964), were themselves Sufis early in their lives (al-Fasi 1931, 2:142; al-Jundi 1965, 32). Both these men played a decisive role in shaping the generation of Moroccans that led the Moroccan nationalist movement. Although they had similar conceptions of Islam, they ultimately played very different political roles: al-Dukkali epitomizing the docile scholar, al-'Alawi the righteous and heroic one—at least in the last decades of his long life.

Al-Dukkali's background demonstrates, once again, that Gellner's distinction between the Protestant orthodoxy of the urban ulama and the anthropolatrous Sufism of rural tribesmen is anachronistic. Al-Dukkali was born and raised in a village of the tribe of al-Dukkala (south of Casablanca), but most of the men of his family were ulama (al-Fasi 1931, 2:142). Al-Dukkali himself, the archetypal Salafi critic of popular Sufism, was a member of the Darqawi Sufi order, to which the men of his family had belonged for generations (ibid.; Cagne 1988, 358). For decades he taught the principles of Salafi Islam in the zawiya of the Nasiri Sufi order in Rabat (al-Jirari 1976, 14; Bargash 1989, 154, 162).

Al-Dukkali may well have eventually quit the Darqawi order and may have preached in the Nasiri zawiya only for lack of an alternative location, for he did sometimes seem to criticize the Sufi orders in general. He once said that the popular Sufi order of the Hamadsha, notorious for the way its adherents slashed their heads while in a trance, was the best of all the orders. When asked how he could make such an incredible statement, al-Dukkali said, "Because the head that is without knowledge and propriety deserves to be broken by its possessor" (Bargash 1989, 154).

The fact remains, however, that al-Dukkali's Salafi reformism was in many respects similar to the orthodoxy embodied by the Darqawi, Nasiri, and Kattani orders—as opposed to the more popular orders like the Hamadsha and the 'Isawa. One thinks, for example, of the famous story about al-Dukkali's having a sacred tree cut down because women would hang amulets, hairs, and pieces of cloth on its branches in the hope that it would grant their wishes (al-Jirari 1976, 30). The destruction of such trees is a classical theme in Islam —sometimes associated with the myth of the righteous man of God. Al-Yusi had praised a Sufi shaykh for having one cut down in the seventeenth century, noting that the Prophet's companions had sought to thwart the worship of the tree under which the first oath of allegiance to Muhammad had been sworn (al-Yusi 1982, 1:99– 101). Al-Dukkali, however, does seem to have gone further in his condemnation of popular Islam than did orthodox Sufis like al-Yusi. It is hard to know just how far he went in this respect, because he conveyed his ideas primarily through teaching rather than writing. When asked why he did not write, he answered, "Moroccans do not read" (Bargash 1989, 175).

As for his political role, the historical al-Dukkali differed from the heroic al-Dukkali of nationalist hagiography (al-Jirari 1976, 83). After studying at al-Azhar University in Cairo and working for about eight years as an scholar in the service of the Sharif of Mecca, al-Dukkali returned to Morocco in 1907, around the time of 'Abd al-Hafidh's revolt (al-Fasi 1931, 2:143). His lectures on the need to return to the Quran and the Sunna attracted large and enthusiastic audiences at al-Qarawiyyin—as well as the new sultan's support. Mulay 'Abd al-Hafidh bestowed money, a house, and eventually a judgeship on al-Dukkali, who stressed the need to avoid a conflict with the French that the Moroccans could not win (ibid.; al-Susi 1983, 47, 64, 86–87; Cagne 1988, 355). When the French forced Mulay 'Abd al-Hafidh to sign a treaty transforming Morocco into a French protectorate in 1912, al-Dukkali did not resign. He was still a judge in Marrakesh when the rebel army of Ahmad al-Hiba entered this city in August 1912 (al-Susi 1960, 148).

THE SCHOLAR AND THE MAHDI

Al-Hiba was the last of Morocco's great mahdis. It is not clear to what extent he actually claimed to be the Muslim messiah, but he was certainly viewed as such by some of his followers (ibid., 123). A sharif, a Sufi, and the son of the famous Saharan shaykh Ma' al-'Aynayn, al-Hiba attracted widespread popular support not only by leading a holy war against the French, but also by saying he would eliminate the powerful qaids who had traditionally oppressed the poor (ibid., 127, 130). Renowned for his puritanism, people said that he would cut off the heads of those who did not pray (ibid., 123). At the same time, it was said that his great baraka enabled him to perform miracles (ibid., 126–28, 150). He was reported to have made the soil of the Sus Valley fertile after it had been barren for years. Tribes that opposed him were said to be afflicted by frogs and lice (Ibn Ibrahim 2:475). It was also said that the cannonballs of his enemies became watermelons, that all the ammunition and provisions of a qaid who had refused to support him suddenly vanished, and that he had a sack of barley that was never empty no matter how many people were fed from it (Ladreit de LaCharrière 1912, 482). Such was the baraka of the imam who was going to drive the unbelievers from Morocco. Criers in the markets of the south warned that those who failed to join al-Hiba's holy war would burn for all eternity in the fires of hell (Ibn Ibrahim 2:474).

Al-Dukkali, who stressed the rational reformist view of Islam as well as the need to avoid wars that could not be won, obliquely criticized al-Hiba's revolt in his sermons. So the mahdi summoned the famous Salafi scholar to his palace in Marrakesh. Sitting behind a screen, al-Hiba listened as his brother and a man named Ibn 'Abd al-'Aziz interrogated al-Dukkali. 'Abd al-'Aziz said of the scholar: "He is the shaykh of Islam known in the east and the west. But he is an apostate!" (lakinahu irtadda) (ibid., 2:479). Al-Dukkali asked Ibn 'Abd al-'Aziz what legal text justified calling him an apostate. Ibn 'Abd al-'Aziz answered, "You curse the mujahidin [fighters of holy war] from the pulpits of the mosques." Al-Dukkali denied he had done this, saying that he had criticized only those mujahids "who cause the occupation of the lands of Islam," men like Bu Hmara and the leaders of the anticolonial resistance in the Chaouia and among the Bani Mtir.[4] At this point, al-Hiba emerged from behind his screen and accused al-Dukkali of trying to weaken the Muslims by saying that they could not defeat the Europeans. Then, in a more conciliatory tone, al-Hiba asked al-Dukkali to urge the leaders of the tribes of al-Dukkala and 'Abda to support him. Al-Dukkali said, "I cannot." Al-Hiba responded, "There will be no blame upon you today. May God forgive you." The interrogation was over (ibid., 2:479–80).[5]

Within the next few weeks, the French had routed al-Hiba's troops and forced them to flee south from Marrakesh. When urged to submit to the protectorate regime by Sidi Muhammad bin 'Abd al-Kabir al-Kattani's brother 'Abd al-Hayy, al-Hiba answered: "I seek only to call you to deliverance and you call me to the fires of hell" (al-Susi 1960, 180). He asserted that those who asked him to submit to the French-controlled government of Sultan Mulay Yusif were asking him to deny God and become an infidel (tad'uni li-akfira billah) (ibid.). Pursued relentlessly by the French and their Moroccan agents in southern Morocco, most of al-Hiba's men did submit, many of them becoming wealthy qaids under the protectorate. But al-Hiba and a handful of followers continued to resist in the far south, surviving on the food brought by local villagers. In 1919, al-Hiba died of illness in the Anti-Atlas mountains, at the age of forty-five (ibid., 211–12, 242). One still hears his name mentioned with awe by old people, even in the popular quarters of northern cities like Tangier.

As for al-Dukkali, his fate was quite different. When the conquering colonial army entered Marrakesh in September 1912, he made a speech welcoming the French commander and praising France's compassion (al-Susi 1983, 96). The French responded by naming him minister of justice, a position he held until 1923 (Ibn Mansur 1979, 1:201). During World War I, while al-Hiba and other marabouts continued to wage holy war against French imperialism in the mountains and deserts, al-Dukkali—along with many other prominent Moroccan ulama—exhorted Moroccans to support the protectorate and oppose the Germans and their Ottoman allies (al-Dukkali 1914). He said that the Ottoman sultan should not be regarded as the caliph of Islam since he was not a descendant of the Prophet. Moroccans should instead obey their true caliph, the sharif Mulay Yusif—installed on his throne by the French after the abdication of Mulay 'Abd al-Hafidh in 1912 (ibid., 365). The great Salafi cited in this respect the famous hadith: "the sultan is the shadow of God on earth and it is with him that all the oppressed find refuge" (ibid.). Al-Dukkali knew that Moroccans referred to Mulay Yusif as "the sultan of the Christians" and that the Germans were assisting the various rural movements seeking to free Morocco from colonial rule (Lyautey 1953–58, 4:105; al-Susi 1960, 104, 121; al-Susi 1983, 104–5).

The contrast between the roles played by al-Dukkali and al-Hiba in the anticolonial resistance demonstrates the anachronism of the tendency to equate Salafi reformism and nationalist anticolonial resistance in the early decades of the twentieth century. By the time of World War II, there was some truth to this equation, but not at the time of World War I. Salafi ulama like al-Dukkali did, of course, resent colonial rule, and they did see the reform of Islam as the key to overcoming it. But most of them never defied the French (or the Spanish in the far north and south), and many of them, like al-Dukkali, benefited enormously from serving the French empire.

After resigning as minister of justice in 1923, al-Dukkali devoted himself to "expanding his vast properties, teaching, and spreading Salafi thought" (Ibn Mansur 1979, 1:201). The French government awarded him the Legion of Honor while Sultan Sidi Muhammad V, enthroned by the French after the death of Mulay Yusif in 1927, honored him with the Moroccan version of this medal, the *Wisam al-'Alawi* (al-Jirari 1976, 10–11). When al-Dukkali became seriously ill in the 1930s, Sultan Muhammad V brought him to live in his palace, where he died on 17 June 1937 (Ibn Mansur 1979, 1:202–3).

Such was the life of the man sometimes called "the Muhammad 'Abduh of Morocco," 'Abduh having been the principal Salafi reformer of early twentieth-century Egypt (Bargash 1989, 148). The comparison is apt insofar as both men were Salafi reformers who actively collaborated with colonial regimes. Both men exemplified the docility of the overwhelming majority of ulama. Al-Dukkali did briefly defy al-Hiba in Marrakesh, but al-Hiba was fighting to free Morocco from colonial rule. One can, of course, point out that in submitting to and serving the French, al-Dukkali, like most of his fellow ulama, was simply being realistic. Yet he does not cut an especially noble figure when compared with those men who risked imprisonment, exile, and death to fight colonialism—men like al-Dukkali's student Sidi Muhammad bin al-'Arbi al-'Alawi.

SIDI MUHAMMAD BIN AL-'ARBI AL-'ALAWI (d. 1964)

Sidi Muhammad bin al-'Arbi al-'Alawi played a pivotal role in transforming the politically passive Salafi reformism of al-Dukkali into the nationalism of younger Salafis like 'Allal al-Fassi (d. 1974). Like his teacher al-Dukkali, but unlike most of his nationalist students, al-'Alawi was born in the countryside (al-Asfi 1986, 25). Also like al-Dukkali, al-'Alawi came from a family of rural ulama and belonged to a Sufi order in his youth—the Tijaniyya (al-'Alawi 1980, 96). He was an 'Alawi sharif and related to the royal family.

In about 1899, al-'Alawi's father took him to study at al-Qarawiyyin in Fez. It was here that he first manifested the obstinacy for which he eventually became renowned. As an 'Alawi sharif, he was expected to marry a woman of sharifian ancestry. Although he was not supposed to marry a nonsharifian woman without the permission of the naqib, or head of the shurafa, he did so anyway, and the naqib therefore had him imprisoned. Mulay 'Abd al-Hafidh, who was sultan at the time, had the young scholar released as soon as he heard of the incident. Decades later, al-'Alawi convinced King Muhammad v to relax the restrictions on sharifian marriages with nonshurafa (Banani 1964, 9–10).

After the imposition of the protectorate and the abdication of 'Abd al-Hafidh in 1912, al-'Alawi briefly taught the former sultan's children in Tangier. He soon returned to Fez, however, where he was appointed a judge by the French in 1915 (al-Asfi 1986, 46). He also taught at al-Qarawiyyin and at several schools, some created by the fledgling Salafi movement after World War I, and one created by the French for the sons of the elite (Banani 1964, 10). Thus, like al-Dukkali and most other ulama who had a chance to do so, al-'Alawi spent decades in the service of the colonial regime. This was to some degree a matter of economic necessity. If the ulama did not accept government appointments—usually as judges, teachers, or notaries, they often had no way to make a living. But unlike most other ulama, al-'Alawi was outspoken in his support for the tribesmen who were waging holy war against the European imperialists in the mountains of Morocco. Indeed, he allegedly sought to join the mujahidin in the Middle Atlas and later in the Rif (al-Asfi 1986, 54–62). However, his important role in the post–World War I period was that of teacher. Through his popular lectures at al-Qarawiyyin, he instilled the ideals of a staunchly anticolonial Islamic reformism in the minds of the young scions of the elite.

Moroccan opposition to the Berber Decree of 1930 marked the convergence of Salafi reformism with modern Moroccan nationalism. (Though the latter was still in an embryonic stage.) This decree declared that Berber tribes would be subject to their customary tribal laws rather than to Islamic law. Al-'Alawi's students convinced many Moroccans that the decree was the first step toward the conversion of the Berbers to Christianity. Although the young students who led the opposition to the Berber decree were motivated by a specifically *nationalistic* resentment of what they saw as the divide-and-conquer tactics of the French, they were able to mobilize widespread support only by portraying the decree as a threat to Islam (Brown 1976, 198–206; Ghallab 1987, 1:103; Hoisington 1984, 29–73). Moroccans' sense of religious identity both transcended and suffused their still inchoate sense of belonging to a Moroccan nation.

Whereas some of al-'Alawi's students were jailed for their active participation in the protests against the Berber Decree, he simply encouraged Moroccans to oppose the law without going so far as to jeopardize his own position in the French protectorate (al-Asfi 1986, 155). At this point in his life, al-'Alawi's behavior (if not his rhetoric) was thus typical of the ulama generally. This remained true for the next fourteen years, during which al-ʿAlawi continued to serve in various positions in the colonial regime. He even became the minister of justice, the position formerly held by al-Dukkali (ibid., 71). But al-ʿAlawi's support for the Salafi-oriented nationalist movement was well known and led to his first open confrontation with the French in 1944.

During the 1930s and early 1940s, the nationalist-cum-Salafi movement had grown from a few secret societies involving a handful of young men from prominent families (mostly from Fez) to a truly national movement. Most of its leaders were still from the urban elite (Ghallab 1987, 2:283, 288–89). Some younger ulama like ʿAllal al-Fassi were active in the movement, but most were docile agents of the colonial regime. One former French administrator in Morocco has said, "The ulama, they were a big joke; the Resident General made them say whatever he wanted" (Tozy 1984, 46).

During World War II, the German occupation of Paris and the American invasion of Morocco in 1942 led many of the nationalists to believe that they could now push for independence rather than simply reforms. This was especially true in the wake of a 1943 meeting between Franklin Roosevelt and Sultan Muhammad V, which was widely interpreted as signifying American support for the nationalist struggle (Ghallab 1987, 1:218). Thus, in January 1944, nationalists associated with the new Istiqlal (Independence) party presented a manifesto to Muhammad V demanding independence. The sultan himself, who had become identified with the nationalist struggle during the past decade, had read and approved the text of the manifesto before it was made public (ibid., 1:223). Al-ʿAlawi, who had become the principal intermediary between Muhammad V and the nationalists, wholeheartedly endorsed the demand for independence. However, all but one of the sultan's other ministers caved in to French pressure and condemned it (ibid., 1:266, 323; al-Asfi 1986, 72). Even the sultan himself was forced to declare to his cabinet that "the word independence must disappear from the hearts and the mouths" (Julien 1978, 191). But al-ʿAlawi refused to submit to the French. The sixty-four-year-old scholar told the Resident General that he was sick and tired of acting "like a carnival monkey that stands when told to stand and sleeps when told to sleep" (Banani 1964, 16). He was removed from office and banished to the Tafilalt. As he was about to leave Rabat, he told a friend that he found solace in the words of the famous reformer Ibn Taymiyya (1263–1328): "If they imprison me, it will mean seclusion. If they exile me, it will mean travel. If they kill me, it will mean death as a martyr" (ibid.). After decades of docility, the righteous man of God had rebelled, not against an unjust sultan, but against a colonial regime he had always considered illegitimate. He now joined the ranks of many of his former students, men like ʿAllal al-Fassi and al-Mukhtar al-Susi, whom he had inspired to oppose colonialism decades earlier (al-Susi 1963, 2:114, 128, 226, 228).

Al-ʿAlawi was allowed to return to Rabat in 1946 and moved to Fez the same year. His immensely popular lectures at al-Qarawiyyin prompted the French general in charge of the city to warn him to avoid political issues. He refused to do so, saying that there was no distinction between religion and politics in Islam (al-Asfi 1986, 77). By the beginning of 1951, he was again exiled by the French, this time to a village in the Middle Atlas. Disturbed by the number of Moroccans who sought to visit him in this village, the French returned him to Fez, where his house was under constant surveillance (ibid., 86).

The early 1950s were a period of extreme tension between the nationalists and the French in Morocco. Exasperated by Muhammad v's increasingly obvious support for the nationalists, the Resident General Juin decided to depose him in 1953. The Pasha of Marrakesh, Tuhami al-Glawi, and the scholar-cum-Sufi ʿAbd al-Hayy al-Kattani agreed to assist the French in getting rid of the nationalist king (Lacouture and Lacouture 1958). (Al-Glawi's brother had organized the revolt of ʿAbd al-Hafidh in 1907; al-Kattani was the brother of Sidi Muhammad bin ʿAbd al-Kabir, the man ʿAbd al-Hafidh had had flogged to death in 1909.)

Whereas his brother and many other Sufi shaykhs like Ahmad al-Hiba had once led resistance to colonial rule, ʿAbd al-Hayy al-Kattani and most other prominent leaders of the Sufi orders now collaborated with the French against the sultan and the nationalist-cum-Salafi movement. The conflict between Salafism and Sufism was now widely equated with the distinction between patriotism and treason—despite the fact that many Moroccans attracted to Salafi reformism did not actively challenge the colonial order, whereas some Sufis—like Sidi Tuhami al-Wazzani—did (Benjelloun 1988, 111–18; Ghallab 1991, 271–81). Some of the most famous Salafi nationalists were themselves from prominent Sufi families, for example, ʿAllal al-Fassi, Muhammad Ibrahim al-Kattani, Muhammad Hassan al-Wazzani, and al-Mukhtar al-Susi, but many of these men were critical of the Sufi tradition with which their families had been associated for centuries (al-Fasi 1948, 139).

In early June 1953, the ulama of Fez sent a telegram to the president of France condemning the French-inspired efforts of ʿAbd al-Hayy al-Kattani and Tuhami al-Glawi to depose the sultan (Julien 1978, 288). Three hundred and eighteen ulama from several cities sent a declaration of loyalty to Muhammad v (Ghallab 1987, 2:553). Al-ʿAlawi, the most respected scholar in the country, called for a jihad to expel the colonialists from Morocco (ibid.). On 20 August 1953, however, the French forced Sidi Muhammad v out of his palace and onto a plane bound for Corsica.

The following day was the feast of sacrifice commemorating Abraham's willingness to sacrifice his son. The name of the reigning imam would be said during the collective prayers, so the French hurried to ensure that the man they had chosen to replace Muhammad v—his cousin Sidi Muhammad bin ʿArafa—would be the "legitimate" sultan before the collective prayers took place. During the night of 20 August, French policemen went to the homes of Morocco's principal ulama, ordering them to gather early the following morning to sign the bayʿa of the new sultan, which almost all of them except al-ʿAlawi did. One scholar from Marrakesh who initially refused was beaten until he changed his mind (Julien 1978, 306–10). The role of the ulama in all of this was reminiscent of their behavior in 1907–08.

The French officer who governed Fez summoned al-ʿAlawi to his office and told him, "Sultan Muhammad bin Yusif is gone." Al-ʿAlawi, by now seventy-three years old, asked, "How so?" The

Frenchman answered, "We deposed him." The scholar said, "How happy I am that you deposed him and that he did not abdicate or do anything that would hurt his reputation or the reputation of his country!" The Frenchman asked al-'Alawi what he thought of the new sultan Ibn 'Arafa. "He should be killed in accordance with our Shari'a, which says that if bay'as are made to two khalifas, the second one should be killed because he is a devil." The officer tried to induce the fiery old man to change his mind, but al-'Alawi declared: "So long as my hand is a part of me, I will not sign his bay'a. If you sever it from my arm, do with it what you wish" (Banani 1964, 17). The Frenchman warned him that he would be imprisoned if he did not sign. Al-'Alawi responded that it would not be the first time his faith had been tested by God. He was banished to Tiznit in the far south of Morocco. Before leaving his house in Fez, he packed a burial shroud in the battered little bag he took with him. If the French planned to kill him, he would be ready (al-Asfi 1986, 99).

Although many of his former students were also in exile or in prison, al-'Alawi's defiance contrasted with the compliance of most Moroccan ulama. Despite the fact that, like most Moroccans, the ulama venerated Sidi Muhammad bin Yusif (Muhammad V) not only as the legitimate sultan, but also as a great national hero, few dared to risk their positions and privileges by confronting the French. Some rural ulama and Quranic school teachers who led the Feast of Sacrifice prayers the day after Muhammad V's deposition simply coughed when they were supposed to mention the reigning sultan (Eickelman 1985, 152; Rabinow 1975, 67). One scholar asked a French administrator if he could invoke the name of Sidi Muhammad in his sermon without specifying whether he meant Muhammad bin 'Arafa or Muhammad V (Montagne 1953, 249). Such temporization exemplified the behavior of most Moroccan ulama—indeed of most Moroccans. Al-'Alawi, however, embodied the myth of the righteous man of God.

Once in exile, Muhammad V became the principal symbol of the nationalist struggle. His father, Mulay Yusif, had been scorned as a puppet of the French—as was Muhammad bin 'Arafa from 1953 to

1955. But Muhammad V was "our Lord" (Siyyidna), the real sultan (Julien 1978, 335). Thousands, if not millions of people, claimed to see his face and the faces of his children in the moon (Lacouture and Lacouture 1958, 108). Just as al-'Alawi had come to personify the ideal of the righteous scholar, so, too, Muhammad V had come to personify the ideal of the just ruler.

The sultan's exile provoked widespread demonstrations as well as attacks on Europeans and Moroccans identified with the colonial regime. In response, the French gathered the leading ulama to legitimate the death sentence for men they called terrorists (Julien 1978, 342). On 22 December 1953, the assembled scholars, many of whom had reaffirmed their loyalty to Muhammad V earlier in the year, decreed that in cases of murder "not motivated by vengeance or personal enmity," the death penalty was obligatory (ibid.). The men who signed this text knew that it was designed to justify the execution of men regarded by most Moroccans as patriotic heroes and fighters in a holy war (mujahidun). Muhammad bin al-'Arbi al-'Alawi was not one of the signatories, nor were other nationalist ulama —many of whom were in prison or in exile (al-Susi 1982).

It would be wrong to suggest that all Moroccan ulama collaborated with the colonial regime during Muhammad V's exile from 1953 to 1955. In August 1954, on the first anniversary of Muhammad V's deposition, forty of the ulama of Fez demanded his return and staged a protest in the sanctuary of Mulay Idris II in Fez. The French barricaded the men in the traditionally inviolable shrine, allowing only one glass of milk a day to be brought to each of the protesting scholars (Ghallab 1987, 2:624). After about a week, the colonial authorities sent in the Black Guard, normally supposed to protect the sultan, to violate the sanctuary of Mulay Idris and force out the ulama (ibid.; Julien 1978, 369). But most ulama did not engage in such protests—at least until it became clear that the widespread popular protests and guerrilla activities were going to result in the sultan's return as the ruler of an independent state (Eickelman 1985, 132-39; al-Jabiri 1988, 57; Tozy 1983, 225).

By the fall of 1955, the French allowed Muhammad V to return to Morocco, after over two years in exile. On 2 March 1956, after

forty-four years of colonial rule, Morocco regained its independence. Sidi Muhammad bin al-'Arbi al-'Alawi became a special
adviser to the sultan with the title of minister of the crown (wazir
al-taj) (al-Asfi 1986, 119). He was seventy-six years old and revered as
one of the great heroes of the Salafi-cum-nationalist movement. It
was generally assumed that he was an aged hero of the past who
would have little impact on politics in independent Morocco. This
did not turn out to be the case.

The early years of independence witnessed a growing split in the
Istiqlal party between the more traditional Salafis and many of the
younger and more secular radicals. In 1959, this culminated in the
radicals' forming a new socialist party called the Union Nationale
des Forces Populaires (UNFP) or al-Ittihad al-watani lil-quwat al-sha'biyya
in Arabic. With respect to the leaders of the factions involved, the
split was to some extent a conflict between the devoutly Islamic
elite and a new generation of French-educated Marxist intellectuals
from relatively humble social backgrounds. Many radicals, however, were themselves the scions of elite families (Ashford 1961;
Waterbury 1970).

After the 1959 split, the Istiqlal began to sound more radical in
order to stop the hemorrhaging on its left, and the UNFP took pains
to stress that its socialism was entirely in conformity with Islam
(Tozy 1983, 231–34). Moreover, many of the UNFP's members were
devout Muslims in their personal lives. But the fact remains that the
Istiqlal always remained an Islamic party representing Salafi reformism, whereas the UNFP represented the essentially secular radical-
ism of the 1960s.

Thus, most Moroccans were amazed to discover, in late December 1959, that Sidi Muhammad bin al-'Arbi al-'Alawi, the quintes-
sential Salafi reformist, had resigned as minister of the crown to
become an active member of the UNFP (al-Asfi 1986, 125). Given
that al-'Alawi, like al-Dukkali, rarely set his ideas down in writing,
his political position in 1959 is not entirely clear. He was certainly
unsympathetic to the Marxism of some of the leaders of the UNFP,
but he was also bitterly disappointed that the Istiqlal had allowed
Muhammad v to circumvent demands for a constitutional monar-

chy and social reform (Ouardighi n.d., 45–46). He was outraged by
the arrests of former members of the anticolonial guerrilla army
who had been accused of plotting to kill Crown Prince Hassan
(Zartman 1964a, 56). Thus it was that al-ʿAlawi quit the government
and went to live in a little house on the outskirts of Fez, where he
lived by selling the milk of his three cows and the eggs of his
chickens (al-Asfi 1986, 125–26). This life obviously enhanced his
image as the archetypal righteous man of God who shuns wealth
and power.

Al-ʿAlawi's criticism of Muhammad v's policies did not erase the
old man's affection and respect for the king who continued to
symbolize the nationalist struggle in the minds of most Moroccans.
When Muhammad v died in February 1961, al-ʿAlawi led the funeral
prayer and wept (ibid., 136–37).

Al-ʿAlawi's affection for the late king did not extend to his successor Hassan ii. When a group of friends visited him to express
their condolences after Muhammad v's death, al-ʿAlawi declared:
"May God have mercy on Muhammad v. As for Mulay al-Hassan, he
should look at what happened in Iraq" (khassu ishuf shnu uqaʿ
fi'l-ʿIraq).[6] Al-ʿAlawi was referring to the 1958 coup that had resulted
in the death of Iraq's King Faysal ii and the elimination of that country's monarchy (Batatu 1978, 764–807). His hostility toward Hassan
ii reflected the attitude of the Moroccan Left in general (Zartman
1964a, 31). The social democratic egalitarianism espoused by the
UNFP and by al-ʿAlawi himself was difficult to reconcile with Hassan
ii's conception of his role as God's shadow on earth.

The conflict between al-ʿAlawi and King Hassan ii soon became
public when the venerable Salafi condemned the king's proposed
constitution of 1962 on the ground that it contradicted Islamic law
on two key points: royal succession by primogeniture and the creation of a legislative assembly. With respect to the first point,
al-ʿAlawi stressed that the caliph was supposed to be elected by the
ulama rather than inherit his position at birth (Tozy 1984, 54). This
was indeed the classical principle and the constitution of 1962 did
violate Islamic law in this regard. It eviscerated the whole idea of
the bayʿa. It was one thing for actual practice to violate Islamic law,

as it usually had throughout most of Moroccan history, but now the law of the land would do so too. Yet Hassan II had no trouble inducing the newly created League of Ulama to endorse his constitution (Ouardighi n.d., 54).

Al-'Alawi also criticized the 1962 constitution for giving the king too much power and the legislature too little, as did many of his UNFP colleagues (Diouri 1987, 173). He told a crowd in Fez the following story:

> It is said that a lion, a wolf, and a fox were hunting and caught a zebra, a gazelle, and a hare. The lion said to the wolf, "Divide the game among us!" "It is very easy," said the wolf. "The zebra will be for your lunch, the gazelle for me, and the hare for the fox." The lion was furious and killed the wolf with one blow. He then asked the fox to proceed with the division of the spoils. "My Lord, answered the fox, the zebra will be for your lunch, the gazelle for your dinner, and the hare will be your snack in between. . . . " The lion asked: "How did you come up with such a division?" "It was the death of the wolf, my Lord, that inspired me." (Ouardighi n.d., 57)

The venerated old nationalist was referring, in the humorous manner for which he was renowned, to the Istiqlal's decision to support the constitution even though it left the lion's share of power in the hands of the king. After years of fighting to wrest the spoils of government from the throne, the Istiqlal had caved in to avoid incurring the wrath of Hassan II, who had no intention of dividing his power with the Istiqlal or anyone else (see Waterbury 1970).

At a rally in support of the UNFP campaign to boycott the referendum on the 1962 constitution, al-'Alawi declared:

> O brothers, we are a Muslim people and our legislation is Islamic. The right that the rulers have given themselves to formulate a constitution and to appropriate for themselves means to make it pass by forcing the people to vote for it are in flagrant contradiction with the principles of Islam and are contrary to the national interest. It is our duty to see to it that the nation elects those who will look after the rights of the people and who are known for their integrity, their competence, and their dedication. As for the secret prefabrication of a constitution which is hurriedly presented to the people, it is a trick.

And as for forcing Muslims to accept it, it is inadmissible by virtue of the fact that this was done by pressure and coercion and all consent obtained by coercion is null and void. (Ouardighi n.d., 57)

This passage is in the tradition of the righteous man of God, despite its novel references to the national interest and elections. Al-'Alawi's repeated allusions to coercion refer to the fact that Hassan II's referenda have always resulted in at least 97 percent approval of whatever it is he wants approved. The constitutional referendum of 1962 was no exception (Palazzoli 1974, 46)

Al-'Alawi died in 1964. He was buried, as he had requested, in the cemetery of the village where he had been born eighty-four years before (al-Asfi 1986, 141–42).

An anachronistic misconception often found in studies of twentieth-century Moroccan Islam is that Salafi reformism was always associated with the nationalist struggle against foreign domination. Early Salafis like al-Dukkali did see Islamic reform as a means of overcoming this domination, but like most ulama, they usually did nothing to oppose colonial rule per se and in fact actively cooperated with it. Marabouts like Ahmad al-Hiba, however, fought colonialism until the day they died. Of course, not all Sufi shaykhs resembled al-Hiba, nor did all Salafi ulama resemble al-Dukkali. By the 1940s, Salafi reformism and nationalist activism had become thoroughly intertwined, and most (but not all) Sufi shaykhs did collaborate with the French and the Spanish. But this was not the case in the early decades of the century. Even in the 1940s and 1950s, most ulama of a Salafi orientation continued to serve their colonial masters just as their fathers had served precolonial sultans. Like al-Yusi and Sidi Muhammad bin 'Abd al-Kabir al-Kattani, Muhammad bin al-'Arbi al-'Alawi did not represent the typical scholar of his time. He exemplified a mythical ideal.

In *Islam Observed*, Geertz recognized what few other scholars have, that Salafi reformism represented, at least to some extent, an ideological and polemical version of Islam. Geertz's assertion that Moroccan scripturalists sought to separate religion from everyday life is mistaken, but his discussion of the process whereby religion becomes polemic is insightful. The apologetic defense of religion in the tracts of reformists (and fundamentalists) should never be confused with religion as it is lived by real people during their everyday lives.

The polemicization of religion and its fusion with nationalism occurred in much of what we now call the third world. This was especially true when the distinction between colonizer and colonized meshed with a religious dichotomy. Thus we find Buddhist, Hindu, and Muslim nationalists all calling for a revival of true Buddhism, Hinduism, and Islam, as opposed to the decadent practices of ordinary people. The revival of religion became the key to the revival of "the nation."

The religion that reformists-cum-nationalists usually sought to revive was always to some extent an invented tradition (Hobsbawm and Ranger 1983). In Ceylon, now Sri Lanka, Buddhist reformists-cum-Sinhalese nationalists educated in British schools assured their followers that true Buddhists used knives and forks when eating, though Sinhalese Buddhists had in fact never done so (Gombrich and Obeyesekere 1988, 215). Time and time again, reformists-cum-nationalists insisted that democracy, socialism, the essence of scientific thought, the equality of men and women, and the Protestant work ethic were all essential components of their religion in its original form. (See Smith 1971.)

But although much of what reformists said about their religion involved obvious imitation of the West, some of it was also rooted in authentic patterns of orthodox revivalism. Something like Gellner's pendulum swing can be found in all the world religions. (Though it does not necessarily take the social forms he attributes to it.) In calling for a return to the Islam of the Quran and the Sunna, the Salafis were echoing what Muslim revivalists had periodically said for over a millennium. One could not imagine a more authentic representative of the myth of the righteous man of God than Muhammad bin al-'Arbi al-'Alawi. So one should not dismiss all Salafi reformism as an invented and ideological form of Islam.

Anthropologists have tended to assume that the popular-orthodox dichotomy they observed during their fieldwork existed throughout Islamic history. It did not. The Salafi movement transformed the nature of this dichotomy in the twentieth century. Through about the 1920s, most of Morocco's urban elite venerated saints and Sufi shaykhs as much as did illiterate tribesmen. 'Allal al-Fassi, the leader of Morocco's Salafi-cum-nationalist movement, was the scion of a family of Sufi shaykhs that had controlled one of the most prestigious Sufi zawiyas in Morocco for centuries. This zawiya was located not on a mountaintop or in a desert, but in the heart of Fez. (The name *al-Fassi* [*al-Fasi*] literally means "someone from Fez.) The people who came to this zawiya for mystical enlightenment included many of the most learned ulama of Morocco, not to mention sultans, government officials, and merchants (Berque 1982, 125–59).

Much of the literature on the relation between popular and orthodox Islam in Morocco reflects the pernicious consequences of the traditional academic division of labor, with historians studying texts and anthropologists people. If anthropologists were familiar with the Moroccan hagiographic tradition represented by Sidi Muhammad bin Ja'far al-Kattani's *Salwat al-anfas*, they would never assert that the Moroccan veneration of saints "was, and is, essentially a tribal phenomenon" (Geertz 1968, 49). Conversely, if historians spent a year or two living with flesh-and-blood Muslims, they would never mistake the Islam of polemical texts for Islam as really lived by people.

Five Holy and Unholy
Kingship in
Twentieth-Century Morocco

Geertz argues that the Moroccan monarchy is not just the pivotal institution in the Moroccan political system, it is also "the key institution in the Moroccan religious system" (1968, 75). He asserts that the power of King Hassan II, who has ruled since 1961, rests "almost entirely on the legitimacy of the Sultanate in the eyes of the masses" (ibid., 88). These assertions demonstrate what happens when students of the political role of religion overlook both the strictly religious aspects of religion and the strictly political aspects of power.

Geertz fails to distinguish between the religion of Islam as it is understood by Moroccan Muslims and the political institutions traditionally legitimated in Islamic terms, and he overlooks the role of force and fear in the Moroccan polity. This is not to deny the importance of the popular belief in the legitimacy of the Moroccan monarchy. But Geertz himself has correctly noted that a Moroccan monarch has to be both "holy man and strong man" (ibid.). In *Islam Observed*, he effectively ignores the strong-man side of things, as he does in his book on Balinese kingship (1980).

THE TANGENTIAL RELIGIOUS SIGNIFICANCE OF THE MONARCHY
IN LATE TWENTIETH-CENTURY MOROCCO

When we look at how Moroccan Muslims actually worship and live their everyday lives, we see that the monarchy is at best a tangential aspect of their religion. (I would argue that this was largely true in earlier periods as well, but for present purposes I focus on only the late twentieth century.) What is tangential from a religious perspective may, of course, be crucial from a political one, but the two need to be distinguished if their relationship is to be understood.

To understand a religion from the believer's point of view, one needs to study the basic rituals in which the believer's basic beliefs and values are articulated and reinforced on a regular basis. Students of sacred kingship often focus on the grandiose rituals of royalty without ever examining the ordinary rituals of ordinary people. The result is a thoroughly skewed picture of the religious significance of kingship. In *Islam Observed*, Geertz does not discuss any Moroccan rituals, though he does stress the importance of ritual in general (p. 100). He discusses the "royal progresses" of precolonial sultans in a later essay, "Centers, Kings, and Charisma: Reflections on the Symbolics of Power" (1983, 121–46), but fails to link these marches around Morocco to the basic religious rituals and beliefs of ordinary Moroccans.

Geertz is not alone in neglecting the basic rituals of Islam. Most anthropologists have—as have most students of the political role of Islam in other disciplines (Graham 1983). The words spoken by Muslims during their most intimate religious experiences are deemed irrelevant to the study of those who rule and rebel in the name of Islam. Such assumptions have led to fundamental distortions in the perception of Islam's political role—as illustrated not only by Geertz's view of the Moroccan monarchy as the key institution in the Moroccan religious system, but also by the widely accepted view that there is no distinction between religion and politics in Islam. This has indeed been among the principal shibboleths of Muslim reformists and fundamentalists. But its implausibility is obvious to anyone who knows how most flesh-and-blood

Muslims actually worship and speak about Islam in everyday life (Ayubi 1991; Loeffler 1988; Munson 1984). I have often heard Moroccan Muslims discuss Islam for hours without ever mentioning anything remotely political, let alone the monarchy.

To convey a sense of how Moroccan Muslims understand their religion and to demonstrate the insignificance of the monarchy in it, we may consider the basic everyday ritual of Islam—prayer.[1] The call to prayer that Muslims hear five times a day consists of the following phrases (each said twice except for the last one):

God is greater [Allahu akbar]
I bear witness that there is no god but God
I bear witness that Muhammad is the messenger of God
I bear witness that there is no god but God
I bear witness that Muhammad is the messenger of God
Come to prayer
Come to success
God is greater
There is no god but God.[2]

In Morocco, as in most of the rest of the Islamic world, most people still think of daily time in terms of this call to prayer, which is chanted at dawn, noon, midafternoon, sunset, and late in the evening. If one asks peasants or peddlers what time it is, they will most often say "the noon prayer has just been called," "the sunset prayer has not yet been called," or something along these lines.

All prayer in Islam must be performed in a state of ritual purity or tahara. (We have already noted the link between this concept and baraka in the popular imagination.) Purity is normally achieved by ablutions with running water. The Muslim begins prayer standing in the direction of Mecca, the spiritual center of the Islamic world, raising the palms of both hands to the back of the ears and saying Allahu akbar, "God is greater." Once the believer has said this phrase, he or she enters a sacred state that will end only when the prayer is over. One then recites the Fatiha, the short opening chapter (sura) of the Quran, which is also the basic prayer of Islam:

> In the name of God, the merciful, the compassionate
> Praise be to God, Lord of the worlds
> The merciful, the compassionate
> Master of the day of judgment
> You do we worship and from you do we seek aid
> Guide us on the straight path
> The path of those whom you have blessed
> Not of those who have incurred your wrath
> Nor of those who go astray.[3]

The worshiper then recites another short chapter of the Quran or several verses of a longer one. This is done while still standing. The chapter of sincere faith (surat al-ikhlas) is the most commonly recited:

> Say he is the one God
> God the eternal
> He has not begotten nor was he begotten
> And no one has ever been comparable to him.

Having completed the recitation of this sura, which like the Fatiha is often said to contain the essence of the Quran as a whole, the believer bows, stands, prostrates himself or herself with forehead on the ground, and sits with legs under the buttocks, saying "Allahu akbar" (God is greater) with almost each movement, as well as the following phrases: "My Lord the great be praised," "God hears those who praise him," "Our Lord, for you is the praise," and "My Lord on high be praised." The worshiper then returns to the standing position, having now completed one rak'a, the basic unit of all Islamic prayer. The five daily prayers consist simply of repetitions of these rak'as: the dawn prayer has two, the noon prayer four (when said individually), the midafternoon prayer four, the sunset prayer three, and the late evening prayer four. After every two rak'as and at the end of prayer, while still seated, the worshiper says the tashahhud, which incorporates a modified form of the attestation of faith, "I bear witness that there is no god but God and I bear witness that Muhammad is the messenger of God":

> Greetings to God, the pure things are for God, the good things are for God, and the prayers [al-salawat] are for God.

Peace be upon you O Prophet and the mercy of God on high and his
    blessings
Peace be upon us
and upon the righteous slaves [ʿibad] of God.
I bear witness that there is no god but God
and I bear witness that
Muhammad is his slave [ʿabduhu] and messenger.

When these phrases come at the end of prayer, the believer, still
seated, asks God to bless Muhammad and his descendants and then
turns his or her face first to the right and then to the left saying,
"Peace be upon you and the mercy of God" (as-salamu ʿalaykum wa
rahmat Allah). These words, which are popularly believed to be
addressed to the two angels that watch over every Muslim, termi-
nate the sacred state of prayer. After saying them, the worshiper is
free to get up and resume everyday life. Many people remain seated,
however, and raise their hands to God, asking for a particular favor
of some kind. This is the personal prayer known as duʿaʾ, or "sup-
plication." There is no mention of the monarchy or any other political institution in any of this.

THE FRIDAY PRAYER

The daily prayers can be said anywhere that is ritually pure. They
are usually said individually. The Friday noon prayer should be said
collectively in a mosque if possible. This is primarily true for men,
women having traditionally been encouraged to pray at home
(Kamal 1978, 31). The largest mosques in cities usually have a relatively small space reserved for women either behind the men or in
a closed-off balcony above the main floor. The collective Friday
noon prayer is led by an imam standing in front of the other worshipers. (It will be recalled that the basic meaning of imam is "he
who stands in front and leads prayer.") The imam can be any adult
male regarded as a good Muslim. He is usually responsible for
delivering the Friday sermon, although this can be done by someone else—again any male recognized as a good Muslim. The Friday
prayer proper takes place after the sermon and consists of the two-

rak'a sequence described above. (Said individually, the noon prayer has four rak'as but said collectively, it has only two.)

The sermon is divided into two parts, between which the preacher sits briefly. It must include exhortations and supplications on behalf of the faithful, recitation of Quranic verses and the attestation of faith, and statements praising God and asking him to bless Muhammad. The plea that God bless Muhammad is usually extended to request that he bless the Prophet's patrilineal descendants as well. It is also customary for the man giving the sermon to ask God to help the local ruler as well as the faithful in general (Antoun 1989, 71–72). *This is the only time that rulers are mentioned in the basic rituals of Islam.* The request that God assist the head of state is an insignificant aspect of Friday prayer in religious terms. When Muslims of several nationalities pray together, as is common among students and workers in Europe and North America, no ruler is mentioned and no one feels that Friday prayer is thereby diminished. But the mention of the ruler was traditionally very important politically. When there were two or more claimants to the throne, asking God to assist one of them was a statement of political allegiance. Sermons can also be significant politically in that the preacher has the right, in principle, to address any issue affecting the Muslim community. The Moroccan government, however, like most Muslim governments, has tried to curb criticism from the pulpit (Claisse 1987, 48; Tozy and Etienne 1986).

Sermons are also given after the collective prayers on the two major Islamic holidays: the feast of breaking the fast at the end of Ramadan, the month of fasting, and the feast of sacrifice when Muslims commemorate Abraham's willingness to sacrifice his son to God. In colloquial Arabic, Moroccans usually call the feast at the end of Ramadan "the little holiday" ('id as-sghir) and the feast of sacrifice "the big holiday" ('id al-kbir). These are the two main Muslim holidays (for Sunnis anyway). Like the Friday prayers, the holiday prayers consist of two rak'as—with the phrase "God is greater" (Allahu akbar) said a few extra times. Thus, in speaking of the five daily rituals of prayer, we are also speaking of the rituals performed on the holiest of the holy days of the Muslim year.

COMBS-SCHILLING ON THE RITUAL CENTRALITY OF
THE MONARCHY

Elaine Combs-Schilling has argued that the monarchy is of fundamental religious significance in Morocco and that "the king is the
center of the most important rituals of the faith" (1989, 21). This is
in the spirit of Geertz's claim that the monarchy is the key institution in the Moroccan religious system. In speaking of the most
important rituals of the faith, Combs-Schilling, like Geertz, ignores
the rituals that are in fact central in Islam—the prayers that are said
five times a day, every Friday, and every holy day. She focuses instead
on specific aspects of weddings, the feast of sacrifice, and the cele-
bration of the Prophet's birthday (al-mawlid). Although the prayers
said five times a day are actually also essential elements of the cele-
bration of the latter two holidays, Combs-Schilling does not discuss
them.

We have already seen that the king is not mentioned in the daily
prayers. He is only mentioned briefly in the sermons at collective
prayer on Fridays and holy days. The monarchy could disappear
tomorrow, and the only difference in the basic Islamic rituals would
be that preachers on Fridays and holy days might ask God to bless a
president—or no one at all. The political role of Islam in Morocco
would, of course, be radically transformed, but Islam as lived by
Muslims in their basic rituals and everyday life would be unaffected.

Combs-Schilling writes that "the legitimacy of the blood-linked
monarchy is written in the most basic substance of existence, in red
blood flowing on ground and bed—the blood of the sacrificial ram
and the blood of the deflowered bride" (1989, 301). She is referring
to the blood that flows from rams when they are slaughtered on the
feast of sacrifice and to the blood that is supposed to be shed by
brides as proof of their virginity. But there is no evidence that Moroccans associate the blood of slaughtered rams and "deflowered"
brides with the legitimacy of the blood-linked monarchy.

Morocco's monarchy is normally neither mentioned nor thought
of during weddings and sacrifices. Pictures of Hassan II must be
displayed in public places all over the country, and if a wedding or a

sacrifice occurs in such a place, it occurs in the presence of the king's picture, as do speeches, soccer matches, and just about everything else that takes place outside of bedrooms and toilets. The king does not thereby become the center of the rituals. The fact that the bridegroom is called a *sultan* at traditional Moroccan weddings does not mean that anyone present thinks of the reigning sultan symbolically severing the bride's hymen himself. The metaphor of the bridegroom as king occurs in many societies where kingship disappeared long ago.[4] It is certainly a significant metaphor, reflecting among other things a homology between the authority of husbands and that of kings. Yet no late twentieth-century Moroccan thinks of the bridegroom "taking on the ruler's persona" because the latter is "the archetypal man" or because the monarchy is an essential feature of the ordinary Moroccan's "definition of self" (Combs-Schilling 1989, 190, 25). All Moroccans I have asked about this agree: the king of Morocco plays no role in traditional Moroccan weddings.

The second holy day Combs-Schilling discusses is the feast of sacrifice, which she describes as "the most important ritual support of the Moroccan monarchy" (1989, 223). She notes that the king's sacrifice is repeatedly shown on television and "is discussed on radio and summarized in newspapers" (p. 227). She fails, however, to mention that *everything* the king does publicly is endlessly covered in the government-controlled media. Such coverage reflects what the government wants people to think, not what they actually do. Although it is true that the king's sacrifice is supposed to occur before any other (Entelis 1989, 57–58), this is not required by Islamic law (see Ibn Anas 1989). One young Moroccan told me that his father used to lead collective prayers and perform the collective sacrifice in a northern town at seven in the morning, "and the king never gets up that early."

On the morning of the feast of sacrifice, women and children anxiously await the return of the men of the house from collective prayer. This is usually held in an open space (*msalla*) much larger than any single mosque. Whoever gives the sermon on this occasion normally sacrifices a sheep after the prayer is over. Once the men return home, they slaughter and skin their own family's sheep or goat. (Some men, including many well-educated ones, have someone else do this.) The women start cooking the liver while the men are still at work. It is eaten right away and the mood at this point is joyous. Other parts of the animal are eaten on the following days, with most of the meat eaten during the next week or so—some being given to relatives, friends, neighbors, and the poor. Nothing said or done during all of this has anything to do with the king as "the great collective sacrificer upon whom the good of the whole depends" (Combs-Schilling 1989, 10).

There used to be a belief that if the heart of the ram sacrificed by the sultan was still beating when it arrived at the royal palace, this was a good omen (Saint Olon 1695, 46–47; Chénier 1788, 197; Combs-Schilling 1989, 226–27; see Ibn Zaydan 1961–62, 1:167). Westermarck notes that this belief still existed in the early twentieth century (1926, 2:126), but he does not suggest that the sultan's sacrifice was of any particular importance to most Moroccans. Indeed, of the fifty-two pages he devotes to the feast of sacrifice in *Ritual and Belief in Morocco*, he refers to the royal sacrifice in only two sentences (ibid., 2:119 and 126). The historian Ibn Zaydan devotes almost half a page to the rules concerning the sultan's sacrifice in precolonial Morocco, but he too does not say that it was of any special significance to Moroccans in general (1961–62, 1:167). The Moroccan anthropologist Abdellah Hammoudi does not even mention the king's ram in his book about sacrifice in twentieth-century Morocco (1988). The fact is, in the late twentieth century at any rate, that the king's sacrifice is no more significant to most Moroccan families than the American president's lighting of "the national Christmas tree" is to Christian families in the United States. One Moroccan woman I know did not even realize that the king sacrificed an animal himself until I told her he did. There may well be an important link between kingship and sacrifice in some societies, but Morocco is not one of them.

With respect to the third holy day Combs-Schilling discusses, that of the Prophet's birthday, she deserves credit for recognizing that it has indeed played an important role in the evolution of the political role of Islam in Morocco, notably as a means of reinforcing the legitimacy of the sharifian Sa'adian and 'Alawi dynasties.[5] Hassan II still uses the holiday this way, making sure that those of his subjects with access to a television see him reading the Quran surrounded by candles and men chanting verses of the holy book for hours on end.

But when Combs-Schilling writes that "the Prophet's Birthday is a straightforward political ritual that legitimates the Moroccan monarchy" (1989, 173), she reduces its religious substance to a political side effect. The men who chant the Quran in mosques on the night of the Prophet's birthday do not think of themselves as participating in a straightforward political ritual legitimating the Moroccan monarchy. Moreover, the late sixteenth-century celebrations of the Prophet's birthday that Combs-Schilling describes are by now largely extinct. This holiday is less significant that the feast of sacrifice and the feast at the end of Ramadan. Moreover, its legitimacy has often been questioned by ulama, reformists, and fundamentalists because it is associated with the popular transformation of the Prophet from a mere mortal who received revelations from God into a divine being (Fuchs and de Jong 1989). For present purposes, the crucial point is that the king and the monarchy are at best of marginal significance in the popular celebrations of the Prophet's birthday in twentieth-century Morocco. Once again, one should not confuse the religious significance attributed to the king by Morocco's government-controlled media with the religious significance attributed to him by ordinary Moroccans.

Combs-Schilling's contention that the king is the center of the most important rituals of the faith—like Geertz's claim that the monarchy is the key institution in the Moroccan religious system—is mistaken. When we examine the basic Muslim rituals, we find that the king is almost never mentioned in them. One has to distinguish between religion as a conceptual system in terms of which believers interpret the world and political institutions legitimated in religious terms. While Geertz himself has noted the importance of this distinction (1966, 42; 1968, 2), his conception of the Moroccan monarchy as being central to the Moroccan religious system illustrates his failure to make it in practice.

In stressing the insignificance of the monarchy with respect to the religious beliefs of the Moroccan people, I do not wish to suggest that these beliefs are insignificant with respect to the monarchy. These are two different issues. As already noted, what may be tangential from a religious perspective may be crucial from a political one. The two must be distinguished if we are to understand how they are related.

THE EVOLUTION OF THE MONARCHY IN
TWENTIETH-CENTURY MOROCCO

When the French imposed their protectorate on Morocco in 1912, they decided to preserve the outward form of the sultanate while draining it of all real power. After forcing Mulay 'Abd al-Hafidh to sign the Treaty of Fez creating the protectorate, they replaced him by his pliant brother Mulay Yusif (1912–27) and then by the latter's son Muhammad v (1927–61), all of this dutifully ratified by the ulama. Thus, during the colonial period, the sultanate was discredited in the eyes of many Moroccans and, as Geertz notes, if Morocco had become independent in the 1930s, it might well have become a republic (1968, 80). This did not happen, because Muhammad v eventually decided to support the nationalist struggle against the French (and against the Spanish in the northern zone). This support, at first tacit but eventually overt, induced the French to depose him in August 1953 and banish him from Morocco until November 1955. As we have seen, this exile transformed the sultan into the symbol of the nationalist struggle. Millions of Moroccans saw his face in the moon when he was under house arrest in Madagascar (Julien 1978, 335). The idea of sacred kingship was thus resuscitated, despite the fact that it was condemned by the very Salafi nationalists who had made its resuscitation possible (Tozy 1984, 99–101). Geertz summarizes Muhammad v's impact on the monarchy well: "Muhammad v made, in his quiet, tenacious, blandly recalcitrant way, a radically new thing out of the Sultanate. A museum piece when its French 'protectors' awarded it to him in 1927, his impact upon it was at least as great as its impact upon him, and

when he died in 1961, he left it a revived and transformed office"
(1968, 75).

During the struggle for independence, Muhammad V repeatedly
said that he shared the nationalists' desire for a constitutional monarchy and real democracy (Ghallab 1987, 2:738, 767). Such a political system was a basic demand of the Salafi nationalists, who went
to great lengths to reconcile the idea of democracy with the idea
that government should ultimately be based on the Quran and the
Sunna (al-Fasi 1963, 213–20). The secular socialists also demanded
democracy and a constitutional monarchy—though many were
unenthusiastic about retaining any monarchy at all (Agnouche 1987,
312; Ben Barka 1968, 87–94). Yet Muhammad V effectively aborted
all efforts to diminish the monarchy's power, as did his son and
successor Hassan II (el-Mossadeq 1987; Waterbury 1970; Zartman
1964a, 1964b, 1987a).

In 1957, one year after independence, the monarch's title was
officially changed from *sultan* to *malik* (king). Throughout most of
Islamic history, the term *malik* was one of opprobrium symbolic of
the transformation of the contractual caliphate into a hereditary
monarchy. In the twentieth century, however, it was embraced by
many Muslim rulers as part of.an attempt to modernize and westernize their governments and thus eliminate the image of Oriental
despotism evoked by the word *sultan* (Ayalon 1991). Ironically, the
nominal transformation of the sultan into a king occurred at a time
when the Moroccan monarch actually had more power than any of
his precolonial predecessors. This was due in part to the French
and Spanish subjugation of the highland tribes that the precolonial
sultans had never entirely controlled. It was also due to Muhammad V's extraordinary charismatic authority as the symbol of the
nationalist struggle.

Even the radical nationalists who regarded kingship as an anachronism revered Muhammad V (Lacouture and Lacouture 1958,
121–22), as did the Salafis who advocated a constitutional monarchy (Tozy 1984, 99–102). Muhammad V became a mythical figure
embodying the ideal of the just ruler. Even in the 1980s, peasants
and the urban poor still said that Muhammad V used to visit popu-

lar quarters, villages, and markets incognito and in shabby clothes
to see how the poor were faring. Such stories are not told of Hassan
II, who succeeded his father in 1961.

THE SACRED KINGSHIP OF HASSAN II

Hassan II has tried to squeeze every possible political advantage out
of the hierocratic dimensions of the monarchy resuscitated by his
father. The constitutions of 1970 and 1972, both tailored to Hassan's
specifications, declare that "the person of the King is inviolable and
sacred" (Tozy 1984, 73). A law passed in 1958, while Muhammad V
was still alive, declared that the king cannot be criticized or represented in a comic manner (ibid., 74). As many Moroccans can
attest, the government takes this law quite seriously. A young poet
was sentenced to fifteen years in prison because a verse of his
describing King Hussein of Jordan as "Hitler II" was interpreted as a
reference to Hassan II (Perrault 1990, 325). Even the king's decrees
are immune from legal challenge, a point that the Moroccan scholar
Abdelatif Agnouche has linked to the Shi'i idea of the pure and
sinless imam (1987, 290). Most dictators enforce similar rules
whether or not they are enshrined in law. Hassan II, however, seeks
to legitimate them by invoking his role as caliph as well as sharif.

In 1978, the king told the members of Morocco's parliament:
"the control of him whom God has entrusted with the mission of
being the Prophet's successor is indispensable for the legislative as
well as the executive branch of government" (Tozy 1984, 84). This
was Hassan II's way of warning the members of the Moroccan parliament not to confuse their role with that of their British counterparts. In 1979, as he officially named a general to head the army's
southern zone, the king declared: "Anyone we entrust with a civil
or military mission must reflect our mission, that of the commander
of the faithful, obliged to serve as the divine shadow on earth. . . .
Therefore, be our sword and our shadow which shelters anyone
who seeks the protection of the commander of the faithful. Be our
sword for defense and combat, to fight those who break the unity
of the ranks and rebel against the order of the commander of the

faithful" (ibid., 85). Such rhetoric is also found in the official discourse of the king's subjects, as in the following bay'a by some
notables of the Western Sahara in 1979:

> We tribes of Oulad Dlim, Ait Lahsen [. . .] among the tribes that
> know best the noble qualities of the king [. . .] have decided by
> general agreement, without exception and with a unanimity that
> excludes all error, to renew our oath of allegiance [bay'a] to the
> commander of the faithful [. . .], the object of which is the same as
> the oath sworn to the Prophet under the blessed tree [shajarat
> al-ridwan], thereby acknowledging his authority, committing ourselves
> to always be obedient and loyally devoted to him. (Tozy 1983, 221)

That such language is still used in the late twentieth century is
certainly significant. However, an analysis of Moroccan kingship
based solely on such rhetoric would be egregiously inadequate.
Even those Moroccans who really do revere the king almost never
speak of him as the "shadow of God" or "commander of the faithful." These terms belong to prescribed public discourse rather than
to the spontaneous speech of real people. Most people know that
the king is called the commander of the faithful, but many do not
realize that this is a caliphal title. If you say the word khalifa to most
Moroccans, they usually think of the local administrative official
who bears this title and serves as deputy to a qaid. The very idea of
the caliphate is not at all clear in the minds of most Moroccans with
little formal education, and roughly two-thirds of all Moroccans
aged fifteen and over were illiterate in 1989 (World Bank 1989, 211).

The king's status as a sharif carries far more weight in the popular
imagination than does his status as caliph. The majority of Moroccans, notably the illiterate and marginally literate, still believe in the
king's sharifian baraka. There are even still people who say that the
prosperity of Morocco as a whole depends on the king's baraka
(Fernea 1976, 223). Yet belief in Hassan II's baraka, though still important, does not have the political significance that some Western
scholars think it does. So long as a ruler remains on his throne,
uneducated Moroccans say he has retained his baraka. As soon as
he is overthrown, these same Moroccans say he has lost it (or much

of it). Such circular reasoning (reminiscent of how some scholars use the notion of *legitimacy*) does not entail any specific loyalty. Most peasants assume that the king is sacred much as they assume that water is wet. The former assumption does not imply much more of a political commitment than the latter.

The passivity of most Moroccans during the coups of 1971 and 1972 is revealing in this respect. During the coup of July 1971, at Hassan II's forty-second birthday party, officers repeatedly broadcast radio messages announcing the king's death and the establishment of a republic (Benoist-Méchin 1972, 357–58). The announcement did not induce the Moroccan people to rush to the monarchy's defense. Even the peasants who by and large still believed in the king's baraka did nothing. In fact, the only initial response was that of the many high school and university students who were ecstatic (Santucci 1985, 35).

Once it became clear that the coup of 1971 had failed and Hassan II was still firmly in control, there were some spontaneous celebrations by the small number of remaining Moroccan Jews who had feared the emergence of a Moroccan Qadhdhafi (Stillman 1988, 17). But there were few such celebrations among the Muslims. The large demonstrations that did occur within days after the foiled coup were carefully orchestrated by the government (ibid.; Palazzoli 1973, 51–53). Most Moroccans were equally passive during and after the abortive coup of 1972 (Santucci 1985, 46).

This passivity illustrates several features of Morocco's "political culture" that are also found in most other third world societies.[6] First of all, the great majority of Moroccans see government as an alien and terrifying entity that affects them but which they cannot affect. Second, when there is a struggle for power, people wait and see who wins before taking a position one way or the other. Political behavior is generally dictated by self-interest rather than by commitment, and self-interest dictates that one do whatever has to be done to avoid incurring the wrath of those in power.

Had the officers of 1971 or 1972 succeeded, the same people who had professed undying loyalty to Hassan II while he was on the throne would have professed undying loyalty to the officer who would have replaced him as head of state. In May 1952, the Egyptian religious scholar Ahmad Hassan al-Zayyat praised Egypt's King Farouq as a "defender of Islam and Arabism." Yet after Farouq was overthrown a few months later, the same scholar called him "a satan who dared transgress the religion of Allah and break all taboos" (Sivan 1985, 53). Similar transformations would be commonplace in Morocco if Hassan II were overthrown.

I used to know an illiterate old woman in a northern city of Morocco who attributed the king's survival of the coups of 1971 and 1972 to his baraka whenever she alluded to these events, which are mentioned more often than the abortive Marxist insurrection of 3 March 1973 (Serfaty 1992, 97–98). In speaking with trusted relatives, however, this same old woman, who was born in a mountain village, often referred to Hassan II as the 'azzi (Negro or nigger), a conventional comical insult in Moroccan popular culture. This old woman's belief in the king's baraka definitely did not imply reverential devotion to him.

The ritual insults of Hassan II that one encounters in most urban social strata are of interest because they are radically unlike the descriptions of the king in the government-controlled media and in the writings of Western anthropologists like Geertz and Combs-Schilling. Such insults are not a new phenomenon. They are hard to find in Moroccan texts, given the danger they could pose for their authors, but we do find them recorded in the texts of foreigners. Thus, according to a Frenchman who spent several decades as a slave in Morocco during the early eighteenth century, the dark-skinned Mulay Isma'il (1672–1727) was called "the son of a black slave woman" by the people of Fez (Varonne 1974, 85). This phrase, wild al-'abda in Arabic, is also said of Hassan II (behind closed doors).

Since so many of the ritual insults of the king concern his dark skin, I should point out that "race" is a sensitive issue in Moroccan popular culture. Until slavery was officially banned during the French protectorate, most black Moroccans were slaves (Brunschvig 1960, 39). The word for "slave," 'abd, remains the standard word for a "black man" (a black woman being an 'abda). Black skin is popularly still seen as intrinsically inferior to white or brown. I have even heard it said that Muhammad V should have been succeeded by his son Mulay ʿAbd Allah rather than by Hassan II simply because the former's skin was lighter than the latter's. Most educated Moroccans ridicule such thinking and often stress that Islam does not tolerate any form of racism (al-ʿunsuriyya). Moreover, Morocco is by no means rigidly stratified along racial lines. Wealthy and powerful men in precolonial Morocco often had black concubines whose children were regarded as legitimate (Aubin 1922, 317–18). One thus finds many dark-skinned Moroccans in the royal family and the elite.

It is not always easy to determine the political significance of the ritual insults referring to the king's skin color. They are said by people who speak openly of their desire to overthrow the monarchy. Yet they are also said by people who would never speak this way. They take on different political meanings depending on who says them and in what context. Nevertheless, in a society where it is a crime to make fun of or insult the head of state, doing so is always more meaningful than it would be in a democracy. Jokes about the king's darkness are always symbolic revolts. They invert the sycophantic reverence the king's subjects must display in public (and the white clothes symbolizing purity that he wears on religious occasions). Most of the people who mock the king's darkness by calling him an ʿazzi would never think of really revolting against the king, or anyone else. They do, however, derive considerable pleasure from doing so rhetorically (and secretly).

Geertz does not mention the ritual insults of Hassan II, which are significant indices of the popular perception of the king (though their significance is not always easy to determine). Nor does he mention the extensive published criticism of the monarchy by Moroccan radicals. In 1960, Mehdi Ben Barka (al-Mahdi bin Barka), the leader of the Union Nationale des Forces Populaires, declared that his party did not want to participate in a government that was theocratic and feudal and trying to "resuscitate the medieval structures of traditional Moroccan society to preserve its former privileges" (Agnouche 1987, 312). Also in the early 1960s, another leader of the UNFP, al-Fqih Basri, declared that "the goal of our movement is to overthrow this rotten regime" (ibid.). At its second congress in 1962, the UNFP passed a resolution referring to the Moroccan monarchy as "an archaic and precolonial" institution that served the interests of neocolonialism (Ben Barka 1968, 81–83). The UNFP was the second most powerful political party in Morocco in the early 1960s (after the Salafi-oriented Istiqlal from which it had emerged), and Mehdi Ben Barka and al-Fqih Basri were two of the country's most influential politicians—the latter being a hero of the anti-colonial "Army of Liberation" (Waterbury 1970). Yet their views of the monarchy are not mentioned in Islam Observed, which was published in 1968.

The educated Moroccans who questioned the legitimacy of the monarchy in the 1960s were certainly a minority of the population as a whole, but, as in most third world countries, they were far more important politically than they were numerically. Educated young people (notably students, teachers, and officers) have always constituted the most conspicuous opposition to Hassan II's regime (Munson 1986b; Santucci 1985; Suleiman 1987; Waterbury 1970). To ignore their views is to ignore a crucial aspect of late twentieth-century Moroccan political life.

HASSAN II AS STRONG MAN

Geertz concedes, in Islam Observed, that the "strong-man" aspect of Moroccan kingship "inevitably clashed with and usually dominated the holy-man aspects" and that this was "both true and, for an understanding of the nature of the Moroccan state, critical" (1968, 53). Having made this important point, however, Geertz ignores it and asserts that Hassan II's power has rested "almost entirely on the legitimacy of the Sultanate in the eyes of the masses" (ibid., 88). This assertion is astonishing in the light of the many famous manifestations of the strong-man dimension of Hassan II's power during the years preceding the publication of Islam Observed.

While still crown prince in the late 1950s, Hassan II orchestrated the suppression of the guerrilla army that had fought the French as well as that of a number of regional Berber revolts (Waterbury 1970).

In 1959, his plane was fired on as he landed to lead some twenty thousand troops in suppressing the most important of these revolts in the Rif (Zartman 1964b, 89–91). Hassan II himself alluded to the severity of this suppression in a televised speech delivered in the wake of the riots of January 1984 (Tessler 1987, 231). Much of the Rif remained under military rule for three and a half years after the revolt of 1958–59 (Hart 1976, 431). None of this is mentioned in *Islam Observed*.

In the early 1960s, Hassan II faced serious opposition from the leftist UNFP, which had widespread support among students, former members of the anticolonial guerrilla army, and educated Moroccans generally. In late 1959 and early 1960, prominent members of this party were arrested on charges of plotting to kill Hassan II while he was still the crown prince (Waterbury 1970, 204, 211). In local elections held in May 1960, the UNFP managed to win a majority of the votes in towns and cities with over ten thousand people (ibid., 220). The government, which was controlled by Hassan II even before he officially became king in 1961, thus began to put more pressure on the Left (Diouri 1972, 45, 50). When the UNFP still managed to win almost 20 percent of the parliamentary seats in the 1963 elections, the government declared that some of the party's most prominent leaders were involved in a plot to kill Hassan II and eliminate the monarchy (ibid., 73, 121). Whether or not such a plot actually existed, it is true that the Marxist Left would have been delighted to see Hassan II dead and the monarchy eliminated. At the collective trial of the alleged plotters in December 1963, one man forced to confess that he had thought of killing the king asked, "What Moroccan hasn't?" (Waterbury 1970, 294). The government's star witness at this trial was supposed to have been Moumen Diouri. But when he took the witness stand, Diouri said the plot was a government hoax and suddenly stripped down to his bloodstained underwear to display where he had been tortured (Diouri 1972, 114–23). None of this is mentioned in *Islam Observed*.

In March 1965, strikes and demonstrations by high school students and teachers in the major cities of Morocco turned into bloody riots involving young men from the poorest neighborhoods of Casablanca. Some witnesses said that government troops killed as many as four hundred people before restoring order (Waterbury 1970, 313). In the wake of the riots, Hassan II dissolved parliament and declared a state of emergency that would remain in effect for five years. The king blamed teachers for encouraging students to protest, declaring: "There is no danger for the state as grave as the so-called intellectual. It would be better if you were all illiterate" (ibid., 311–13). None of this is mentioned in *Islam Observed*.

In October 1965, Mehdi Ben Barka, the leader of the UNFP, was kidnapped and assassinated in France. Charles de Gaulle, France's president at the time, later told a French scholar that Hassan II had had Ben Barka killed (Balta 1990, 117). In January 1966, the French issued arrest warrants for Morocco's minister of the interior, Muhammad Oufkir, and another Moroccan official named Ahmed Dlimi, thus provoking a serious crisis in Franco-Moroccan relations (Muratet 1967, 289). (Both men were later killed for trying to overthrow the king.) In July 1967, after a lengthy trial that attracted worldwide attention, a French court sentenced Oufkir, in absentia, to life imprisonment for his role in the murder of Ben Barka (Violet 1991). None of this is mentioned in *Islam Observed*.

In the early 1970s, Hassan II's rule was threatened by the very institution he had always used to eliminate threats—the army. He barely survived the coup attempts of 1971 and 1972, and he had General Oufkir killed for his involvement in the latter (Pédron 1972). The king was by now haunted by the idea of a coup, and rumors spread that the keys to Morocco's military arsenals had been given to Frenchmen since there were no Moroccans the king could trust (Daure-Serfaty 1992, 32). In December 1972, Hassan II told his subjects: "God has placed the king on his throne to safeguard the monarchy and to do this the Maliki school of Islam [which prevails in Morocco] stipulates that he must not hesitate, if necessary, to eliminate the third of the population infected by evil ideas to protect the two-thirds of the population not so infected" (Agnouche 1987, 27). This may well be the single most famous sentence Hassan II has ever uttered. Yet it is never quoted in anthropological studies of Morocco's sacred kingship.

The traumatic 1971 and 1972 coups were followed by an unsuccessful Marxist guerrilla insurrection in 1973. Although Hassan II suppressed it easily, it was obvious that he had to do something to overcome the opposition of the educated middle-class and educated army officers. Spain's decision to withdraw from the Western Sahara, which was claimed by Morocco, provided him with a perfect solution. In 1975, he led a "Green March" of hundreds of thousands of unarmed Moroccans into the Sahara, thereby initiating a costly war with the Polisario guerrillas, who demanded an independent Saharan state (Bookin-Weiner 1979; Damis 1983). The king told the Moroccan people that God had given him the idea for this march while he was praying at the shrine of Mulay Idris II in Fez (Cherifi 1988, 48–49). The war in the Sahara, which dragged on into the early 1990s, served to rally all the major Moroccan political parties around the king (Damis 1987, 1990). The king thus allowed parliamentary and local elections to take place in the late 1970s for the first time since the early 1960s. The ministry of the interior, however, determined the outcome of these elections long before a single vote was cast (Claisse 1987).

The Iranian revolution of 1978–79 generated widespread enthusiasm—and concern—in Morocco. Morocco's fundamentalists had hitherto been inconsequential. They were now taken most seriously (see chap. 6). The shah himself sought refuge in Morocco in 1979. Widespread student protests and graffiti like "the king is the shah's dog" induced Hassan II to ask him to leave (Lamchichi 1989, 285; Ockrent and de Marenches 1986, 257). Hassan II used the ulama, docile as always, to reinforce his Islamic legitimacy and discredit that of his Islamic opposition (Souriau 1983, 378).

Then in 1981, Morocco was shaken by the worse riots since 1965—riots sparked by the International Monetary Fund's (IMF) demands that the government reduce the subsidized prices of basic foodstuffs. Somewhere between six hundred and a thousand were reportedly killed during the suppression of these riots (Clément 1986, 7: Le Monde, 27 June 1981).

Less than three years later, and less than a year after yet another abortive coup that resulted in Ahmed Dlimi's death, large-scale rioting occurred again in January 1984 (Clément 1990, 67–68). These riots were precipitated by the government's decision to raise the cost of a fee paid by high school students as well as by further price increases demanded by the International Monetary Fund (Seddon 1984). In Marrakesh, high school students attacked banks, government buildings, and many stores (Paul 1984, 5). Student strikes, protests, and eventually riots then spread to the north, where young blue-collar workers often joined the students, especially in the Rif and the northwestern city of Tetuan (Seddon 1984). A dozen or so young men were killed as they tried to occupy the residence of the governor of the Rifian province of Nador (El País, 24 Jan. 1984). In Tetuan, crowds overran a police station and army barracks. Five thousand troops had to be flown in to Tetuan to reinforce local army and police units in order to suppress what amounted to an insurrection (Paul 1984, 6). In a televised address on 22 January, Hassan II explained to the people of Morocco that all of this was the result of a "Communist, Zionist, and Khomeinist" plot (El País, 24 Jan. 1984). Referring to his role in the harsh repression of the Rif revolt of 1958–59, he said, "inhabitants of the north who knew yesterday's crown prince very well should know what to expect from King Hassan II" (Tessler 1987, 231).

The king was violently condemned during the uprisings of 1984. Rioters tore up his pictures and smeared excrement over them (del Pino 1990, 156). Graffiti appeared warning the monarch "we are going to eat you for dessert" (ibid.). In the Rif, protestors are reported to have chanted: "Enough prisons and palaces, [we want] universities and schools," "One, two, three, we're going to kill the king, four, five, six, we're going to kill his son," "Muhammad V was our father, but you, who are you," "Down with Hassan II," and "Long live the republic" (Clément 1986, 23, 30). Other sources speak of protestors carrying pink parasols "to express their disdain for royal pomp and their indignation at the excesses of the king and the elite" (Tessler 1991, 12). By the time the protests-cum-riots-cum-insurrections of January 1984 were suppressed, Western observers estimated that over two hundred people had been killed and over fourteen thousand arrested (Clément 1986, 6–8; El País, 26 Jan. 1984).

None of this is mentioned in Elaine Combs-Schilling's 1989 book on Morocco's sacred kingship.

Further rioting occurred in Morocco's large cities in December 1990. Once again, the employment problems of the young were among the underlying causes (Tessler 1991, 16). Already in 1982, almost three-fourths of the officially unemployed Moroccans were under thirty (Lahlou 1991, 487). The problem of the unemployed young became even more acute during the following decade (Bessis 1992). It was in this context that a general strike called for by two labor unions in December 1990 led to violence in many of Morocco's cities (Le Monde, 16–17, 18 Dec. 1990). Young men from the poor neighborhoods of Fez attacked symbols of wealth such as luxury hotels. One Moroccan doctor told a foreign reporter that "on the basis of hospital and morgue registers, there must have been one hundred dead and two hundred wounded" (New York Times, 17 Dec. 1990).

The next major domestic crisis Hassan II faced was brought about by the Gulf War of 1991, during which Moroccan troops participated in the American-led coalition against Iraq (Daoud 1991). During a massive pro-Iraqi demonstration in Rabat on 3 February 1991, in which somewhere between two hundred thousand and five hundred thousand people participated, the crowds chanted "Shame! Shame! Treason is in the house," "Bush is a murderer, Mitterand his dog, Fahd [the king of Saudi Arabia] his donkey!" and "Iraq is at the front, the traitors are with the Americans" (Soudan 1991b, 31; Le Monde, 5 Feb. 1991). Hassan II, who had sent about twelve hundred troops to Saudi Arabia in August 1990, would not have tolerated such slogans in normal times. But he had not foreseen to what extent Moroccans and Morocco's political parties would sympathize with Iraq (al-Ahnaf 1991).

Moroccans, especially the educated ones, saw the war as an attempt to maintain American hegemony over the Arab world (Daoud 1991a; al-Manjra 1991). They identified with the Iraqis, whereas the Kuwaitis were routinely depicted as feudal potentates who served the interests of Western imperialism. This is precisely how leftist and fundamentalist Moroccans portray Hassan II (Agnouche 1987, 312; Dhaouadi and Ibrahim 1982, 57–59; Yasin 1974).

After the war broke out in January 1991, the king had to backtrack from his early support for the American position to a more neutral one, declaring that the Moroccan troops in Saudi Arabia were there for strictly defensive purposes and that "our heart is with Iraq even though our mind is against it" (Daoud 1991). In his televised address to the Moroccan people on 15 January 1991, the king banned all demonstrations and all criticism of any Arab governments "whatever side they are on." He eventually tolerated the demonstration of 3 February, probably fearful of the consequences of trying to stop it. Two days earlier, he had warned Moroccans not to criticize the Saudis or their king Fahd, saying "all of us Moroccans love them, not just me" (Soudan 1991b, 31).

Hassan II was especially sensitive to criticism of the Saudi (and Kuwaiti) royal families because he knew, as all educated Moroccans knew, that criticism of them was criticism of him. When the marchers of 3 February did condemn the Saudis, they deliberately mocked Hassan II saying: "The Saudi princes are traitors, we do not love them, and we have no use for their love" (Le Monde, 5 Feb. 1991). Others chanted "can love be commanded?" (Soudan 1991b, 31). Moroccans assumed that the king tolerated such defiance because he could not stop it. Many other demonstrations against the war, however, were broken up by police (U.S. Congress 1991, 94).

The popular outrage provoked by the Gulf War represented a serious challenge to Hassan II's regime. Some two thousand Moroccan troops reportedly went to Algeria in the hope of being sent to fight alongside the Iraqis (Diouri 1992, 15–16; Libération, 11 Feb. 1991). Thousands more would probably have refused to fire on antiwar demonstrators had they been ordered to do so. The king was lucky Saddam Hussein's army was routed in "a hundred hours." He might not have survived a protracted war, with protracted Moroccan exposure to images of Muslim Iraqis being bombed by non-Muslim Americans, Europeans, and "feudal" Saudis. The war reinforced Hassan II's image as "a puppet of American imperialism."

HASSAN II AND HUMAN RIGHTS

In addition to the Gulf War and the difficult economic situation facing Morocco in the early 1990s, Hassan II also had to confront growing domestic and international criticism of his regime's use of arbitrary imprisonment and torture. Moroccan survivors of Hassan II's prisons have described these practices in numbing detail (Bouissef Rekab 1989; Diouri 1972, 1987; Laâbi 1982, 1983; Serfaty 1986; Souhaili 1986). The king largely ignored criticism of his government's treatment of political prisoners until the late 1980s when the deluge of reports by Western human rights groups threatened to block the flow of American and European aid upon which Hassan II's regime depends (Parker 1990, 372; U.S. Congress 1991, 102; Waltz 1991).

On 20 December 1989, when asked about human rights abuses in Morocco on a French television program, Hassan II declared "If 1 percent of what I am accused of were true, I could not sleep or kiss my children or shake the hands of heads of state" (Daure-Serfaty 1992, 129). On 13 February 1990, the king assured two representatives of Amnesty International that the human rights situation in Morocco was not as bad as they thought and that they should bear in mind that every head of state had a "secret garden" (*The Economist*, 29 Oct. 1990). This was Hassan II's metaphor for the prisons where he kept his political prisoners. When the human rights group issued a harsh critique of Hassan II's secret garden a week later, the Moroccan government bought space in major American, French, and British newspapers to respond. Stung by the growing foreign criticism of his regime's use of torture, especially in France where over half a million Moroccans work, Hassan II established an official "Royal Consultative Council on Human Rights" in May 1990 (U.S. Congress 1991, 14). Moroccan intellectuals contend that this council is ultimately powerless. Yet its existence does reflect a new awareness of the human rights issue.

Moroccan government officials often blame international criticism of the human rights situation in Morocco on a foreign conspiracy organized by François Mitterand's wife Danielle, who is head of the French human rights group "France Libertés." The king himself has suggested that European criticism of his regime's human rights abuses is part of a French attempt to "destabilize" his regime (Soudan 1991c, 31–32). Hassan II often resorts to such conspiratorial explanations, the most famous example being the previously mentioned assertion that the riots of January 1984 were the result of a Communist, Zionist, and Khomeinist plot. A less well-known example is the king's explanation of Watergate as "an affair planned by two Soviet agents" (Montbrial 1986, 21). This penchant for conspiratorial theories is by no means a royal idiosyncrasy. In 1991, a young Moroccan woman (a university student of a Marxist orientation) assured me that the king could not be held responsible for the use of torture in Morocco because he was simply obeying his American masters. She said that the CIA would simply have Hassan II killed and replaced by his son if he were ever foolish enough to stop torturing the Moroccans the CIA wanted tortured.

One book did more to focus international attention on the human rights situation in Morocco than all the reports of Western human rights groups (see Amnesty International 1982, 1990, 1991 and Middle East Watch 1990, 1991). This was the French journalist Gilles Perrault's best-selling *Notre ami le roi* (Our Friend the King), published in September 1990. The Moroccan government helped publicize the book by condemning it (Sada 1990). The king was so outraged by it, and the French government's failure to prohibit its publication, that he canceled an extravagant year-long series of exhibits and performances celebrating Moroccan culture that had been scheduled to begin in Paris on 22 October 1990 (Vals-Russell 1990). Much the same scenario was reenacted on a lesser scale in 1991, when the Moroccan government tried to prevent the publication of a book about Hassan II's personal fortune by a Moroccan living in France—the same Moumen Diouri who had stripped to his bloodstained underwear to show where he had been tortured in the early 1960s (Diouri 1991).[7]

One reason for the tremendous impact of the Perrault book was its chilling account of the plight of the wife and children of the man who had orchestrated the 1965 kidnapping of Mehdi Ben Barka and the foiled coup of 1972—General Muhammad Oufkir. Hassan II had Oufkir killed after the coup, although the official story is that he committed suicide (Pédron 1972, 272–73). After his death, Oufkir's widow, his six children, and a cousin who lived with the family were imprisoned. They spent most of the next fourteen years and four months in a guarded farmhouse separated from each other in perpetually dark rooms without lights or windows. Only the youngest boy, 'Abd al-Latif, was allowed to remain in the same cell with his mother. He was three years old when he and his family were forced into police vans on 23 December 1972 (Perrault 1990, 331–35).

During the night of 19 April 1987, four of the Oufkir children escaped, led by the oldest daughter Malika who was by now thirty-four. The mother, the cousin, and two of the daughters (Sukayna and Myriam) were left behind because they were too weak to move. Malika, Ra'uf, 'Inan, and 'Abd al-Latif, now eighteen, managed to run through deserted fields at night and reached a highway, where they caught a ride to Casablanca on the back of a truck. Every friend and relative they contacted was too afraid to shelter them. So they fled north to Tangier. By now police were looking for them all over Morocco and dozens of former friends of the Oufkirs were being questioned (ibid., 329–36; *Libération*, 7 May 1987).

The four Oufkir children reached the Hotel Ahlen, about a dozen kilometers south of Tangier, where they hid in a grove of eucalyptus trees. Having been warned not to visit by a friend of her mother's in Tangier, Malika Oufkir called the local station of Radio France Internationale on 22 April 1987. French reporters recorded her description of their situation and broadcast part of it. On 24 April, however, the Moroccan police found the Oufkir children, and they were once again temporarily cut off from the outside world (Perrault 1990, 336–40). Four years later, in response to international pressure, especially from the French government, Hassan II finally freed them on condition that they not leave the country or discuss their ordeal with anyone (*Le Monde*, 27 July 1991; U.S. Congress 1991, 40).

In the wake of the uproar caused by Perrault's book, as well as the Gulf War, the king released a number of Morocco's other famous political prisoners in 1991, notably Abraham Serfaty (Daure-Serfaty 1992, 175). The Moroccan government even shut down the notorious prison at Tazmamart and released most of its prisoners (ibid., 61, 183–84;, *Le Monde*, 9 Jan. 1992). It is sometimes suggested that these improvements in the human rights situation were due to pressure exerted by Secretary of State James Baker before Hassan II's trip to the United States in September 1991 (Soudan 1991d, 29).

THE ROLE OF TERROR IN MOROCCO'S POLITICAL CULTURE

Gilles Perrault is, of course, a muckraking journalist, not a scholar. But in *Notre ami le roi*, he captures a fundamental feature of Moroccan political life that most anthropological studies of Moroccan kingship have ignored—the terror. The friends and relatives who shut their doors in the face of the Oufkir children did not do so because of their belief in the king's baraka. They were afraid. Every Moroccan is. Yet one would never know this from reading the descriptions of Hassan II's regime by Geertz and Combs-Schilling. Force and fear are not the sole sources of the king's power, but to ignore them is to distort the nature of Moroccan politics.

The only anthropologist who *has* mentioned the pivotal role of fear in Morocco is Kevin Dwyer, who was the director of Amnesty International's Middle East department for six years. Dwyer quotes a young Moroccan university graduate who says:

> Take Qsar al-Bhar, the section of Rabat where I live. A large part of the population there feels like a piece of wood—they feel unable to do anything because at any moment the police may pick them up and do with them what they will.... As it exists today, the state's project includes imposing its will through violence.... The problem is that to a great degree fear dominates ... whatever it [the regime] tries to introduce, it does so through violence.... Intellectuals themselves participate in this despotic project sometimes despite themselves, sometimes quite consciously. (Dwyer 1991, 137, 139)

Dwyer situates the pervasive fear in Morocco in the context of Morocco's political culture by quoting the following comments on some Moroccan proverbs by the well-known Moroccan sociologist Muhammad Guessous (presumably a distant relative of 'Abd as-Slam Guessous, the scholar killed by Mulay Isma'il in 1709 for refusing to legitimate the enslavement of free men):

> Generally political power is seen essentially as a source of evil and harm, and those who hold power tend to be unjust, to break the law, and to play with other people's lives. Generally the tone of the proverbs is quite bitter, they convey a sense of fear and betrayal. Injustice is the rule, the abuse of power is the rule; the proper, adequate use of power is the exception.
>
> ... the proverbs seem to show a longing for a strong power. For example, 'The stick is the only thing that will prevent rebellion and dissidence'; or, 'An unjust government is better than bad citizens'; or 'Starve your dog and it will follow you.' So the general rule seems to be: if you are going to be eaten, let yourself be eaten; but if you can eat others, then eat them. . . .
>
> What we see here then is fertile ground for despotic behavior, because society can't do without rulers. And we need strong rulers, because otherwise things are likely to go berserk. (ibid., 120–121)

Guessous's remarks, and the proverbs he discusses, echo some classical themes of Islamic political theory, notably the idea that those who hold power are typically unjust and brutal, but even an unjust and brutal king is better than the disorder that occurs in the absence of a strong ruler (see Lambton 1981; Lewis 1988). If fear of Hassan II's secret garden is a key source of his power, so is the fear of the chaos that might ensue if he were overthrown. This point is often raised by relatively traditional Moroccans when their younger, more educated relatives advocate the elimination of the monarchy.

At the same time, however, many of the classical themes associated with the myth of the righteous man of God are also echoed in popular Moroccan proverbs:

> The oppressor will not be helped by God
> [Ad-dalim ma i'inu Allah]
> The oppressor is cursed by God and despised by the people
> [Ad-dalim 'and Allah mal'un wa 'and an-nas maghbun]

There is no protection from the call of the oppressed to God
[Ad-da'wa dal-madlum 'and Allah ma fiha hjub].
(Westermarck 1930, 124, 255)

These proverbs do not contest the idea that power should be concentrated in the hands of one man, they simply stress that this man should be just as well as strong. As Guessous notes, there are no proverbs advocating a democratic diffusion of power (Dwyer 1991, 122). Democratic ideals are embraced by most educated Moroccans, but they have yet to take root in the popular culture. The absolute power of Hassan II does not, in and of itself, outrage the typical Moroccan peasant, peddler, or shopkeeper the way it does the typical lawyer, professor, or student. For many Moroccans, the king's harsh suppression of those who oppose him is seen as a sign that he is the kind of strong ruler Morocco needs.

The belief that rulers must be tough to maintain order is rooted in a more general view of human nature expressed in the following proverb: "If the slave does not taste the stick from Sunday to Sunday, he says there is no one like him" (al-'abd ida ma yakulshi al-'asa min al-had nil-had, kayqul ma f-halu had) (Westermarck 1930, 132). The word 'abd in this proverb means "slave" in the literal sense as well as "slave of God," the standard metaphor for a human being. As we have seen, 'abd is also the standard word for "black man." This proverb is most often used with respect to children in the sense of spare the rod and spoil the child. More generally, it means that every human being has to taste the stick to be kept in line. One Moroccan woman living in the United States told me, "I hate that proverb, it is awful." Indeed, many educated Moroccans hate it, not only because of the memories of childhood beatings it often evokes, but because of the more general Hobbesian conception of human nature it embodies.

One also sees this conception reflected in the proverb "If you are a mallet, hit, if you are a peg, submit patiently" (Ida kunti mirzab, duqq, ida kunti utad, sbar) (Westermarck 1930, 123; cf. Dwyer 1991, 123). All forms of hierarchy are seen as involving hitting and being hit. As Guessous suggests, this idea is also often expressed in terms of the metaphor of eating. Those in power "eat" their subordinates, who do the same to the people beneath them. Those who do the eating are often likened to lions, as in al-'Alawi's story cited in the last chapter, and as in the proverb "Who dares to tell the lion that the lion's mouth smells?" (Dwyer 1991, 121).

People in power are also often likened to sultans. The Jbalan peasants of northwestern Morocco joke that the local qaid that rules them is "like a sultan" (f-hal sultan). Peasants and the urban poor still use the word *sultan* even though the Moroccan monarch's title was officially changed to *malik*. As we have seen, bridegrooms are also called sultans. They too will possess absolute power over their wives and children.[8] Virtually every man in a position of power (women are not usually in such positions) is a little sultan. The big one is simply the most obvious examplar of a conception of power that pervades much of the society as a whole.

SLAVERY AS SYMBOL OF THE RELATION BETWEEN SUBJECT AND KING

Al-Yusi once wrote to Mulay (Mawlay) Isma'il saying: "who shall have pity on us if our sultan does not, for we are his slaves ('abiduhu) and his children (awladuhu)" (1981, 2:612). This image of subjects as the slaves of kings was a common one in earlier periods of Morocco too (Kably 1986, 259–60). One could, of course, argue that this was simply a meaningless figure of speech, a mere nicety of language (Robertson Smith 1927, 68–69). But Hassan II does not see it that way. Once, when he angrily scolded one of his ministers, the man responded humbly, "Your Majesty, I am your slave." The king then shouted, "It is not enough to say it! You must be it! This is what I expect from those who serve me" (Perrault 1990, 212). Most educated Moroccans would find such a statement utterly contemptible and completely contrary to the egalitarian ethos of Islam. But the king's conception of his relationship to his subjects is still found among many of his subjects. There is a well-known story that one day the king was hunting in the Middle Atlas when he saw a beautiful young woman who had a husband and two small children. The day after the king saw her, a car came and took her and the children to the royal palace. Her husband never saw her again (ibid., 214; Ariam 1986, 141). I asked several Moroccans in the United States how peasants would react to such a story. They said most would shrug their shoulders and say, "we belong to him" (hna diyalu). One Moroccan woman recalled how her illiterate mother used to say that families felt honored when their daughters were selected for the king's harem. Educated Moroccans tend to see things somewhat differently now.

The confusion of possession and power inherent in the word malik persists in the minds of many relatively traditional Moroccans. The word is derived from the verb malaka, which means "to possess, control, rule." The related noun mulk can be translated as "power, kingship, right of possession," or "property" (Wehr 1976, 922). We see this same confusion of power and property in the pastoral metaphor used to describe rulers as shepherds of their "flock" (ra'iyya). The latter term remains the principal word for "subjects" in Arabic (Lewis 1988, 18, 61). (The word for "citizen" muwatin, is a neologism that is rarely heard in spontaneous speech.) No matter how vehemently Moroccan intellectuals may condemn the idea that rulers in some sense possess as well as govern their subjects, the idea continues to play an important role in Moroccan politics.

None of this is meant to suggest that Islam or Moroccan society is inherently authoritarian. Most of the distinctive features of Moroccan political culture reflect a level of social development rather than immutable traits of religion or "national character." The idea that rulers own their subjects has existed in many societies, both Muslim and non-Muslim (Geertz 1980, 127–29; Milner 1983, 31). In Morocco, as in the rest of the Islamic world, it has always been confronted by contrary notions, notably that of the equality of all believers and the contractual conception of the caliphate.[9] Moreover, the authoritarian values exemplified by the Moroccan monarchy have been seriously eroded by the transformation of Moroccan society in the twentieth century. More and more educated young Moroccans regard them, like the monarchy itself, as anachronistic.

In a society where everyone is forced to manifest reverential loyalty to a ruler, it is hard to know if any of it is real. In Morocco, some of it undoubtedly is, but many of the sycophantic displays of devotion to Hassan II that one sees on Moroccan television reflect fear rather than reverence, servile submission rather than real loyalty. In May 1992, I asked a university-educated Moroccan what percentage of his compatriots genuinely supported the king. He answered, "On camera, 90 percent; off camera, 5 percent." The four other university-educated Moroccans present laughed and concurred, although one of them was rather nervous about doing so in the presence of an American scholar he had never met before. Actually, these estimates are inaccurate. Slightly more than half of all Moroccans still lived in rural areas in 1989 (World Bank 1989, 210). The overwhelming majority of peasants still support the king, as do many people in the popular quarters of Morocco's cities. Moreover, even many of the educated Moroccans who scoff at the idea that the king is sacred still support the monarchy as a source of stability.

Anthropologists, like many other Western observers, have tended to exaggerate both the religious and political significance of Hassan II's sanctity while completely overlooking his use of force and fear. We have seen that Geertz refers to the monarchy as "the key institution of the Moroccan religious system" (1968, 75). Were it not for Muhammad v's decision to support the nationalist cause, however, Moroccan kingship would not have survived independence. The Moroccans' religious system would have been unaffected by its demise.

Belief in Hassan II's baraka remains widespread, but it is not a central feature of popular religious belief. Nor does it imply a strong political commitment. The Moroccans who still believe in the king's sanctity, notably the peasants, are by and large passive observers of Moroccan politics. For them, politics is a spectacle they watch from afar. For politically conscious, educated Moroccans, the idea that the king is sacred is a relic of the precolonial past artificially preserved by French colonialism. Even the many Moroccans who support the king and the monarchy for fear of the alternatives no longer take these beliefs seriously. To discuss kingship in late twentieth-century Morocco without mentioning these facts is to present a thoroughly distorted picture of Moroccan political life.

Six Fundamentalism
in Late Twentieth-Century
Morocco

During the 1960s, the most serious opposition faced by Hassan II came from the socialist Left. The king was able to cripple this opposition by force and by portraying it as atheistic and hostile to Islam. During the course of the 1970s, however, several movements emerged to oppose Hassan II in Islamic terms. The people in these groups demanded the creation of a truly Islamic state (and society) and scorned the politically ineffective Salafi reformism of the Istiqlal party. Some of them were seemingly no more radical than the Istiqlal, while others openly advocated an Islamic revolution against the Moroccan monarchy. These are the kinds of people commonly referred to in the West as *fundamentalists*.

WHY USE THE TERM *FUNDAMENTALIST*?

Many Muslims and Western specialists on the Islamic world disapprove of the word fundamentalist because of its Protestant rather than Muslim origin and because of its connotations of bigotry and fanaticism. I use it for a number of reasons. First, it has become so entrenched, in the English-speaking world at least, that any attempt to avoid it is futile. Second, words often transcend their original meanings; one thinks, for example, of *zealot* and *puritan*. Third, I have yet to come across an adequate alternative. Some scholars use the term *political Islam*, which is fine, except that Salafi reformism was also political, as is the official Islam of the Moroccan government, which portrays the king as "the shadow of God on earth." Moreover, Muslim fundamentalists claim that Islam is inherently political and would thus regard the term *political Islam* as redundant.

The late twentieth-century advocates of a strictly Islamic polity often call themselves *Islamiyyun*, and the English translation of this, *Islamists*, is sometimes used by scholars. Aside from being an inelegant neologism, however, this term obscures the similarities between the twentieth-century advocates of a strictly Islamic state and twentieth-century advocates of comparable polities in other religions (Antoun and Hegland 1987; Kepel 1991; Lawrence 1989; Marty 1988; Marty and Appleby 1991). While it is important to view revivalist movements in their historical context, there is a great deal to be learned from also viewing them in comparative terms. This is the most important reason why it is useful to speak of Muslim *fundamentalists* as opposed to *Islamists*.

Twentieth-century fundamentalists, whatever their religion, typically argue that the ills of the present are due to deviation from the righteous path of virtuous ancestors. God is (or the gods are) punishing them for this deviation. As soon as believers once again conform to their sacred scriptures, God or the gods will deliver them from evil. This is, of course, a classical theme in Islam. Although the righteous men of God who defied sultans often argued along these lines, twentieth-century fundamentalists tend to interpret such classical themes in novel ways.

Fundamentalists, although often critical of nationalism as a secular ideology, are usually themselves intensely nationalistic. Iran's Islamic revolution was as much a nationalist revolution against foreign domination as it was a fundamentalist revolution against secularism (Munson 1988a). Nationalistic fervor pervades the rhetoric of Israel's Gush Emunim, as opposed to that of the more truly traditional Haredim (Aran 1991; Heilman and Friedman 1991). This fusion of fundamentalist and nationalist zeal is obvious in most fundamentalism, even though there are major differences between the nationalism of a Christian fundamentalist like Jerry Falwell and that of most third world revivalists. The latter are haunted by Western domination in a way that American fundamentalists are not.

The nationalistic dimension of most twentieth-century fundamentalism relates to broader issues. Like countless revivalists throughout history, twentieth-century fundamentalists advocate a return to the true form of their religion, but their conception of their religion is always to some extent an invented one. They typically incorporate bits and pieces of the secular ideologies they condemn into their interpretation of sacred scripture. Over and over again, for example, we are told that the true form of a religion does not permit any form of social injustice or even inequality. The fact that until recently all the world religions tolerated slavery and countless other forms of injustice and inequality is ignored. Rather, we are presented with images of a utopian golden age. All the believers have to do is return to their sacred scriptures, and the golden age will return. Of course, the fundamentalist image of the golden age varies in different religions. The kinds of social grievances often stressed in third world fundamentalisms are irrelevant to most Christian fundamentalists in the United States or to Israel's Gush Emunim.

Late twentieth-century fundamentalism is typically a politicized revival of tradition very different from tradition itself. Fundamentalists usually stress that their religion is an all-encompassing system governing politics and economics as well as what is conventionally thought of as religion (Aran 1991, 296, 307; Juergensmeyer 1990, 58). This ideological view of religion is far removed from how traditional believers believe. As noted in an earlier chapter, the distinction between the ideological defense of religion and religion itself is the most important point Geertz makes in *Islam Observed* (1968, 62). It is directly relevant to most late twentieth-century fundamentalism. We find, however, considerable variation in this respect, as we shall see in the Moroccan context. Some people who demand a strictly Islamic state are relatively traditional, like the Moroccan al-Fqih al-Zamzami. Others are far more ideological, like Morocco's 'Abd as-Slam Yasin. Rather than representing a rigid dichotomy, these men represent points on a continuum.

Twentieth-century fundamentalists usually have a Manichaean worldview. They often seem obsessed by hatred of their foes. Their rhetoric tends to have a shrill ranting tone rather than a religious one. Religion becomes a means to an end rather than an end in itself, a stick with which to beat the enemy rather than a source of spiritual solace. And the enemy is everywhere. Fundamentalists forever celebrate spirituality, yet their own rhetoric tends to be more polemical than spiritual. They thus often turn out to be remarkably irreligious defenders of religion.

Some readers will dismiss such characterizations of fundamentalism as biased. Indeed, among the most common objections to the term *fundamentalist* is that it is "value-laden" and implies a hostile stance toward that which it describes. Of course it does. (Although Christian fundamentalists wear the label proudly.) The words we use to describe social and political phenomena are almost never neutral. One thinks of the choice between *terrorist* and *guerrilla*, or between *capitalism* and *free market economy*. Sometimes we make such choices on strictly logical and empirical criteria. More typically, we do so on the basis of our own sympathies, sympathies largely determined by who *we* are.

As far as my decision to use the word *fundamentalist* is concerned, I have tried to present some of the logical and empirical criteria upon which it is based. But it definitely does reflect my own hostility toward fundamentalism of any kind. I would argue that any reasonable person, regardless of his or her religious background, ought to take a critical and hostile stance toward fundamentalism. Many Muslims do. For example, Rachid Boudjedra and Rachid Mimouni, two of Algeria's most famous novelists, have vehemently condemned that country's Islamic Salvation Front. Both men use the French version of the term *fundamentalist* (Boudjedra 1992, 63; Mimouni 1992, 132), as do many Muslim scholars who have studied the Islamic movements of the late twentieth century (Lamchichi

1989, 47–48; Rouadjia 1990, 92). The term is also commonly used in studies of Buddhism, Hinduism, and Judaism (see Swearer 1991; Gold 1991; Aran 1991). This is not to say it is ideal, but it is less inadequate than the alternatives.

Having attempted to justify my use of a term that many scholars consider ethnocentric, I shall now describe fundamentalism in late twentieth-century Morocco. I focus on three points on a continuum ranging from the most traditional and least ideological to the least traditional and most ideological: (1) the traditionalistic fundamentalism represented by al-Fqih al-Zamzami; (2) the mainstream fundamentalism represented by ʿAbd as-Slam Yasin; and (3) the radically ideological fundamentalism represented by ʿAbd al-Karim Mutiʿ and the left-wing factions of his group, al-Shabiba al-islamiyya (Islamic Youth). I shall discuss the first and last of these movements before discussing that of ʿAbd as-Slam Yasin, which is by far the most important of the three. There are two other groups sometimes associated with Morocco's Islamic opposition of the late twentieth century, notably the Pakistani-based Jamaʿat al-Tabligh waʾl-Daʿwa (the Society for Communication and the Call to God) and the Butshishiyya Sufi Order. Members of both have sometimes evolved into politically active fundamentalists, but these groups themselves are apolitical (Ahmad 1991; Tozy 1984, 267–80, 307–45).

AL-FQIH AL-ZAMZAMI AND THE SUNNI MOVEMENT

Among the least ideological and most authentically traditional of Morocco's Islamic movements is that exemplified by the late Fqih al-Zamzami (d. 1989) of Tangier and his sons. In literary Arabic, the word faqih means scholar, but in Morocco, a fqih is usually a man who teaches the Quran to children (traditionally boys). Al-Zamzami would not be considered a scholar by most Moroccan ulama, though he is viewed as one by his admirers. (When no other source is indicated, my information about al-Zamzami comes from conversations with a prominent activist in his movement in the summers of 1987, 1988, and 1990.)

When I spoke briefly with al-Zamzami at his home in 1987, he was a frail old man in his late seventies. His turban and long white beard made him look very much like a prophet. He was the scion of a famous sharifian family that has produced some of the most important shaykhs of the Darqawi Sufi order in northern Morocco. He underwent a transformation from Sufi to puritanical reformist in the 1950s. His sons and followers call themselves Sunnis, that is, followers of the Prophet's Sunna. In Morocco, the term Sunni is widely used to refer to Muslims who advocate a strictly Islamic way of life but are not directly involved in political activities. It can, of course, also refer to Sunni Muslims in general, but it is not usually used in this sense in everyday Moroccan speech (see al-Ftuh 1990). Al-Zamzami's followers are sometimes also called Wahhabis, the name often given to the puritanical revivalist movement that led to the creation of Saʿudi Arabia, but they do not like the label.

Al-Zamzami began condemning Sufism as a perversion of Islam while still preaching in his family's Sufi zawiya in Tangier. This did not endear him to his relatives, with whom he was not on speaking terms from the late 1950s until his death in 1989. Whereas the more radical and ideological fundamentalists were largely unknown in the popular quarters of Tangier in the late 1980s, virtually everyone knew of al-Fqih al-Zamzami. Most ulama, like the late ʿAbdallah Gannun, regarded him as an ignorant rabble-rouser (interview, 27 Aug. 1987). One prominent Moroccan religious scholar once asked me, "Would you want to be governed by someone like al-Zamzami?" I conceded that I would not. In the popular quarters of Tangier, however, both young and old generally still speak of al-Zamzami with awe. One young jeweler told me that people thought of the fqih as having been "like a prophet" (f-hal nabi). Yet high school and university students often ridicule al-Zamzami and his followers as old-fashioned Muslims unwilling to confront the regime of King Hassan II. This is especially true of students sympathetic to the more radical fundamentalism of ʿAbd as-Slam Yasin (as many are).

Yasin laughed when I mentioned al-Zamzami to him in June 1987. His daughter Nadia suggested that al-Zamzami was actually a government agent. (He was still alive at the time.) Yasin himself said that regardless of his intentions, al-Zamzami helped the government by focusing attention on matters of ritual and dress rather than on the need for a fundamental transformation of Moroccan society. Al-Zamzami's sons respond to such statements by condemning Yasin as a wild-eyed revolutionary. A close associate of al-Zamzami's praises the Iranian revolution for having shown "the true face of Islam," but says that unlike Yasin, the Fqih wanted to change people rather than overthrow a government (interview, 17 July 1987). It is true that al-Zamzami never advocated revolution in his writings, but he was more political than people like Yasin claim.

Al-Zamzami's ideas, like those of similar preachers, have been disseminated through cassette tapes of his sermons and lectures as well by his books and pamphlets (Tozy and Etienne 1986, 27). While many of his publications were pamphlets with titles like "How to Fulfill the Obligation of Prayer," some were critical of the present social and political order in Morocco. We may consider, for example, al-Zamzami's tract *Mawqif al-Islam min al-aghniya' wa'l-fuqara'* (The Position of Islam vis-à-vis the Rich and the Poor), the second edition of which was published in 1979–80 (1400 A.H.). This 91-page opus is banned in Morocco, and I was given my copy in a manner that might have been imagined by Ian Fleming.

Al-Zamzami begins this book by stressing that Islam does not allow people to possess wealth beyond what they need to live on. To support his critique of the rich, al-Zamzami cites a hadith that says, "I saw hell and most of the people in it were women and the rich" (p. 18). Al-Zamzami goes on to say that the rulers and the rich of the present age squander vast sums on worldly goods even though this is forbidden by Islam (pp. 20–21). Although by referring to "the rulers and the rich of the present age" (*al-hukkam wa'l-aghniya' fi hadha'l-waqt*) al-Zamzami avoids direct criticism of King Hassan II, most Moroccans would interpret his words as such. The Fqih fulminates against the rulers and the rich as follows:

> We find that they squander more than even the kings and the rich of the infidels!!
> And their goal is eminence, and the display of fake greatness and pageantry!
> They oppress "the weak" and devour the rights of the poor in order

to live in luxury and to increase their enjoyment of the pleasures of the world. (p. 21)

This is the traditional rhetoric of the righteous man of God.

Al-Zamzami says that the exploitation of the poor by the rulers of the present serves to strengthen and legitimate communist attempts to overthrow them (pp. 21–22). He contends that the professional imams and muezzins of Morocco's mosques are paupers living on the crumbs from the tables of the wealthy bureaucrats in the ministry of al-awqaf, or religious endowments (p. 22). One room in the house of a former minister of al-awqaf was so big, says al-Zamzami, that one could barely see who was sitting at the opposite end (p. 23).

One of al-Zamzami's favorite themes is corruption:

> The aid provided to the poor by "foreign countries" does not reach them [the poor] and they know of it neither much nor little. For those in charge take from it what they please. If anything remains —and it is only flour—they distribute it to the poor by way of the government employees, whose wages for this consist of "the flour of national cooperation" [tahin al-ta'awun al-watani]!
>
> As for sugar, oil, butter, chocolate, cheese, and similar wholesome foodstuffs [al-mawadd al-ghidha'iyya al-nafi'a], they are among the things selected by those in charge for themselves! (pp. 25–26)

A good example of al-Zamzami's ability to condemn corruption by means of concrete and comical anecdotes goes as follows:

> It is said that a king gave the prime minister a thousand dinars and told him to spend it on the illumination of the capital on a certain night. The prime minister took half the money for himself and gave the rest to the mayor of the capital. The mayor kept half of this and gave the rest to the head of the muqaddims in charge of the city's neighborhoods. The head of the muqaddims kept all of this money for himself and told the inhabitants of the city that the king had ordered them to illuminate the capital on such and such a date.
>
> On the designated night, the king observed the city and saw that it was indeed illuminated as he had ordered by means of the money he had given to the prime thief [ra'is al-surraq]. (pp. 26–27)

Al-Zamzami writes *ra'is al-surraq*, or "prime thief" instead of *ra'is al-wuzara'*, "prime minister." It should be noted that al-Zamzami carefully avoids criticism of the king himself in this passage.

In the 1980s, al-Zamzami protested the fact that women were being forced to show their hair when photographed for a national identity card (*bitaqa wataniyya*). He wrote the minister of the interior demanding that this practice be ended. Also in the 1980s, al-Zamzami's sons led a campaign against the way the poor were treated at public hospitals in Tangier. This is the sort of reformist rather than revolutionary behavior that was typical of al-Zamzami.

The governor of the province of Tangier once sent a representative to al-Zamzami's house in the old city asking him to speak at a ceremony celebrating the anniversary of a famous speech by Muhammad V. Al-Zamzami refused. On another occasion, the governor invited him to have dinner with him and some other guests. Again al-Zamzami refused. A close associate of his told me in 1987 that the Fqih "does not eat the food of government officials because it is derived from the sweat of the people." As we have seen, this is a classical motif of the myth of the righteous man of God (Goitein 1968, 207). In many respects, al-Zamzami exemplified this myth, but he was not a real scholar in the eyes of most ulama and he never defied a sultan as directly as did men like al-Yusi or Muhammad bin al-'Arbi al-'Alawi.

The most influential of al-Zamzami's sons, 'Abd al-Bari' bin al-Siddiq, used to preach in a popular mosque of Tangier. In 1983, he delivered a sermon that provoked the local authorities to arrest him. The day after the sermon, policemen surrounded the al-Zamzami home in Tangier's old city. 'Abd al-Bari' was detained and spent one month blindfolded in a house in Casablanca, where he was also tortured.[1] Soon after his release, 'Abd al-Bari' began preaching again, in Casablanca. But he now avoided direct criticism of the government in public. Like Muhammad bin al-Madani Gannun over a century earlier, he had come to understand the consequences of incurring the sultan's wrath. Henceforth he was careful not to do so again.

The Sunni movement exemplified by al-Zamzami appeals to shopkeepers and many blue-collar Moroccan workers employed in Europe, though 'Abd al-Bari' bin al-Siddiq in Casablanca appeals to more educated young Moroccans as well. By the late 1980s, the impact of this Sunni tendency could be seen in all the cities of Morocco—in clothing, wedding styles, and rhetoric. For most of the people involved, there is nothing explicitly political about all of this. Nor do most of the people who call themselves Sunnis have any organizational link to al-Fqih al-Zamzami's sons. (There are other similar preachers, see Tozy and Etienne 1986.)

Even at the cultural level, the Sunni tendency does not always run very deep. I recall one evening in a house in Tangier when three young women who always wore Sunni garb outside their home complained because their mother would not let them watch a Moroccan rock-and-roll singer on television. There was, to say the least, nothing Islamic about the singer's performance. Al-Zamzami would never have allowed his family to watch such a program. One hears many stories about young women who cover their hair and bodies in Sunni fashion simply to avoid being harassed by men in public. I have also heard men boast of sexual relations with women who wear the *hijab* (that covers everything but the face and hands). As 'Abd as-Slam Yasin himself stressed when I interviewed him in 1987, it would be a serious mistake to assume that all women wearing Sunni clothes are committed to the goal of an Islamic revolution.

The Sunni movement with which al-Zamzami is identified is actually a diffuse religious and cultural tendency rather than an organized political group. Al-Zamzami sometimes criticized the government in a manner reminiscent of the classical righteous man of God, but he never advocated revolution. A close associate of his tells me that al-Zamzami (like most Muslim fundamentalists) believed that the very idea of monarchy was contrary to Islam, but he never openly criticized Hassan II. His fundamentalism was much more traditional and much less ideological than that which has generally appealed to students and other educated young Moroccans.

'ABD AL-KARIM MUTI' AND THE SHABIBA AL-ISLAMIYYA

If al-Zamzami represents the most traditional wing of the Islamic opposition faced by King Hassan II in the late twentieth-century, 'Abd al-Karim Muti' and his group Islamic Youth represents its most radical one. The following passage is taken from an editorial in the first issue of a review published (in Belgium) by a faction of al-Shabiba in 1981:

> Our present and our future are caught between the hammer of American imperialism and the anvil of its agents represented by the corrupt monarchical regime and those who support it. . . .
>
> Your review appears in these circumstances to be, God willing, in the vanguard of an authentic Islamic revolution in Morocco; a revolution that enlightens the horizons of this country and liberates its people to bring them back to the Islam of Muhammad and those of his people who have known how to follow him—not the Islam of the merchants of oil and the agents of the Americans. (Dhaouadi and Ibrahim 1982, 57)

The merchants of oil in this passage are the Saudis and the other potentates of the Gulf. These people, like King Hassan II himself, are routinely condemned as agents of the Americans by the more radical fundamentalists. This rhetoric draws heavily on that of the Marxist tradition. Al-Zamzami would not have spoken of a "vanguard of an authentic Islamic revolution."

The same group that published the review in which the above passage appeared printed an open letter to the king after he told people not to sacrifice an animal for the feast of sacrifice in the early 1980s, because drought had decimated Morocco's flocks of sheep and goats:

> We have known you ever since you abrogated God's Book in its entirety and became yourself a god who makes laws, forbidding that which is permitted and permitting that which is forbidden; making blood flow and spreading dishonor. The cancellation of the feast of sacrifice only crowns the thirst for Pharaonism and tyranny that controls the core of your vile soul. . . . We say to you: Fear God in his religion and the religion of his prophet before he changes you into a monkey, after having changed you into a drunkard and an opium addict.

> We say to our people, Muslim and believing: Enough humiliation! Enough cowardice and shame! Revolt against this tyrant who wants to turn your country, beloved Muslim Morocco, into a land of debauchery and libertinism for the Jews who impoverish and starve its inhabitants at leisure. You have in your Quran and the Sunna of your prophet the best support. (Harbi 1991, 159).

This is an "ideologized" version of the classical tradition of the *nasiha* (frank counsel) given by righteous men of God to sultans. This is illustrated by its anti-Semitism. Contempt rather than obsessive hatred was the typical Muslim attitude toward the Jew before the twentieth century (see Lewis 1984, 33, 85; Stillman 1977, 80). This remains true today in Moroccan popular culture.[2] The charge that Jews impoverish and starve the Muslims of Morocco reflects the influence of European anti-Semitism on Muslim fundamentalists. By 1990, all but a few thousand of Morocco's Jews had left the country, which had a total population of about 25 million (Escallier 1991; Laskier 1990).

'Abd al-Karim Muti', who founded al-Shabiba al-islamiyya was at one time an inspector in the ministry of education and active in Morocco's teachers' union and in the Union Socialiste des Forces Populaires (USPF) (the principal offshoot of the Union Nationale des Forces Populaires, which split in two in 1972). He is reported to have undergone his transformation into an Islamic activist while on a pilgrimage to Mecca in the late 1960s when he was in his thirties. Under his leadership, al-Shabiba al-islamiyya began to attract supporters in Morocco's high schools and universities in the early 1970s. Clashes between his followers and Marxists were common (Munson 1988b, 340–42; Shahin 1989, 203–15).

On 18 December 1975, 'Umar Ben Jelloun, editor of the socialist newspaper *al-Muharrir* and one of the most prominent of Morocco's Marxist intellectuals, was assassinated. The government claimed that the murderers were members of al-Shabiba al-islamiyya. This is denied by the group, which claims that the government planned the murder to get rid of both Ben Jelloun and Muti' at the same time (al-Shabiba al-islamiyya 1984, 16, 35). Muti' left Morocco three days after Ben Jelloun's murder to attend a conference in Cordoba, according to some accounts, and he has not been back since. He is said to have been involved in the seizure of the Great Mosque of Mecca in 1979 (Burgat 1988, 141).

Muti' tried to retain a great measure of control over al-Shabiba after leaving Morocco in 1975. In some cases, his followers could not travel or marry without his permission (Tozy 1989, 38). Resentment of his authoritarian leadership was one of the causes of the fragmentation of the movement into mutually antagonistic groups in the late 1970s and early 1980s. One rebellious faction of al-Shabiba rejected Muti''s advocacy of the use of force against "those members of the community who have been led astray" (ibid., 351).

Another reason for the fragmentation and decreasing influence of al-Shabiba al-islamiyya in the 1980s was repression and cooptation by the Moroccan government. In 1984, seventy-one members of al-Shabiba received sentences ranging from four years imprisonment to death. Even before this, a number of activists in the organization had decided that it was too dangerous to challenge the current regime. So some of them left al-Shabiba and established groups and publications that continued to advocate a strictly Islamic polity but refrained from any direct criticism of the government and, above all, the king. The best-known of these groups is led by 'Abd al-Ilah Ben Kiran. It has repeatedly tried and failed to win recognition as a political party. Radical fundamentalists contend that Ben Kiran receives a regular stipend from the government to spread his message of nonrevolutionary revivalism. Al-Zamzami's son 'Abd al-Bari' bin al-Siddiq has close ties to such former militants.

Al-Shabiba al-islamiyya effectively ceased to exist during the 1980s, though some of its offshoots remain significant in Morocco's high schools and universities and among Moroccan students in Europe. Even among students, these offshoots are less significant than the movement inspired by the most influential Moroccan fundamentalist of the late twentieth century—'Abd as-Slam Yasin.

'ABD AS-SLAM YASIN AND THE MAINSTREAM ISLAMIC OPPOSITION

Yasin's movement is more radical and ideological than that of al-Zamzami but less so than that of al-Shabiba al-islamiyya. It is also the most politically significant of the three. Like the members of al-Shabiba al-islamiyya, Yasin's followers originally tended to be students. In the summer of 1987, I asked dozens of people I had known for years in several popular quarters of Tangier if they had ever heard of Yasin. The only one who had was a university student whose father had been a factory worker in Belgium. (He revered him.) In the late 1980s and early 1990s, however, Yasin attracted a growing amount of support from young people unable to find work, even some with no more than an elementary school education. He has had little or no success in mobilizing peasants and the urban poor (see Munson 1986b, 1986c, 1988b, 1991a; Wahbi 1987).

In person, Yasin exudes a spiritual aura as well as a gentleness that comes as a shock to anyone familiar with the stridency of his published polemics. He has a scraggly beard and twinkling eyes that suggest grandfatherly benevolence rather than religious fanaticism. He was about sixty years old when I interviewed him at his home on 26 June 1987, at which time he looked thin and frail. (When other sources are not indicated, information about Yasin is derived from this interview, during part of which we were joined by Yasin's daughter Nadia.)

Yasin studied at the traditional Islamic al-Yusifiyya University in Marrakesh and became a teacher of Arabic and then an inspector in the ministry of education, a position he held when Morocco regained its independence in 1956. He was a devout Muslim in the 1950s, praying the five daily prayers and fasting during Ramadan. He says, with a grin, that his Islam at this time was gentle and apolitical. Yet his way of life was highly westernized. He sent his children, including his famous daughter Nadia, to French schools. (While he was in prison, Nadia spoke on his behalf.) Nadia used to wear T-shirts and jeans as a teenager. She now wears a scarf over her hair and a *jillaba* (or burnous) that covers everything but her face and hands.

In 1965, at the age of thirty-eight, Yasin had what he calls a spiritual crisis, which he concedes some people could not distinguish from a nervous breakdown (Yasin 1974, 5). In speaking with me, Yasin observed that many great religious leaders have had such crises around the age of forty, and he cited the case of the Buddha! (The Prophet Muhammad also had such a crisis.) After reading a wide range of mystical texts, Yasin joined the Sufi brotherhood of the Butshishiyya, becoming a follower of Shaykh al-Hajj al-'Abbas, who died six years later. After this, Yasin claims he was dismayed by the materialism that prevailed in the brotherhood and left it. A prominent member of the Butshishiyya tells me that Yasin actually left the order in 1971 because he wanted to turn it into a political movement and was unable to do so. But while Yasin quit the Butshishiyya order, he never renounced Sufism and repeatedly refers to it in his writings. This is in sharp contrast to the antipathy toward Sufism characteristic of most twentieth-century Muslim fundamentalists (Burgat 1988, 16–20).

Yasin's attitude toward Islam was politicized in the early 1970s, in part as a result of reading the Egyptian writers Hassan al-Banna and Sayyid Qutb. (Yasin speaks of his realization that Islam is inherently political rather than of the politicization of his conception of Islam.) In 1974, he decided to write a *risala* (epistle or letter) to King Hassan II entitled *al-Islam aw at-Tufan: risala maftuha ila malik al-Maghrib* (Islam or the Deluge: an open epistle to the king of Morocco). This text is a conscious attempt to revive the classical tradition of *nasiha* (see pp. 1, 8–9). The epistle is 114 pages long, 114 being the number of chapters in the Quran. After sending a copy for the king to the governor of Marrakesh province, Yasin is reported to have prepared his burial shroud (Soudan 1991a, 39). Whether or not this is true, it certainly fits the myth of the righteous man of God. Muhammad bin al-'Arbi al-'Alawi too had prepared a burial shroud after defying the French.

Yasin begins his open letter to the king by saying: "My epistle to you is not like all epistles for it demands an answer." (p. 1). He repeatedly addresses the king as "O my brother" (*ya akhi*) or "O my beloved one" (*ya habibi*), terms never used by Moroccans in addressing Hassan II (pp. 11, 16–17). Yasin identifies himself as "the son of a poor Berber peasant and an Idrissi sharif by descent" seeking to guide a "frightened and confused king" (pp. 8–9). He suggests that the king is frightened because of the attempted coups of 1971 and 1972 and declares that "today we in Morocco are ruled by police terror that translates the terror of the king" (yusaytir ʿalayna al-ruʿb al-bulisi yutarjim ruʿb al-malik wa halaʿahu) (p. 11). He also says that "the king is on a volcano about to erupt" (p. 12).

Yasin frequently uses the word umma, which, as we have seen, can be translated as "the Islamic community" incorporating all Muslims all over the world. When Yasin uses this word, the context makes clear that he is actually referring primarily to the Moroccan people, as in the following passage: "Shall I tell the umma what everyone knows, namely that after the incident of Skhirat [the attempted coup of 1971] the king added a palace in France to his other palaces and sent to it his most valuable possessions and furniture so that he would be prepared in the event of an emergency? Or shall I inform people that the king has sold and is selling his properties and lands that cover an important part of Morocco?" (p. 11).

Yasin goes on to discuss a speech in which the king said that he did not like to see beggars: "Islam gives him who spends the night hungry the right to bear arms against him who has deprived him of the bounty of God. . . . Your palaces, your properties, and the opulent class in the land all explain the presence of beggary and misery" (p. 12). Yasin notes that after the king had informed his subjects of his sentiments regarding mendicants, the police removed Morocco's beggars from the streets so that "our Lord [Mawlana] would not be vexed by a painful sight." After elaborating further on the lamentable state of Morocco's economy, which he says is dominated by foreigners and "Zionist wealth" (p. 12), Yasin assures the king that "the solution to all these problems can be summed up in one word: Islam" (p. 13).

Yasin contends that Hassan II simply camouflages his Western "liberal" ideas with religion when he feels it is politically expedient to do so (p. 14). He tells the king that his "playing with Islam" has convinced young Moroccans that religion is indeed "the opium of the people and mere trickery by means of which hypocritical rulers exploit the gullibility of the masses and enslave them" (p. 18). (Al-Zamzami also argued along these lines, although less bluntly.) "You do not realize that you are the ally of communism in our country and that your senseless and deranged actions are manifest proof of the accuracy of what is claimed by the enemies of God [the Marxists]! How will you face God you so-and-so? [Bi ayyi wajhin talqa Allah ya hadha?] Tell me how if you are [truly] a believer! [Qul li bi ayy wajhin in kunta mu'minan!]" (p. 18). It is hard to convey a sense of how shocking this language is in the Moroccan context. In the official rhetoric of the government-controlled media, Hassan II is the commander of the faithful and the shadow of God on earth. Yet Yasin questions whether he is, in fact, a Muslim at all.

Yasin says the coups of the early 1970s were warnings from God (p. 21). He ridicules the king's claim to have survived these coups thanks to his baraka (p. 19). God saved him, not his baraka, but Hassan II failed to heed God's warnings and became more of a tyrant than ever (p. 21). Yasin's epistle represents the king's last chance. It too is a warning from God. If Hassan II heeds it and repents, he can still be saved. If not, "Who will there be to protect you?" (p. 21).

Yasin likens himself to Sidi Muhammad bin 'Abd al-Kabir al-Kattani, as well as to the two most famous fundamentalists of twentieth-century Egypt: Hassan al-Banna and Sayyid Qutb (pp. 2, 123). He notes that three years after killing al-Kattani, 'Abd al-Hafidh lost his throne after surrendering Morocco to the "infidel enemy" (p. 22). Similarly, King Farouq of Egypt was overthrown and ended his life "in the taverns of Rome" after having Hassan al-Banna killed. Soon after executing Sayyid Qutb in 1966, Nasser was defeated "by the vilest and most contemptible people on the face of the earth" (akhass al-nas wa ardhalahum fi wajhi'l-ard) (pp. 22–23). This is Yasin's view of the Six-Day War.

After thus warning Hassan II that he too will incur the wrath of God if he does not repent and return to the path of righteousness, Yasin then laments the transformation of the caliphate into a hereditary and absolute monarchy (pp. 26–30). Yasin reviles most of the rulers of the Umayyad and 'Abbassid dynasties but cites the

Umayyad caliph ʿUmar bin ʿAbd al-ʿAziz (717–20) as the arche-typal just ruler (pp. 30–31). Yasin describes most ulama as the sycophants of sultans (pp. 25–31).

Yasin contends that Hassan II seeks to imitate the governments of jahili societies, by which he means the governments of the West (p. 108). As we have seen, this term basically means "ignorant," with particular reference to the ignorance that prevailed before Islam. It is used in twentieth-century fundamentalist literature to refer to non-Muslim societies, including those societies in the Islamic world that are not governed according to Islamic law. Such societies, says Yasin, are "animalistic because they do not think of the reason why God created humanity and sent the prophets" (ibid.). In contrast to the jahili policies of the king and his government, says Yasin, the hearts of the oppressed masses (al-mustadʿafin), are full of real faith (iman). The king must get rid of his jahili advisers and surround himself by believers, as did the just ruler ʿUmar bin ʿAbd al-ʿAziz. "They will be the seed of good and around them will be built a society of believers based on a reciprocal oath of allegiance [al-mubaʿaya] instead of the bayʿa that is forced on the people by kings" (ibid.).

In summarizing his message, Yasin tells the king he can still save himself by implementing the following five conditions:

1. Announce publicly and clearly your repentance [tawbaka] and your intention to renovate Islam. [ibid.]
2. Reform what you have corrupted and all that has corrupted you, especially the wealth and honor you have unjustly taken. . . . Bring your fortune back to Morocco. Sell your palaces. [pp. 108–9]
3. Swear allegiance to a council elected in an Islamic manner that will be guided by men of the call to God [rijal al-daʿwa] after you have banned the political parties. [p. 109]
4. Gradually discard both liberalism and the illusory socialism that enriches [those] around it and create an Islamic economy based on these three principles: the [equitable] distribution of rights and duties . . . government use of wealth with freedom and courage for the sake of general prosperity . . . and the elimination of social injustice and the poverty of the umma. [pp. 109–10]

5. A general repentance . . . Islamic kindness [al-rifq] is the only alternative to the class violence and civil war that threatens us . . . and
general repentance can occur only under a repentant ruler and under
a renovated form of reciprocal allegiance [mubaya'a mujadadda]. [pp.
110–11]

Yasin concludes with a verse from the Quran that is also said in
daily prayer: "Praise be to God Lord of the worlds" (p. 114).

The basic message of Yasin's epistle is simple and familiar. The
Muslims' problems are due to their having deviated from Islam. If
they return to the laws of God and stop imitating the West, the
oppression of the poor by the rich will vanish. The domination of
Morocco by the West will vanish. The state of terror in which Moroccans now live will vanish. Poverty will vanish. The squatter settle-
ments ringing Morocco's cities will vanish. The caliph will be a man
of the people instead of a potentate living indolently in his palaces.
Everything that is bad will be good.

To some extent, Yasin's rhetoric in this epistle is thoroughly traditional and reminiscent of what righteous men of God have said to
sultans throughout Morocco's Islamic history. One is especially
struck by the similarity to what the Kattanis were saying at the
beginning of the twentieth century. One thinks, for example, of Sidi
Muhammad bin 'Abd al-Kabir al-Kattani's lament: "How could they
[the Christians] not defeat us when we have forsaken the practices
of our Prophet and filled our time with their practices, their
machines, their goods, their trinkets, and their novelties?" (al-Kattani
1962, 37).

If one compares Sidi Muhammad bin Ja'far al-Kattani's Nasihat ahl
al-Islam of 1908 with Yasin's epistle of 1974, the similarity is incredible, even with respect to the more traditional aspects of the earlier
text. This is true, for example, with respect to Yasin's emphasis on
the importance of sharifian descent. He stresses that both he and
the king are shurafa (p. 9). Yasin repeatedly refers to the king as a
"descendant of the Prophet" (pp. 1, 8, 16–17) and alludes to the
traditional belief that God commanded all Muslims to love "the
people of the house" of the Prophet (p. 19).

One does not find this traditional language in most Salafi and fundamentalist literature, where the equality of all Muslims is stressed, as it is in most of Yasin's publications (see Yasin 1973, 1979a, 1982). I asked Yasin how he reconciled his references to sharifian descent in his epistle with the egalitarianism he usually stresses. He said that he had mentioned his sharifian identity only so that the king would regard him as an equal and listen to his message. It is because of their common descent from the Prophet, says Yasin, that he often addressed Hassan II as his brother in the epistle. Yet one gets the sense that Yasin takes great pride in his (alleged) sharifian ancestry, as do many other educated Moroccans who claim to scoff at the traditional veneration of the descendants of the Prophet.

Yasin's repeated references to Sufism in his epistle (pp. 5–7, 19) also have a traditional ring to them. There has been a Sufi revival of sorts in Morocco since the 1980s, and many educated Moroccans have joined the Butshishi order, to which Yasin belonged for six years. (This has resulted in the publication of a new Sufi journal, al-Murid.) In the eyes of most educated Moroccans of the late twentieth century, however, Sufism remains a tainted vestige of the past. Yasin's Sufi proclivities are vehemently condemned by many Moroccan fundamentalists, as one would expect (Burgat 1988, 24).

Another surprisingly traditional aspect of al-Islam aw al-Tufan is Yasin's reference to Sidi Muhammad bin 'Abd al-Kabir as a saint (wali Allah) as well as "a Sufi shaykh" (pp. 22–23). Twentieth-century fundamentalists generally condemn the popular veneration of saints, as does Yasin himself in some of his later writings (Yasin 1979b, 121). One could argue that in his epistle, Yasin is using the term wali Allah in the specifically Sufi sense of one who is mystically close to God (Cornell 1989), but most Salafi reformists and fundamentalists would have a hard time accepting even this.

Warning rulers of their fate on the day of judgment, as Yasin does in his epistle, is a traditional feature of the nasiha genre, at least in its more radical forms (al-Manuni 1979, 228). But most twentieth-century Moroccans familiar with Yasin's epistle cannot believe he dared speak this way to Hassan II. Even al-Yusi never went this far with Mulay Isma'il—although Ibn Tumart did with 'Ali bin Yusif in the twelfth century (Ibn Abi Zar' 1860, 245; Lévi-Provençal 1928, 17–18). Fliers printed by the more militant factions of al-Shabiba al-islamiyya in the 1980s criticized Hassan II more violently than did Yasin in his epistle, but they were written anonymously.

Yasin's condemnation of the transformation of the caliphate into an absolute monarchy is thoroughly traditional, as is his emphasis on the reciprocal obligations of both the ruler and the ruled (al-Yusi 1981, 1:249–55). This is simply the classical model of the contractual caliphate that one finds in most of the great nasiha texts of the past. The suggestion that the king turn over much of his power to a council, however, is novel.

Yasin's insistence on the contractual nature of the caliphate should not be confused with a commitment to democracy. Yasin's conception of an ideal Islamic polity is a thoroughly authoritarian one, with the masses seen as being in need of a "just imam" to guide them on the path of righteousness. Unlike many Salafi reformists, not to mention Morocco's principal political parties, Yasin ridicules democracy and advocates a "council elected in an Islamic manner" *after all political parties have been banned* (p. 109). "The party of Satan," as Yasin calls people who advocate a secular form of government (1981, 4), would not be allowed to participate in the elections for this council. Yasin contends that those who reject the idea of a strictly Islamic polity are entitled to "firm but humane solicitude" (1982, 57). That is to say that they have the right to be taught the error of their ways.

In June 1987, Yasin told me that he wanted to establish an Islamic party to participate in Moroccan elections. Given his published criticism of the very idea of democracy, however, this appears to have been a ploy resulting from his movement's inability to overthrow the regime of Hassan II. His contempt for elections is not simply the result of the well-known fact that Moroccan elections are rigged. It reflects a more basic hostility to the idea of a government based on the will of the people—as opposed to one based on the laws of God. This is a common theme in the fundamentalist literature (see al-Ahnaf, Botiveau and Frégosi 1991, 85–99).

Yasin says that "general repentance" (*al-tawba al-'amma*) can occur only "under a repentant ruler" (pp. 110–11). This illustrates to what extent Yasin's vision of an Islamic polity revolves around a wise and just ruler. God, not the people, will select such a ruler (Yasin 1973, 862–63). Yasin has repeatedly stressed that the truly Islamic state he envisions will not be a democratic one (ibid., 870–79; 1982, 29–30). Despite his condemnation of Hassan II's authoritarianism, Yasin's conception of the proper political role of the people is ultimately not that different from the king's. Both see the masses as a flock of sheep in need of a shepherd. They disagree only as to the identity of the shepherd.

Yasin's epistle of 1974 is among the most traditional texts he has written, but even here we see the ideologization characteristic of most twentieth-century fundamentalism in his references to liberalism, socialism, "Zionist wealth," and the elimination of all social inequality—all notions that would have been unintelligible to Sidi Muhammad bin Ja'far al-Kattani in 1908. In his 1973 book al-Islam ghadan (Islam Tomorrow), Yasin discusses Mao Tse Tung at some length, suggesting that he lacked the one ingredient that would have made his revolution work—Islam (pp. 340–50). In an article published in 1979, Yasin speaks of the "dependence" of secular Moroccan intellectuals on Western thought, while his choice of words reflects his own dependence on Western dependency theory (Yasin 1979, 12). In this same article he says "the poor oppressed people groan under the oppression of the oppressor class" (al-sha'b al-mustad'af al-maskin ya'innu taht dhulm al-tabaqa al-dhalima), and he says that "Islam is a call of love, but there is no love but by the elimination of social distinctions in wealth and access to education, health, and security" (ibid., 49). One finds lots of talk of oppression in al-Yusi's epistle to Mulay Isma'il and Muhammad bin Ja'far al-Kattani's Nasihat ahl al-Islam, but one does not find references to an oppressor class or to the elimination of social distinctions in wealth and access to education, health, and security. Like most twentieth-century fundamentalists, Yasin borrows the rhetoric of the secular ideologies he condemns.

Hassan II was, of course, infuriated by Yasin's epistle and asked the late 'Abdallah Gannun, head of Morocco's League of Ulama, how he should respond to it. When I interviewed Gannun on 27 August 1987, he said that he told the king that Yasin should be put in a psychiatric hospital since only a lunatic could address Hassan II as Yasin had. This is, in fact, what many Moroccans say, not necessarily because they think what Yasin says in the epistle is crazy, but because they know what happens to people who criticize the king. In discussing al-Islam aw al-Tufan with Moroccans, one often hears comments about Yasin's insanity coupled with praise of his courage. He dared to say what others only think. This has always been one of the principal sources of the appeal of the righteous man of God. Many of al-Yusi's peers undoubtedly thought that he, too, was insane to criticize Mulay Isma'il.

Yasin spent three and a half years (1974–77) in an insane asylum because of his epistle. He told me, with a chuckle, that "they did to me what the communists do in Russia." But he may have suggested this strategy in al-Islam aw al-Tufan when he acknowledged that some people had mistaken his spiritual crisis of 1965 for a nervous breakdown (p. 5). Most Moroccans aware of Yasin's epistle of 1974 cannot believe that Hassan II did not have him killed. His relatively lenient sentence was undoubtedly due to the king's fear of turning Yasin into a martyr. Had Yasin been a Marxist rather than a modern version of the righteous man of God defying an unjust sultan, he would have been less threatening and would therefore have been punished more severely.

Once released from the asylum, Yasin resumed his campaign for a strictly Islamic polity in Morocco, but he no longer criticized the king directly. In 1979, he began publishing an Islamic review entitled al-Jama'a, "The Group," of which no more than three thousand copies were ever published (Tozy 1984, 394). The government had obstructed the publication of this review for at least a year before the first issue was published. It was banned after the eleventh issue appeared in 1983. The government also forbade Yasin from preaching in mosques. In December 1983, he tried to publish another newspaper entitled al-Subh, "The Dawn," but this too was immediately banned and he was sentenced to two years in prison. He was released in January 1986.

From 1986 until 1989, Yasin's home in Salé became the center of his movement, even though policemen always guarded it and often questioned visitors. Like al-Zamzami, Yasin the fundamentalist critic of the popular veneration of saints became somewhat of a saint himself, and his home became a shrine to which supporters from all over Morocco came on pilgrimage. A schoolteacher arrested in January 1990 told the police: "'Abd as-Slam Yasin is for me a saint. I prefer him to my father and even to my soul. I am devoted to him and his ideas and works body and soul" (Gendarmerie Royale de Kenitra, 1990, 6). The two Rifian schoolteachers who visited Yasin while I was interviewing him seemed to view him the same way. The advocate of the contractual caliphate turns out to be a hierocratic imam.

Despite his break with the Butshishiyya Sufi order, Yasin's movement, now known as "Justice and Benevolence" (al-'Adl wa'l-Ihsan) is itself reminiscent of a Sufi order. In 1981, Yasin told a depressed young schoolteacher from Fez to read a collection of sermons by the twelfth-century Sufi 'Abd al-Qadir al-Jilani as well as a book by the twentieth-century Syrian fundamentalist Sa'id Hawwa (ibid., 21). Like a Sufi shaykh, Yasin is regularly referred to as a murshid, or "guide," by his followers. Like a shaykh, he stresses the importance of prayers involving "the remembrance of God" (dhikr Allah). And like some Sufis, Yasin's followers are allegedly expected to chant "there is no god but God" three thousand times a day and "God bless our Lord Muhammad" three hundred times a day (ibid., 13). As I have noted, this Sufi aspect of Yasin's movement is unusual and condemned by some fundamentalists.

In December 1989, the police stopped allowing visits to Yasin's house, where he remained under house arrest. The following month, six leaders of Yasin's Justice and Benevolence movement were arrested (Le Monde, 16 Jan. 1990). The trial of these six men sparked a demonstration of some two thousand people in May 1990. The center of Rabat was paralyzed for about three hours before the police finally dispersed the protestors, most of whom were university students (ibid., 5 May 1990). The fact that this demonstration was Yasin's most dramatic political success demonstrates just how unsuccessful his movement has been. In February 1991, his follow-ers did participate in the huge rally against the Gulf War, but they constituted a small minority of the hundreds of thousands of pro-testors (*New York Times*, 4 Feb. 1991). In April 1992, Yasin's followers occupied the medical school at the Université Hassan II near Casa-blanca after one of them was killed in a clash with police. Many students, however, were outraged that the fundamentalists prevented them from taking their exams as scheduled (Lévy 1991).

Even in the high schools and universities, where they are strong-est, Yasin's followers face opposition from the radical Left and from many other students unsympathetic to their politicized form of Islam. In October 1991, violent clashes between fundamentalist and Marxist students in Oujda resulted in three deaths (*Maghreb-Machrek*, Jan.–March 1992, p. 123).

WHY SO STRONG?

Unlike the Sunni movement exemplified by al-Zamzami and the Islamic Youth movement exemplified by 'Abd al-Karim Muti', Yasin's Justice and Benevolence movement could eventually pose a real threat to the regime of King Hassan II. In addition to his student support, Yasin has a growing number of followers among the edu-cated young people unable to find work. Yet he and his followers have had nothing like the impact of the fundamentalists of Algeria in 1990–91, let alone the success of the fundamentalists in Iran in 1978–79 (see al-Ahnaf, Botiveau, and Frégosi 1991; Entelis 1992; Roberts 1991; Munson 1988a).

This could change. The Iranian fundamentalists were deemed politically insignificant until 1978. Their Algerian counterparts were viewed the same way until the late 1980s. The growing number of unemployed or marginally employed young people in Morocco are increasingly desperate, and Yasin promises them utopia in an appeal-ing Islamic idiom (Akesbi 1991; Lahlou 1991). In 1990, one young Algerian explained his support for Algeria's Islamic Salvation Front (*Front islamique du salut*, or FIS) as follows: "In this country, if you are a young man . . . you have only four choices: you can remain unemployed and celibate because there are no jobs and no apartments to live in; you can work in the black market and risk being arrested; you can try to emigrate to France to sweep the streets of Paris or Marseilles; or you can join the FIS and vote for Islam" (Tessler 1991, 17). Such reasoning is beginning to take root in Morocco. I know one young man from a popular quarter of Tangier who did not complete high school and never had a real job. He never seemed especially religious. In fact, he had a reputation as a "ladies' man." By 1991, he had become a zealous advocate of an Islamic state!

It is not just unemployed young men who get excited about the idea of such a state. A well-paid Moroccan civil servant once assured me that "Islam does not tolerate oppression (dhulm). If Muslims conformed to Islam, oppression would not exist." On another occasion, a university-educated young Moroccan woman told me that all the solutions to Morocco's problems lay in the Quran. Such views are widespread. Mohamed Tozy undertook a survey of four hundred Moroccan university students in 1984 and found that 55 percent endorsed the idea that "the backwardness of our society is due to our renunciation of the true Islamic religion" and 62 percent agreed that the precepts of the Quran should be emphasized "to reconstruct the cultural identity of Moroccans" (Tozy 1984, 248–52). Such beliefs do not in and of themselves entail a commitment to the idea of an Islamic revolution, but they create a receptive audience for the rhetoric of people like Yasin.

Another factor that has helped the fundamentalists is the relative weakness of Morocco's secular Left, which was once the principal source of opposition to the regime of Hassan II. The Left never managed to overcome the perception that it was hostile to Islam. (The king has exploited this perception, but he did not create it.) Nor was the Left ever able to recover from the harsh repression of the 1960s and 1970s and the divisions it engendered. The Left has also been discredited by the failure of communism in eastern Europe and that of socialism in the Arab world, especially in Algeria. The Union Socialiste des Forces Populaires remains popular among many intellectuals, students, schoolteachers, and some union activists. The related labor union (the Confédération Démocratique du Travail) also remains powerful. Nonetheless, the Left as a whole has lost much of its credibility.

The king has always excelled at using both carrots and sticks to tame his opponents. Critics of Hassan II's regime are imprisoned on the slightest pretext. If, however, they are considered influential, they are told that if they renounce their objectionable beliefs and express their loyalty to the throne, the king will pardon them and reward them with a good job and the good life that goes with it (Waterbury 1970, 271). Such pardons are routinely announced on holidays so that the families and friends of political prisoners anxiously watch and listen to the news on these occasions. Individuals fortunate enough to be forgiven by Hassan II are reminded that they could be yanked back to the king's secret garden at a moment's notice. In this way, they are made to feel utterly dependent on Hassan II—as children are on their father. (The king often speaks of himself as his subjects' father.) Hassan II has used this method so often to pull the Left's teeth that it now bites with its gums. Anyone who regularly watches the evening news in Morocco can name men who once dreamed of leading a Marxist revolution but now extol the king's virtues. Women have rarely undergone such transformations because they are not usually considered politically significant enough to warrant cooptation.[3]

The king has used similar methods to control the Istiqlal party associated with Salafi reformism, but this party has generally been so tame since the 1960s that it has not had to taste the stick as much as the Left has. The Istiqlal's shibboleths about the need to return to the pristine Islam of the Prophet have to a large extent been appropriated by fundamentalists like Yasin, who, unlike the leaders of the Istiqlal, are not tainted by decades of collaboration with the king. Although by no means dead, the Istiqlal is generally seen as the king's toy rather than as a serious alternative to the status quo. This is basically true of all the established political parties with the partial exception of the USFP (which is divided into moderate and radical wings).

WHY SO WEAK?

Given the weakness of the USFP, the Istiqlal, and Morocco's other political parties, one might well ask why Yasin and his followers have not been more successful. One reason often given is the religious legitimacy of the monarchy, which is undoubtedly a factor. A pious Moroccan scholar once said to me: "Why do these people demand an Islamic state? We already have one." As I tried to show in the last chapter, however, the political significance of the Islamic dimension of the monarchy has been greatly exaggerated. The king has stressed his role as commander of the faithful more than ever before because of the fundamentalist threat. He has tried to enhance the political role of the ulama, who say what he wants them to say (Bowen 1985); he has served as head of the Committee for the Liberation of Jerusalem, organized by the Islamic Conference of Ministers of Foreign Affairs (Lamchichi 1989, 174); and he has built the most expensive mosque in the world, the "Hassan II Mosque" in Casablanca (Gouzi 1991). But none of this has had much of an impact on public opinion except for the mosque, which for some Moroccans has actually become a symbol of the monarchy's illegitimacy.[4]

A more significant cause of the fundamentalists' weakness has been, once again, the harsh repression to which they, like all critics of Hassan II's regime, have been subjected. Countless young Moroccans have been imprisoned and tortured for involvement in fundamentalist groups (Amnesty International 1982, 1990, 1991). Others have also been coopted by the government in the manner I have described. According to Yasin, many former militants receive government subsidies to publish magazines or newspapers that advocate a return to the Islam of the Prophet without questioning the political status quo in Morocco. Yasin himself is reported to have rejected the government's offer to make his movement a legally recognized party in return for his public declaration of allegiance to the throne (Lévy 1991, 26).

Another less obvious reason for the weakness of the fundamentalists is that their politicized version of Islam differs radically from the more strictly religious ways in which most Muslims understand their religion. As I have pointed out, the conventional wisdom that Islam does not distinguish between religion and politics does not reflect Islam as it is understood by most Muslims. Much of the ideological rhetoric of the fundamentalists is as far removed from the beliefs and values of ordinary Moroccan Muslims as is the caliphal rhetoric of the king. The very fact that the fundamentalists feel compelled to stress constantly that religion and politics are inseparable in Islam illustrates that this is not how most Muslims perceive their religion. We do not find the fundamentalists stressing that Muhammad was the last of God's prophets or that people will eventually go to heaven or hell, because they know that Muslims take these things for granted. Fundamentalists themselves readily concede that most Muslims do not think of Islam in political terms, but they attribute this to ignorance (al-Banna 1965, 228; Burgat 1988, 16).

The gap between popular belief and the ideologized Islam of the fundamentalists is demonstrated by the popularity of the Moroccan television show "The Mufti's Corner" (Rukn al-Mufti), on which ulama answer viewer's questions, sent in by mail, about everyday matters like sex, marriage, inheritance, and ritual obligations. Fundamentalists dismiss this show as a circus designed to prevent Moroccans from understanding the political dimensions of Islam, but most devoutly religious Moroccans love it and would be shocked by the suggestion that it does not represent true Islam. (This is certainly true of the working-class Moroccans with whom I have watched the program.)

Khomeini and the Shiʻi ulama of Iran were able to overcome the gap between popular and politicized Islam in part because of the tremendous authority of the Shiʻi ulama (Munson 1988a). In the Sunni world, especially the twentieth-century Sunni world, the ulama lack this authority and do not have much impact on popular belief. Anyway, the ulama have by and large not been involved in the fundamentalist movements of Morocco or the rest of the Sunni world.

The teachers and other civil servants who have generally led the

radical or revolutionary Sunni fundamentalist movements have had
a hard time mobilizing large numbers of supporters outside the
ranks of students and the educated middle class (Ayubi 1991, 159;
al-Jabiri 1988, 67). Yasin too has had this problem. Contrary to what
is often asserted in the literature on "the Islamic revival," people
who migrate to cities from rural areas have not been active in Muslim
fundamentalist movements, nor have peasants or blue-collar workers (Munson 1988a, 100–2). The gap between such people's religion of saints and spirits and Yasin's ideological Islam is enormous
(even though Yasin is less divorced from popular belief than some
other fundamentalists). Algeria and Iran have demonstrated that
this gap can be bridged—at least to some extent and for brief
periods—but Yasin has yet to build such a bridge in Morocco.

Another source of the fundamentalists' weakness in Morocco is
that many Moroccans fear them even more than they do Hassan II.
The electoral successes of Algeria's Islamic Salvation Front in 1990
and 1991 had a double-edged effect in Morocco. On the one hand,
they revived interest in the notion of Islamic revolution, which had
lost some of its luster during the decade following the Iranian revolution of 1978–79. On the other hand, they scared many Moroccans of the middle class and the elite into reluctant acceptance of
Hassan II as the lesser of two evils. Better a Moroccan shah than a
Moroccan Khomeini. People who have fought for democracy all
their adult lives now find themselves worrying that democratiza-
tion could result in a fundamentalist state.

No one really knows if people like Yasin could win free elections
in Morocco. He has never actually threatened Hassan II's regime in
the past. But a major reason for this has been the government's
effective repression of his movement. Although Yasin's politicized
version of Islam does differ from how Islam is understood by most
Moroccans, it nonetheless articulates widespread grievances in a
basically familiar and appealing idiom, and Yasin does evoke the
classical image of the righteous man of God who dares to defy an
unjust sultan. These factors, and the absence of appealing alternatives, could well induce a majority of Moroccans to vote for people

like Yasin in free elections. This possibility has led some Moroccans to conclude that autocracy may be preferable to democracy after all—in the short run at least. Fear of the fundamentalists has thus reinforced the traditional fear of the chaos that might ensue in the absence of a tough ruler.

Seven Conclusion:
Rethinking Geertz

Throughout this book, I have looked at the relation between religion and power in Morocco by focusing primarily on a series of clashes that embodied the myth of the righteous man of God who dares to defy an unjust sultan. I have tried to avoid generalization divorced from what real people do as well as the description of events severed from the structures that shape them. Like Geertz, I have tried "to find in the little what eludes us in the large" (1968, 4). I have leapt back and forth between event and structure in a manner ostensibly similar to Geertz's "dialectical tacking between the most local of local detail and the most global of global structure" (1983, 69). These similarities are not coincidental. Like most other American anthropologists born since World War II, I have been strongly influenced by Geertz's theoretical writings.

While I have tried to demonstrate the need for a less ethereal alternative to Geertz's approach to the social history of the imagination, as represented by *Islam*

Observed, I nonetheless consider this an important book. In addition to being one of the earliest attempts by an American anthropologist to bridge the gap between the *histoire des mentalités* and anthropology, it includes several valuable theoretical points, notably the idea that religion as a symbolic system in terms of which believers view the world should be distinguished from "the sorts of social apparatus" which have been associated with it (1968, 2). In practice, Geertz often fails to make this distinction and thus ends up saying things like the Moroccan monarchy is "the key institution in the Moroccan religious system" (ibid., 75). However, the theoretical point does not lose its value simply because Geertz fails to implement it himself.

The most important contribution Geertz makes in *Islam Observed* is his discussion of the ideologization of religion. Although many of the specific points Geertz makes about Moroccan scripturalism are mistaken, he saw what few other scholars did—that reformist Islam was more than just another swing of the pendulum between popular and orthodox Islam. It was, to some extent at least, an ideological transformation of orthodoxy. It involved the transformation of religious symbols from "imagistic revelations of the divine, evidences of God, to ideological assertions of the divine's importance" (ibid., 62).

In an earlier book, I discussed the contrast between the spontaneous innate fundamentalism of traditional Muslims and the self-conscious ideological fundamentalism of political activists (Munson 1984, 20–23). The distinction I sought to make in these terms was in the spirit of Geertz's contrast between religiousness and religious-mindedness (1968, 61–62), and Mannheim's distinction between traditionalism and conservatism (1953, 94–115). All three dichotomies are attempts to contrast the spontaneity of people who simply take their traditional beliefs for granted with the deliberate, self-conscious defense of traditional beliefs by people who feel that they are in some way threatened. I would emphasize that such contrasts should be seen as involving points on a continuum. Not all defenses of tradition are equally ideological, as we can see by comparing the fundamentalism of al-Zamzami with that of Yasin.

Islam Observed was published before Geertz's celebrated interpretive essays of the 1970s, notably "Deep Play: Notes on the Balinese Cockfight" (1972) and "Thick Description: Toward an Interpretive Theory of Culture" (1973, 3–30). Geertz's interpretations of the folktales about al-Yusi in *Islam Observed*, however, illustrate both the strengths and the weaknesses of the approach he advocates in his later work.

A basic problem with Geertz's attempts to understand religions and cultures by means of interpreting little stories is his failure to situate them in the context of the structures in which they are embedded. In "Thick Description," he asserts that symbols "draw their meaning from the role they play (Wittgenstein would say their 'use') in an ongoing pattern of life, not from any intrinsic relationships they bear to one another" (1973, 17). But symbols do derive much of their meaning from the systems of which they are a part (Schneider 1980, 125–29). They do not suddenly become meaningful during the course of being used. Any attempt to understand isolated symbols without reference to the broader structures in which they are embedded leads to confusion.

It is true that many structuralist analyses are elegant fantasies unrelated to the world views they allegedly depict. It is also true that we need to study symbols in terms of how they are actually used by real people living their everyday lives. Such study, however, does not preclude the analysis of structure. On the contrary, it entails it. As Geertz has himself noted, one cannot make sense of snippets of action on a baseball diamond without some awareness of the game's overall structure (1983, 69). Nor can one make sense of a religious concept without reference to the conceptual system of which it is a part.

If Geertz had studied Moroccan Islam as a religious system embodied in its basic rituals and if he had carefully distinguished between Islam the religion and the political institutions associated with it, he would never have said that the Moroccan monarchy is "the key institution in the Moroccan religious system" (1968, 75). He would have recognized that the monarchy is, in fact, a tangential aspect of Islam as understood by most late twentieth-century Moroccan Muslims.

Geertz has correctly warned that when "the political, economic, stratificatory realities within which men are everywhere contained" are ignored, one runs the risk of "turning cultural analysis into a kind of sociological aestheticism" (1973, 30). Yet that is precisely what he himself tends to do. The most striking example of this in *Islam Observed* is Geertz's claim that the power of Hassan II in the 1960s was based "almost entirely on the legitimacy of the Sultanate in the eyes of the masses" (1968, 88). Hassan's use of force had been front-page news in much of the world during the years before these words were written. Yet this aspect of Moroccan kingship is effectively ignored in *Islam Observed*. Geertz has criticized Western political theory for its tendency to reduce power to its coercive and violent dimensions (1980, 134). But an analysis that ignores these dimensions is as inadequate as one that ignores everything else.[1]

In studying the relation between religion and power, one has to avoid reducing either to the other. If we focus only on the explicitly political facets of a religion, we cannot understand how it is seen from the believer's point of view. We therefore cannot understand its real political significance. Conversely, if we ignore the secular facets of power, such as brute force and the fear it inspires, we end up attributing to religion greater political significance than it really has. *Islam Observed* demonstrates how the relation between religion and power can be distorted by the neglect of both the strictly religious aspects of religion and the strictly political aspects of power.

Geertz has played a key role in the convergence of history and anthropology, and his notion of the social history of the imagination represents a laudable attempt to transcend the artificial boundaries that fragment the human sciences. One cannot, however, reconstruct the collective imagination of seventeenth-century Morocco on the basis of twentieth-century folktales and the writings of French Orientalists. One has to study the texts written by the people whose imagination one is trying to reconstruct (assuming that such texts exist).

The traditional academic division of labor has perpetuated the illusion that the folk tradition studied by anthropologists in villages and the great tradition studied by Orientalists are autonomous.

There undoubtedly are differences between the two, but they are rooted in the basic imagination. In Morocco, for example, one finds the myth of the righteous man of God who defies an unjust sultan in the historical texts of the past as well as the folktales of the present. A social history of the imagination should take both into account.

Those anthropologists inclined to dismiss texts as being unrelated to what real people think and do are as misguided as the indigenous literati who dismiss popular belief as a bundle of superstitions unrelated to real religion. Had Geertz read al-Yusi's writings, he would have realized that the man he dismissed as a restless zealot was, in fact, a brilliant social historian and ethnographer whose reflections on religion, language, society, and politics enable us to understand how seventeenth-century Moroccans saw the world and lived their everyday lives. Such understanding is precisely what Geertz strives for in *Islam Observed*, and yet he ignores the very sources that can provide it.

Readers familiar with current debates in anthropology and related disciplines will undoubtedly have noticed a few similarities between my criticism of Geertz and that of the postmodernists (see Clifford 1983; Crapanzano 1986). The similarities, however, are minor when compared with the differences. The postmodernists complain that "despite Geertz's occasional acknowledgements of the ineluctability of fictionalizing, he has never pushed that insight very far" (Rabinow 1986, 243). As far as I am concerned, Geertz has pushed that insight too far, and the postmodernists have pushed it to the point of absurdity.

The most interesting and influential of the postmodernist theorists, the philosopher Richard Rorty, has argued that texts are "made as they are interpreted" and that "a text just has whatever coherence it happened to acquire during the last roll of the hermeneutic wheel, just as a lump of clay only has whatever coherence it happened to pick up at the last turn of the potter's wheel" (1992, 97). This is wrong. It is true that texts, like events and cultures, are interpreted in different ways by people whose perspectives have been shaped by different social historical contexts. But they are not invented ex nihilo every time they are interpreted, and to say they have no coherence or meaning of their own is ludicrous, as are the related notions that all interpretations are equally plausible and equally fictional. (See Eco 1992, 23–25, 40, 43.) Would Rorty seriously suggest that an interpretation of Plato's *Republic* by a renowned scholar of classical Greek philosophy and one by a semiliterate high school student were simply two equivalent turns of the hermeneutic wheel?

It is, of course, true that there are generally no uniquely correct interpretations of texts or events. All are partial and skewed. But some are more plausible than others. I have tried to demonstrate, for example, that my interpretation of al-Yusi's conflict with Mulay Isma'il is more plausible than Geertz's. I do not claim that mine is uniquely correct. I do claim, however, that the evidence I have set forth demonstrates that it is more credible than Geertz's, and that anyone offering an alternative interpretation should assess it in terms of the evidence I have adduced to support my own. If we are all free to spin the hermeneutic wheel as we wish without any attempt to assess our interpretations empirically, why should anyone take us seriously? If all we write is fiction, then why not leave the task to those who really do it well?

Notes

CHAPTER 1: Al-Yusi as Exemplar

1. Geertz, *Islam Observed*, 25, 114. Geertz writes *Lahcen Lyusi* following colloquial pronunciation.
2. Geertz's neglect of indigenous texts has often been noted with respect to his work on Indonesia (Koentjaraningrat 1985, 427; Nakamura 1983, 173; Ricklefs 1983; Schulte Nordholt 1981, 474; Tambiah 1985, 331; Woodward 1989, 245–47).
3. Rabinow's *Reflections on Fieldwork* is among the best-known examples of the "reflexivist" ethnography advocated by the postmodernists (see Clifford 1983; Clifford and Marcus 1986). The advocates of this approach stress, among other things, the importance of describing the social situations from which ethnographies emerge and the need to record precisely what informants say in specific contexts. These are good points. Unfortunately, however, reflexivist ethnographies often end up telling us too much about the anthropologists' personal experiences and too little about the culture they are ostensibly studying. Rabinow's *Reflections on Fieldwork* is a case in point.
4. Muhsin Mahdi, in commenting on an earlier oral version of this chapter, noted that in the Quran, *ahl al-bayt* ("people of the house")

actually refers only to the Prophet himself and his immediate family. Most Muslims have, however, understood the term to include the patrilineal descendants of 'Ali and Fatima (see Gibb and Kramers 1953, 529–33; Sebti 1986, 440.)

The role of the Prophet's daughter Fatima in reckoning descent from the Prophet is anomalous in an otherwise strictly patrilineal system. Her significance is demonstrated by the fact that although both 'Ali and his brother Ja'far were the sons of the Prophet's father's brother (Abu Talib), only the patrilineal descendants of 'Ali and Fatima are generally regarded as "people of the house."

5. In commenting on an earlier oral version of this chapter, both Fawzi Abdulrazaq and Muhsin Mahdi objected to my linking the concepts of *baraka, tahara,* and *'isma.* Insofar as orthodox Sunni Islamic theology and jurisprudence are concerned, the three terms are certainly unrelated. As already noted, *tahara* in the legal codes of both Shi'i and Sunni Islam refers to ritual purity. The concept of *'isma,* however, is especially important in Shi'i Islam, where it used to refer to the pure and sinless Shi'i Imams. But when we look at how these terms (and their derivatives) are actually used in everyday life and a wide variety of Moroccan texts from the twelfth through the twentieth century, we find them to be intertwined—no matter how heretical this may seem from the perspective of a twentieth-century Sunni Muslim theologian.

I should stress, however, that Moroccan Muslims are not usually *consciously* aware of the links between the concepts represented by the words *baraka, tahara,* and *'isma.* For most Moroccans with little formal education, the most common meaning of *tahara* is "circumcision." As for *'isma,* the term is not one that most twentieth-century Moroccans with little education would understand. The concepts represented by these words are nonetheless very much a part of the popular imagination in twentieth-century Morocco as they were in al-Yusi's day. I believe the evidence I present in this chapter demonstrates this.

6. The pure and sinless imams have tended to supplant the Prophet as intercessors in Shi'i Islam. (See Hegland 1983, 221; Munson 1988a, 22–25.)

7. I have not altered Geertz's English version of Berque's French translation (Geertz 1968, 31; Berque 1958, 20), except to replace the incorrect transliteration *Halfun* by *Khalfun.* Berque's version is an

abbreviated excerpt of a longer poem in al-Yusi's *al-Muhadarat* (1982, 1:338).

8. The dates of Moroccan dynasties are somewhat arbitrary since the families in question often ruled certain regions long before and after ruling Morocco as a whole. The 'Alawis ruled much of south-western Morocco by the 1640s, then conquered the northern capital of Fez in 1666, but did not control most of Morocco until 1668, when Mulay Rashid defeated the forces of the zawiya of al-Dila'—as well as those of the Shabanis in Marrakesh and of al-Khidr Ghaylan in Asila. So one could date 'Alawi rule from 1666 or 1668, or from 1664 when Mulay Rashid defeated his brother Mulay Mhammad to become the undisputed sultan of those parts of Morocco under 'Alawi control. I have chosen 1668 since the defeat of the zawiya of al-Dila' eliminated the 'Alawis' principal competitors. (See Berque 1982; Hajji 1988; al-Ifrani 1888; al-Qadiri, vols. 1–2.)

9. See Brunel 1926, 38–41, 55–56; Cornell 56, 64, 108, 128–29, 137–39, 242, 244, 259–60; Crapanzano 1973, 32–36, 40–43; Jamous 1981, 234–36; de Prémare 1985, 104–05; Touati 1989, 1224–25. We find this same image of the saint as defender of the oppressed in Moroccan Jewish hagiography. (See Ben-Ami 1990, 51–52, 115, 120–24, 150–54, 160, 174, 184.)

10. Ibid. The word *faqir* has a range of meanings. The basic meaning is "pauper." From this, one gets the idea of a Sufi mendicant who begs as a means of overcoming pride and the self. Here, al-Yusi uses the word as a standard form of self-abasement, but the Sufi dimension is nonetheless present (as it is throughout al-Yusi's writings).

CHAPTER 2: Scholars and Sultans

1. Munson, *Islam and Revolution*, 16–17, 141. In speaking of Shi'ites in this book, I am generally referring to the principal sect of "Twelver" Shi'ism found in Iran, Iraq, Lebanon, and sprinkled around the Persian Gulf. The Zaydi Shi'ism found in Yemen is closer to Sunni Islam (Dresch 1989).

2. In their book *God's Caliph: Religious Authority in the First Centuries of Islam* (1986), Patricia Crone and Martin Hinds reject this traditional Sunni view. But my concern here is with myth, not history; I am concerned with what Sunnis believe to have happened, not with what actually happened.

3. The four principal "schools" (madhahib) of Sunni Islam are the Hanafis, the Malikis, the Shafi'is, and the Hanbalis. Except for the extremely puritanical Hanbalis, the differences between these schools are relatively minor. The ordinary Moroccan peasant or laborer does not realize they exist. The Maliki school, named after Malik ibn Anas, has prevailed in the Maghrib (Northwest Africa) since the eleventh century (Cottart 1991, 280).

4. On the idea of nasiha, see Berque 1982, 26, 238, 245, and Tozy 1984, 355. Nikki Keddie's *Scholars, Saints, and Sufis* (1972) presents an excellent overview of the Muslim ulama generally, especially with respect to differences between Sunni and Shi'ite Islam. (See also Munson 1988a, 29–38.)

5. Although, as we have seen, Geertz's folktale about al-Yusi and Mulay Isma'il conforms in its basic structure to the classic theme of the virtuous saint overcoming an unjust ruler, I do not recall ever coming across the cemetery-as-refuge motif, except in these accounts of Ibn Tumart's clash with 'Ali bin Yusif. This may simply reflect my inadequate familiarity with Moroccan hagiography and oral folklore (the two being rooted in the same mythic themes), but Fawzi Abdulrazak, who is in charge of the Arabic collection at Harvard's Widener Library, tells me that he too cannot think of other instances of the cemetery motif. It is possible that Geertz's informants deliberately imitated the stories about Ibn Tumart. This seems unlikely, however, because only educated Moroccans in the Sefrou region where Geertz worked would have been likely to know of the stories about Ibn Tumart. Educated Moroccans in the 1960s would probably have deleted much of the miraculous material in the folktale about al-Yusi—unless they prefaced the folktale by saying, "This is what the peasants believe," or something to that effect. Unfortunately, Geertz gives us no clue as to the educational or social background of his informants.

CHAPTER 3: Al-Kattani and the Ulama (1904–1909)

1. There are differing accounts of the accusations. See al-Fasi 1931, 1:46–47; al-Mu'aqqit 1932, 166–70; al-Kattani 1962, 77–88; Ibn Ibrahim 1977, 7:157–58 (which repeats al-Fasi 1931), and 7:163–68.

2. René-LeClerc, Les débuts du règne de Moulay Hafid, 43. The Moroccan historian Ibn Zaydan says the bay'a of Marrakesh took place on

Friday, Rajab 6, 1325, or 15 Aug. 1907 (1929–33, 1:448). But Rajab 6 was a Thursday, so I use the date of Friday, 16 Aug. usually given by French sources (see Arnaud 1952, 238; Cagne 1988, 284).

3. A similar tax had sparked a similar revolt by the tanners of Fez in 1873–74. (See Cagne 1988, 427; Laroui 1977b, 130–31; al-Manuni 1985, 1:381–83; al-Nasiri 9:129–33, 136–39.)

CHAPTER 4: Popular Religion, Orthodoxy, and Salafi Scripturalism

1. I have discussed Gellner's conception of Moroccan tribalism elsewhere (see Munson 1981, 1989, 1990, 1991b, 1993).

2. Like all translations, this one fails to capture the nuances involved. The word *akyas*, the plural of *kayyis*, could be translated "the skillful ones," "the smart ones, "the wise ones", "the elegant ones," or "the handsome ones" (Wehr 1976, 849). The word *sulaha*' literally means "the virtuous and pious ones" or "the righteous ones," but in Moroccan usage it is a standard literary term for "saints."

3. Fawzi Abdulrazak, personal communication, 18 July 1991. From 1865 to 1871, six books were lithographically printed in Morocco, with an average print run of about 300 copies per title (Abdulrazak 1990, 124, 224).

4. Bu Hmara's revolt, which had a mahdist dimension, is discussed in Burke 1972b, 1976; Dunn 1981 and 1991; Ibn Mansur 1979, 1:303–97; and Maldonado 1949. The resistance of the Chaouia and the Bani Mtir are discussed in Burke 1976 and Vinogradov (Rassam) 1974.

5. For a slightly different and briefer version of this encounter, see al-Susi 1960, 148.

6. I was told this story, twice, by a member of the group visiting al-'Alawi. I cannot reveal his name.

CHAPTER 5: Holy and Unholy Kingship in Twentieth-Century Morocco

1. Geertz has argued that the Arabic word *sala* (*salat*) should not be translated as "prayer" since it is "fixed not only in time but also in form and content" (1960, 216). This objection is not persuasive since prayer in most religions is largely fixed in terms of time, form, and content. (See, e.g., Bunzel 1932, 493.) It is, of course, true that the Muslim *sala* is not a prayer in the sense of being a specific

personal request (which Muslims can make after the *sala* is over). It is rather worship focused on the praise of God.

2. In the call to the dawn prayer, the phrase "Prayer is better than sleep" is said twice before the final "There is no god but God." The call to prayer, like the daily prayers themselves, is essentially the same throughout the Islamic world. Shi'is, however, add the phrases "Come to the best of deeds" and, optionally, "I bear witness that 'Ali is the representative of God" (Ghaffari 1975, 49). In discussing both the call to prayer and the prayers themselves, I have relied on my own observations and the following handbooks for Moroccan Muslim children: Abdelmajid Ben Abdessadek's *Initiation à l'Islam*, vol. 1 (Casablanca: Dar Attakafa, 1990), and Muhammad 'Atiyya's *Al-ta'lim al-dini lil-atfal* (Religious Education for Children, n.p.). The minor differences between the Maliki rules of prayer that prevail in Morocco and those of the three other Sunni schools (Hanafi, Hanbali, and Shafi'i) are discussed in Ibrahim 1970.

3. All translations of Quranic passages are my own.

4. Susan Miller tells me that grooms and brides were traditionally called "king" and "queen" (*melekh* and *malka*) in Ashkenazi Jewish weddings. Yadida Stillman tells me that she believes the metaphor of the bridegroom as king or sultan is still used by relatively traditional Moroccan Jews in Israel, as it was in Morocco (see Ben-Ami 1974, 14; Zafrani 1983, 84). Cynthia Mahmood informs me that Hindu grooms are dressed as princes in traditional Hindu weddings. (See Babb 1975, 85; Van Gennep 1960, 141.)

5. For the history of al-mawlid in Morocco, see al-Qabli 1978, 13-15; al-Manuni 1979, 265–86; Salmi 1956; Shinar 1977.

6. I use this term to refer to the beliefs that shape political behavior. These are, to a large extent, shaped by social structure. The controversy surrounding the concept of political culture is discussed in Almond and Verba 1989.

7. According to *Fortune* magazine (7 Sept. 1992, 122), Hassan II was worth $1.4 billion in 1992. See Diouri 1992; Leveau 1987.

8. I do not wish to suggest that there are no other reasons why the groom was traditionally called a *sultan*, but this is the reason Moroccan women have cited when I have asked them about the groom's royal title. For differing views of the role of men in the Moroccan family, see Chraibi 1954, Davis 1983, D. Dwyer 1978; H. Geertz 1979; Maher 1974; Mernissi 1987; Munson 1984; Rassam 1980; van der Yeught 1989.

9. Egalitarian values prevailed in many precolonial highland tribes. See Hart 1976; 1981; 1984; 1989.

CHAPTER 6: Fundamentalism in Late Twentieth-Century Morocco

1. This information is from a close associate of al-Zamzami's who witnessed 'Abd al-Bari''s arrest and his condition after his release. Moroccan political prisoners are usually blindfolded when tortured, presumably to prevent them from knowing the identity of their torturers. (See Amnesty International 1991, 25–32; Diouri 1972, 79, 88–89; Middle East Watch 1990, 2.)

2. For various views of Muslim-Jewish relations in Morocco, see Deshen 1989; Kenbib 1984; Meyers 1982; Rosen 1970, 1984; Schroeter 1988; Shokeid 1985; Stillman 1977, 1978, 1979.

3. Politics, including leftist politics, remains a primarily male domain in Morocco. Fatima Mernissi, the famous Moroccan feminist, notes that "because we women are a small minority in public spaces, and because we're still often uncomfortable there, we are manipulated. Even by the left. I went to some labor union meetings for a time in the 1970s, but for me it was like a mosque" (Dwyer 1991, 183). Mernissi is referring to the fact that women are either excluded from mosques or restricted to a segregated area in the back or to a balcony where they cannot be seen by men.

4. I have heard Moroccans of various social backgrounds complain bitterly that they were forced to "donate" a portion of their salaries to build the Hassan II Mosque, which the king could easily have paid for by selling a palace or two. I have also heard a number of Moroccans say that the millions of dollars spent on the king's mosque should have been used to provide work for Morocco's unemployed. One young Moroccan woman, apparently sympathetic to the fundamentalists, told me that Hassan II would someday be astonished to find the mosque full of his worst enemies—the "real Muslims" of Morocco. Yet I have also heard two prominent ulama say that all Moroccan Muslims are proud of their king's mosque, which has the highest minaret in the world and extends ten meters out over the Atlantic Ocean (Gouzi 1991).

CHAPTER 7: Conclusion

1. My critique of Geertz's neglect of the coercive and violent aspects of Moroccan kingship parallels some classical critiques of the "Apollonian" anthropological tradition represented by Benedict, Mead, and Redfield (see Freeman 1983; Goldfrank 1945; Lewis 1951; Stocking 1989). My own orientation, however, is ultimately closer to Geertz's (at least as represented by his theoretical statements) than it is to that of scholars like Esther Goldfrank, Oscar Lewis, or Derek Freeman.

Glossary

'abd Literally "slave." The phrase 'abd Allah, or "slave of God," is the standard way of speaking of a Muslim and a human being. 'Abd also means "black man," a black woman being an 'abda.

'azzi An insulting colloquial term meaning "Negro" or "nigger"

baraka Blessedness, holiness

bay'a Oath of allegiance, normally to a ruler

hadith A report or tradition concerning the Prophet Muhammad and his companions

imam One who stands in front and leads Muslim prayer. By extension, a leader of the Islamic world. Shi'is believe in a series of pure and sinless imams, the last of whom disappeared and will return as the messiah (al-mahdi). Sunnis call their caliphs imams. Prominent religious leaders are also called imams.

Islam Literally "submission" to God (Allah)

'isma Purity, sinlessness, impeccability, infallibility

jihad Holy war. One who fights in a holy war is a mujahid.

jnun The colloquial Moroccan word for "spirits," derived from classical jinn

khalifa Caliph, thought of as successor to the Prophet or as deputy to God. The local government official bearing this title is the deputy of a qaid.

mahdi The Muslim messiah

marabout French version of Arabic *murabit*. Used in Western sources as a synomym for "saint."

maʿsum Pure and sinless. See *ʿisma*.

al-mawlid The holiday commemorating the birth of the Prophet Muhammad

Mulay From classical *Mawlay*, "my Lord," or "my Master." (*Mawlana* means "our Lord.") Moroccan Muslims use this term to address Allah, great saints, and shurafa, including sultans. In hadiths, the root word *mawla* often refers to the owner of a slave.

murabit Originally one who lived in a *ribat* and fort for Islam. Then it came to mean a patrilineal descendant of a saint who was not a descendant of the Prophet Muhammad.

Muslim Literally, "one who submits" to God (*Allah*)

nasiha The frank counsel or advice that religious scholars were supposed to give rulers

qaid A local government official. In precolonial Morocco, a rural qaid (*qa'id*) was often a powerful tribal leader.

qutb Axis, axle, pivot, pole (of the spiritual universe in a mystical sense). The Sufis use this term to refer to the greatest saints.

ribat Originally a quasi-monastic garrison where men prepared for holy war. The word later came to refer to a place where Sufi mystics studied under a mystical teacher, i.e., a *zawiya*.

Shariʿa Islamic law

sharif A patrilineal descendant of the Prophet by way of his daughter Fatima and her husband ʿAli

shaykh An elderly man. This is an honorific title used for important people in religious, tribal, and modern administrative hierarchies. A Sufi shaykh is a mystical master, or guru.

shurafa Plural of *sharif*

siyyid The most common colloquial word for "saint," derived from classical *sayyid*, "lord" or "master"

Sunna The customary practice of the Prophet Muhammad embodied in the *hadith*-s

Sunni A member of the dominant Sunni sect of Islam, the members of which believe in the four rightly guided caliphs. In Morocco, the term is also used by members of relatively traditional Islamic revivalist movements who shun the more radical and ideological fundamentalism of people like 'Abd as-Slam Yasin.

tahara Ritual purity.

turuq (Plural of *tariqa*) Sufi orders

ulama (Plural of *'alim*) Religious scholars

umma The Islamic community, all Muslims

Wahhabi Common term used to refer to members of the revivalist movement that led to the creation of Sa'udi Arabia

zawiya A Sufi lodge that usually includes a saint's shrine and rooms or buildings for prayer and study.

Bibliography A

SOURCES IN ARABIC

The Arabic definite article *al-* is ignored for purposes of alphabetical order.

al-ʿAlawi, Mhammad (Amhammad) bin Hashim. 1980. *Min wara' al-sudud aw al-haraka al-wataniyya bi-Fas 1937–1944*. 2d ed. Cairo: Dar al-Thaqafa lil-Tabaʿa waʾl-Nashr.

al-ʿAlawi al-Madghari, ʿAbd al-Kabir. 1989. *Al-Fqih Abu ʿAli al-Yusi: namudhaj min al-fikr al-maghribi fi fajr al-dawla al-ʿalawiyya*. Muhammadiya: Matbaʿa Fadala.

al-Asfi, Muhammad al-Wadiʿ. 1986. *Al-Salafi al-munadil al-shaykh Muhammad bin al-ʿArbi al-ʿAlawi*. Casablanca: Dar al-Nashr al-Maghribiyya.

ʿAtiyya, Muhammad. n.d. *Al-taʿlim al-dini lil-atfal lil-madaris al-ibtidaʾiyya waʾl-awwaliyya waʾl-alzamiyya*. Al-juzʾ al-awwwal lil-banin. Casablanca: n.p. (Bought in a bookstore in Rabat in 1990.)

Banani, Ahmad. 1964. Jawanib min shakhsiyyat shaykhna Ibn al-ʿArbi al-ʿAlawi. *al-Iman*, no. 10, 8–18.

al-Banna, Hasan. 1965. *Majmuʿat rasaʾil al-imam al-shahid Hasan al-Banna*. Beirut: Dar al-Andalus.

Bargash [Barkash], ʿAbd al-Hakim. 1989. *Al-Shaykh Abu Shuʿayb al-Dukkali.*

Apparently printed at the author's expense at the Matba'at al-Ma'arif al-Jadida in Rabat.

al-Bu 'Ayyashi, Ahmad. 1975. *Harb al-Rif al-tahririyya wa marahil al-nidal*. 2 vols. Tangier: 'Abd al-Slam Jasus and Sochepresse.

al-Bu Zidi, Ahmad. 1988. *Al-tarikh al-ijtima'i lil-Dar'a (matla' al-qarn 17– matla' al-qarn 20)*. Rabat: Bahth li-nayl diblum al-dirasat al-'ulya fi'l-tarikh, Jami'at Muhammad al-Khamis, Kulliyat al-adab wa'l-'ulum al-insaniyya.

Dawud, Muhammad. 1956–79. *Tarikh Titwan*. 8 vols. Most of these volumes were printed by al-Matba'a al-Mahdiya in Tetouan, but vol. 8 was published by al-Matba'a al-Malikiyya in Rabat in 1979.

al-Du'ayyif, Muhammad bin 'Abd al-Slam. 1986. *Tarikh al-Du'ayyif*. Ed. Ahmad al-'Amari. Rabat: Dar al-Ma'thurat. (Ms. finished 1818.)

al-Fasi, 'Abd al-Hafidh). 1931. *Mu'jam al-shuyukh al-musamma riyad al-janna aw al-mudhish al-mutrib*. 2 vols. Fez: al-Matba'a al-Jadida.

al-Fasi, 'Allal. 1948. *Al-Harakat al-istiqlaliyya fi'l-Maghrib al-'arabi*. Cairo: Lajnat al-Thaqafa al-Wataniyya li-Hizb al-Istiqlal (Marrakush). (I have actually used an undated reprint printed in Tangier by 'Abd as-Slam Jassus. I bought this reprint in 1990 and suspect it was printed in the 1980s.)

———. [1952] 1979. *Al-Naqd al-dhati*. Rabat: Lajnat Nashr Turath Za'im al-Tahrir 'Allal al-Fasi.

———. 1963. *Maqasid al-shari'a al-islamiyya ma makarimuha*. Casablanca: Makatabat al-Wahda al-'Arabiyya.

———. 1967. *Da'iman ma'a al-sha'b*. Rabat: Matba'at al-Risala.

———. [1935] 1979. Abu 'Ali al-Yusi (1040–1102): shakhsiyyatu, hayatuhu, dirasa mujaza li-atharihi. *Al-Manahil* 6(15): 1553.

al-Ftuh, 'Abd al-Bari'. 1990. Fi dhikra wafat al-'allama Muhammad bin al-Siddiq al-Zamzami. *al-Furqan* 20 (Feb. 1990): 6-9.

Gannun [Kannun], 'Abd Allah. 1975. *Al-Nubugh al-maghribi fi'l-adab al-'arabi*. 3d ed. 3 vols. bound in 1. Beirut: Dar al-Kitab al-Lubnani.

Ghallab, 'Abd al-Karim. 1987. *Tarikh al-haraka al-wataniyya bil-Maghrib: min nihayat harb al-Rif ila bina' al-jidar al-sadis fi'l-sahra'*. 2 vols. 2d ed. Rabat: Matba'at al-Risala.

———. 1991. *Al-mahidun..al-khalidun*. Casablanca: al-Matba'a al-Najah al-jadida. (Part of a series published by the Moroccan newspaper *al-'Alam*.)

Gharrit, Muhammad. 1928. *Fawasil al-juman fi anba' wuzara' wa kuttab al-zaman*. Fez: al-Matba'a al-Jadida (1346 A.H.).

Hajji, Muhammad. 1988. *Al-zawiya al-dila'iyya wa dawruha al-dini wa'l-'ilmi wa'l-siyasi.* 2d ed. Casablanca: Matba'at al-Najah al-Jadida.

Ibn 'Ajiba, Sidi Ahmad bin Muhammad (d. 1809). 1982. *Mi'raj al-tashawwuf ila haqa'iq al-tasawwuf.* Tetouan: Matba'a al-Marini.

Ibn 'Askar, Muhammad al-Hasani ash-Shafshawani. 1977. *Dawhat al-nashir li mahasin man kana bi'l-Maghrib min masha'ikh al-qarn al-'ashir,* ed. Muhammad Hajji. Rabat: Dar al-Maghrib.

Ibn Ibrahim, 'Abbas. 1974–83. *Al-I'lam bi-man halla Marrakish wa Aghmat min al-a'lam.* 10 vols. Rabat.

Ibn Mansur, 'Abd al-Wahhab. 1979. *A'lam al-Maghrib al-'arabi.* 2 vols. Rabat.

Ibn Zaydan, 'Abd al-Rahman. 1929–33. *Ithaf a'lam al-nas bi-jamal akhbar hadirat Maknas.* 5 vols. Rabat: al-Matba'a al-Wataniyya.

———. 1937. *Al-Durar al-fakhira bi-ma'athir al-muluk al-'alawiyyin bi Fas al-zahira.* Rabat: al-Matba'a al-Iqtisadiyya.

———. 1961–62. *Al-'Izz wa'l-sawla fi ma'alim nudhum al-dawla.* Rabat: al-Matba'a al-Malikiyya. 2 vols. (First vol. published in 1961, the second in 1962.)

Ibrahim, Muhammad Isma'il. 1970. *Al-Salat kama waradat fil-kitab wa'l-sunna wa 'ala al-madhahib al-arba'a.* 3d ed. Cairo (?): Dar al-Fikr al-'Arabi.

al-Ifrani, Muhammad al-Sughayyir. 1888. *Nuzhat al-hadi bi akhbar muluk al-qarn al-hadi.* Paris: Ernest Leroux.

———. 1962. *Rawdat al-ta'rif bi mafakhir Mawlana Isma'il bin al-Sharif.* Rabat: al-Matba'a al-Malikiyya.

al-Jabiri, Muhammad al-'Abid. 1988. *Al-Maghrib al-mu'asir: al-khususiyya wa'l-huwiyya. al-hadatha wa'l-tanmiyya.* Casablanca: Dar al-Nashr al-Maghribiyya.

al-Jirari, 'Abbas. 1981. *'Abqariyyat al-Yusi.* Casablanca: Dar al-Thaqafa.

———. 1986. *Falsafat nidham al-hukm fi'l-Islam wa ahammiyyat al-bay'a.* In *Nadwat al-bay'a wa'l-khilafa fi'l-Islam. Al-juz' al-thalith.* al-Muhammadiyya: Al-Mamlaka al-maghribiyya, wizarat al-awqaf wa'l-shu'un al-islamiyya.

al-Jirari, 'Abd Allah. 1976. *Al-Muhaddith al-hafidh Abu Shu'ayb al-Dukkali.* Casablanca: Matba'at al-Najah al-Jadida.

al-Jundi, Anwar. 1965. *Al-Fikr wa'l-thaqafa al-mu'asara fi shamal Ifriqiya.* Cairo: al-Dar al-Qawmiyya lil-Taba'a wa'l-Nashr.

al-Kababi, Muhammad 'Aziz. 1989. *Al-Salafiyya: raji'iyya am taqaddumiyya?* In *Al-Harakiyya al-salafiyya fi'l-Maghrib al-'arabi.* Asila: Jam'iyyat al-Muhit al-thaqafiyya bil-ta'awun ma'a al-Jam'iyya al-Maghribiyya lil-tadamun al-islami.

Kably, Mohamed (See al-Qabli, Muhammad below and Kably, Mohamed, in Bibliography B.)

al-Kattani, 'Abd al-Hayy. 1908. *Mufakahat dhawi al-nubl wa'l-ijada hadrat mudir jaridat al-Sa'ada.* Fez: Ahmad al-Azraq.

———. [1928] 1982. *Fahras al-faharis wa'l-ithbat wa mu'jam al-ma'ajim wa'l-mashyakhat wa'l-musalsalat.* 3 vols. Beirut: Dar al-Gharb al-islami. (First published Fez: al-Matba'a al-Jadida, 1928.)

al-Kattani, Idris. 1989. Madkhal (Introduction). In M. J. al-Kattani [1908] 1989, pp. 19–81.

al-Kattani, Muhammad al-Baqir. 1962. *al-Shaykh Muhammad al-Kattani al-shahid.* Rabat: Maktabat al-Talib.

al-Kattani, Muhammad bin Ja'far. 1899. *Salwat al-anfas wa muhadathat al-akyas bi-man uqbira min al-'ulama' wa'l-sulaha' bi-Fas.* 3 vols. Fez: Ahmad al-Azraq.

———. [1908] 1989. *Nasihat ahl al-Islam: Tahlil islami 'ilmi li-'awamil suqut al-dawla al-islamiyya wa 'awamil nuhudiha.* Rabat: Maktabat al-Badr.

al-Kattani, M. I. [Muhammad Ibrahim]. 1989. Taqdim (Preface). In M. J. al-Kattani [1908] 1989, pp. 3–17.

al-Manjra, al-Mahdi. 1991. *Al-Harb al-hadariyya al-ula: mustaqbal al-madi wa madi'l-mustaqbal.* Casablanca: 'Uyun.

al-Mansur, Muhammad. 1989. Tasawwuf al-shurafa': al-mumarisa al-diniyya wa'l-ijtima'iyya lil-zawiya al-wazzaniyya min khilal manaqibiha. In *al-Tarikh wa adab al-manaqib,* pp. 15–27. Rabat: Manshurat 'Ukkadh. (No editor indicated.) (See El Mansour in Bibliography B.)

al-Manuni, Muhammad. 1979. *Waraqat 'an al-hadara al-maghribiyya fi 'asr Bani Marin.* Rabat: Manshurat Kulliyat al-adab wa'l-'ulum al-insaniyya, Jami'at Muhammad al-Khamis.

———. 1985. *Madhahir yaqdhat al-Maghrib al-hadith.* 2 vols. 2d ed. Casablanca: Sharikat al-nashr wa'l-tawzi' al-madaris and Beirut: Dar al-Gharb al-islami.

al-Mu'aqqit, Muhammad bin Muhammad bin 'Abd Allah. 1932. *al-Rihla al-Marrakshiyya aw mir'at al-masawa al-waqtiyya, al-juz' al-awwal.* Cairo: Mustafa al-Babi al-Halabi wa awladuhu.

al-Nasiri, Ahmad ibn Khalid. [1894] 1954–56. *Istiqsa' li-akhbar duwal al-Maghrib al-aqsa.* 9 vols. Casablanca: Dar al-Kitab. (First published in Cairo, 1894.)

al-Qabli, Fatima Khalil. 1981. Muqaddimat al-dirasa. In al-Yusi, *Rasa'il Abi 'Ali al-Hasan bin Mas'ud al-Yusi* 1:11–122.

al-Qabli, Muhammad. 1978. Musahama fi tarikh al-tamhid li-dhuhur dawlat al-Sa'adiyin. *Majallat Kulliyat al-Adab* 3–4, 7–59. (*See* Kably in Bibliography B.)

al-Qadiri, Muhammad bin al-Tayyib (d. 1773). 1977–86. *Nashr al-mathani li-ahl al-qarn al-hadi 'ashr wa'l-thani.* Ed. Muhammad Hajji and Ahmad al-Tawfiq. Rabat: Manshurat al-Jam'iyya al-Maghribiyya lil-Ta'lif wa'l-Tarjama wa'l-Nashr. Nashr wa tawzi' Maktabat al-Talib.

al-Shabiba al-islamiyya. 1984. *al-Mu'amara 'ala al-Shabiba al-islamiyya al-maghribiyya: khalfiyat ightiyal Bin Jallun bi'l-watha'iq wa murafa'at al-difa'.* (Printed in Holland by al-Shabiba al-islamiyya al-maghribiyya.)

al-Sughayyir, 'Abd al-Majid. 1988. *Ishkaliyyat islah al-fikr al-sufi fi'l-qarnayn 18/19.* Rabat: Dar al-Afaq al-Jadida.

al-Susi, Muhammad al-Mukhtar. 1960. *Al-Ma'sul.* Vol. 4. Casablanca: Matba'at al-Najah.

———. 1963. *Al-Ilghiyyat.* 3 vols. Casablanca: Matba'a al-Najah.

———. 1966. *Iligh qadiman wa hadithan.* Rabat: al-Matba'a al-Malikiyya.

———. 1982. *Mu'taqal al-Sahra'.* Vol. 1. Rabat: Matba'at al-Sahil.

———. 1983. *Hawla ma'idat al-ghada'.* Rabat: Matba'at al-Sahil.

al-Tazi, 'Abd al-Hadi. 1979. Bitaqa fi muntaha al-taqa yarfa'uha Abu al-Hasan al-Yusi ila al-sultan Mawlay Isma'il. *al-Manahil* 6(15): 287–310.

Wahbi, Muhammad. 1987. *Al-Usul al-ijtima'iyya lil-harakat al-islamiyya: "namudhaj al-talaba."* Bahth li-nayl al-ijaza fi shi'bat al-falsafa takhassus 'ilm al-ijtima'. Fez: Kulliyat al-adab wa'l-'ulum al-insaniyya, Jami'at Sidi Muhammad bin 'Abd Allah.

al-Wazzani, al-Tuhami. 1942. *Al-Zawiya: al-juz' al-awwal.* Tetuan: Matba'at al-Rif.

Yasin, 'Abd as-Slam. 1973. *Al-Islam ghadan.* Casablanca: an-Najah.

———. 1974. *Al-Islam aw al-Tufan: risala maftuha ila malik al-Maghrib.* Marrakesh. (Privately printed.)

———. 1979a. Da'wa ila Allah. *al-Jama'a* 2:11–50.

———. 1979b. Nadi al-talaba. *al-Jama'a* 2:116–26. (This is a regular section of *al-Jama'a* in which Yasin responded to letters from students.)

———. 1981. Iftitahiyya. *al-Jama'a* 9:3–11.

———. 1983. Iftitahiyya. *al-Jama'a* 11:3–8. (*See* Yasin in Bibliography B.)

al-Yusi, Abu 'Ali al-Hasan bin Mas'ud (d. 1691). 1981. *Rasa'il Abi 'Ali al-Hasan bin Mas'ud al-Yusi.* 2 vols. Ed. Fatima Khalil al-Qabli. Casablanca: Dar al-Thaqafa.

————. 1982. *Al-Muhadarat fil-adab wa'l-lugha.* 2 vols. Ed. Muhammad al-Hasan bin Mas'ud *al-Yusi.* 2 vols. Ed. Fatima Khalil al-Qabli. Casablanca: Dar al-Thaqafa.

————. 1982. *Al-Muhadarat fil-adab wa'l-lugha.* 2 vols. Ed. Muhammad Hajji and Ahmad al-Sharqawi al-Iqbal. Beirut: Dar al-Gharb al-islami.

al-Zamzami, Muhammad. 1979–80. *Mawqif al-Islam min al-aghniya' wa'l-fuqara'.* Tangier: Matabi' al-Bughaz.

Znibir, Muhammad. 1979. Al-Yusi: fikr qawi wara'a shakhsiyya qawiyya. *al-Manahil* 6(15): 260–86.

Bibliography B

SOURCES IN WESTERN LANGUAGES

EI² = Encyclopaedia of Islam, 2d ed., Leiden: E. J. Brill

Abdulrazak, Fawzi A. 1990. The Kingdom of the Book: The History of Printing as an Agency of Change in Morocco between 1865 and 1912. Ph.D. dissertation, Boston University.

Abrahamian, Ervand. 1982. Iran between Two Revolutions. Princeton: Princeton University Press.

Abun-Nasr, Jamil. 1963. The Salafiyya Movement in Morocco: The Religious Bases of the Moroccan Nationalist Movement. St. Antony's Papers (Middle Eastern Affairs) 16:90–105.

———. 1965. The Tijaniyya: A Sufi Order in the Modern World. New York: Oxford University Press.

Afrique française (le Bulletin du Comité de l'Afrique française).

Agnouche, Abdelatif. 1987. Histoire politique du Maroc: Pouvoir-légitimités-institutions. Casablanca: Afrique Orient.

Ahmad, Mumtaz. 1991. Islamic Fundamentalism in South Asia: The Jamaat-i-Islami and the Tablighi Jamaat. In Fundamentalisms Observed, ed. Martin E. Marty and R. Scott Appleby.

Al-Ahnaf, Mustafa. 1990. L'opposition maghrébine face à la crise du

Golfe. *Maghreb-Machrek* 130 (Oct.–Dec.): 99–114.

Al-Ahnaf, Mustafa, Bernard Botiveau, and Franck Frégosi. 1991. *L'Algerié par ses islamistes.* Paris: L'Harmattan.

Akesbi, Najib. 1991. Maroc: Des déséquilibres inquiétants. In *L'état du Maghreb,* ed. Lacoste.

Almond, Gabriel A., and Sidney Verba, eds. 1989. *The Civic Culture Revisited.* Newbury Park: Sage Publications.

Amnesty International. 1982. *Report of an Amnesty International Mission to the Kingdom of Morocco, 10–13 February 1981.* London: Amnesty International Publications.

———. 1990. *Morocco: "Disappearances" of People of Western Saharan Origin, A Summary of Amnesty International's Concerns.* Submission to the United Nations Human Rights Committee. New York: Amnesty International USA.

———. 1991. *Morocco: A Pattern of Political Imprisonment, "Disappearances" and Torture.* New York: Amnesty International USA.

Antoun, Richard T. 1989. *Muslim Preacher in the Modern World: A Jordanian Case Study in Comparative Perspective.* Princeton: Princeton University Press.

Antoun, Richard T., and Mary E. Hegland, eds. 1987. *Religious Resurgence: Contemporary Cases in Islam, Christianity and Judaism.* Syracuse: Syracuse University Press.

Aran, Gideon. 1991. Jewish Zionist Fundamentalism: The Bloc of the Faithful in Israel (Gush Emunim). In *Fundamentalisms Observed,* ed. Marty and Appleby.

Ariam, Claude. 1986. *Rencontres avec le Maroc.* Paris: La Découverte.

Arjomand, Said Amir. 1984. *The Shadow of God and the Hidden Imam.* Chicago: University of Chicago Press.

———. 1988. *The Turban for the Crown: The Islamic Revolution in Iran.* New York: Oxford University Press.

Arnaud, Louis. 1952. *Au temps des mehallas ou le Maroc de 1860 à 1912.* Casablanca: Atlantides.

Ashford, Douglas. 1961. *Political Change in Morocco.* Princeton: Princeton University Press.

Ashmead-Bartlett, E. 1910. *The Passing of the Shareefian Empire.* London: Blackwood.

Aubin, Eugène. 1922. *Le Maroc d'aujourd'hui.* Paris: Librairie Armand Colin.

Ayalon, A. 1991. Malik. EI^2. 6:261–62.

Ayubi, Nazih N. 1991. *Political Islam: Religion and Politics in the Arab World.* New York: Routledge.

Babb, Lawrence. 1975. *The Divine Hierarchy: Popular Hinduism in Central India.* New York: Columbia University Press.

Balta, Paul, with Claudine Rulleau. 1990. *Le grand Maghreb: Des indépendances à l'an 2000.* Paris: La Découverte.

Barrada, Hamid. 1987. Les révélations explosives du "Fqih" Basri. *Jeune Afrique*, 8 July 1987, 4–12.

Batatu, Hanna. 1978. *The Old Social Classes and the Revolutionary Movements in Iraq.* Princeton: Princeton University Press.

Beck, Herman L. 1989. *L'image d'Idris II, ses descendants de Fas et la politique sharifienne des sultans marinides (656–869/1258–1465).* Leiden: E. J. Brill.

Ben Abdessadek, Abdelmajid. 1990. *Initiation à l'islam*, vol. 1. Casablanca: Dar Attakafa.

Ben-Ami, Issachar. 1974. Le mariage traditionnel chez les Juifs marocains. In *Studies in Marriage Customs* (Folklore Research Center Studies 4), ed. Issachar Ben-Ami and Dov Noy. Jerusalem: Magnes Press.

———. 1990. *Culte des saints et pèlerinages judéo-musulmans au Maroc.* Paris: Maisonneuve and Larose.

Ben Barka, El Mehdi. 1968. *The Political Thought of Ben Barka.* Havana: Tricontinental.

Benedict, Ruth. 1932. Configurations of Culture in North America. *American Anthropologist* 34:1–27.

Benjelloun, Abdelmajid. 1988. *Approches du colonialisme espagnol et du mouvement nationaliste marocain dans l'ex-Maroc khalifien.* Rabat: OKAD.

Benoist-Méchin. 1972. *Deux étés africains.* Paris: Albin Michel.

Bensusan, Samuel Levy. 1904. *Morocco.* London: Adam and Charles Black.

Berque, Jacques. 1958. *Al-Yousi: Problèmes de la culture marocaine au dix-septième siècle.* Paris and La Haye: Mouton.

———. 1982. *Ulémas, fondateurs, insurgés du Maghreb, dix-septième siècle.* Paris: Sindbad.

Bessis, Sophie. 1992. Comment désamorcer la bombe sociale? *Le Monde Diplomatique*, April, p. 15.

Bloch, Marc. [1924] 1983. *Les rois thaumaturges.* Paris: Gallimard.

Bookin-Weiner, Jerome B. 1979. The Green March in Historical Perspective. *Middle East Journal* 33:20–33.

———. 1990. The "Sallee Rovers": Morocco and the Corsairs in the Seventeenth Century. In *The Middle East and North Africa: Essays in Honor of J. C. Hurewitz*, ed. Reeva S. Simon. New York: Columbia University Press.

Boudjedra, Rachid. 1992. *FIS de la haine.* Paris: Denoël.

Bouissef Rekab, Driss. 1989. *A l'ombre de Lalla Chafia*. Paris: L'Harmattan.

Bourdieu, Pierre. 1987. *Choses dites*. Paris: Minuit.

Bourouiba, Rachid. 1973. La doctrine almohade. *Revue de l'Occident Musulman et de la Méditerranée* 13–14:141–58 (special issue).

Bowen, Donna Lee. 1985. The Paradoxical Linkage of the 'Ulama' and Monarch in Morocco. *Maghreb Review* 10(1): 3–9.

Brett, Michael. 1980. Mufti, Marabout and Mahdi: Four Types in the Islamic History of North Africa. *Revue de l'Occident Musulman et de la Méditerranée* 29:5–15.

Brignon, Jean, Abdelaziz Amine, Brahim Boutaleb, Guy Martinet, Bernard Rosenberger, with Michel Terrasse. 1967. *Histoire du Maroc*. Paris: Hatier, and Casablanca: Libraire Nationale.

Brives, A. 1909. *Voyages au Maroc (1901–1907)*. Algiers: Adophe Jourdan.

Brown, Kenneth L. 1972. Profile of a Nineteenth-Century Moroccan Scholar. In *Scholars, Saints, and Sufis*, ed. Nikki R. Keddie.

———. 1976. *People of Salé: Tradition and Change in a Moroccan City, 1830–1930*. Manchester: Manchester University Press.

Brown, Leon Carl. 1966. The Role of Islam in Modern North Africa. In *State and Society in Independent North Africa*, ed. Leon Carl Brown. Washington, D.C.: Middle East Institute.

Brunel, René. 1926. *Essai sur la confrérie religieuse des Aissaouas au Maroc*. Paris: Geuthner.

Brunschvig, Robert. 1960. ʿAbd. EI^2 1:24–40.

Bunzel, Ruth. 1932. Introduction to Zuni Ceremonialism. *Forty-Seventh Annual Report of the Bureau of American Ethnology, 1929–1930*, 467–544. Washington, D.C.: Smithsonian Institution.

Burgat, François. 1988. *L'islamisme au Maghreb: La voix du Sud*. Paris: Karthala.

Burke, Edmund III. 1972a. The Image of the Moroccan State in French Ethnological Literature: A New Look at the Origin of Lyautey's Berber Policy. In *Arabs and Berbers: From Tribe to Nation in North Africa*, ed. Ernest Gellner and Charles Micaud. Lexington: Lexington Books.

———. 1972b. The Moroccan Ulama, 1860–1912: An Introduction. In *Scholars, Saints, and Sufis*, ed. Keddie.

———. 1976. *Prelude to Protectorate in Morocco: Precolonial Protest and Resistance, 1860–1912*. Chicago: University of Chicago Press.

Cagne, Jacques. 1988. *Nation et nationalisme au Maroc*. Rabat: Dar Nashr al-Maʿrifa. 1988.

Chaudhuri, Nirad. 1979. *Hinduism: A Religion to Live By*. New York: Oxford University Press.

Chenier, Louis de. 1788. *The Present State of the Empire of Morocco*. London: G. G. J. and J. Robinson.

Cherifi, Rachida. 1988. *Le Makhzen politique au Maroc: Hier et aujourd'hui*. Casablanca: Afrique Orient.

Chraibi, Driss. 1954. *Le passé simple*. Paris: Denoël.

Cigar, Norman. 1978. Conflict and Community in an Urban Milieu: Under the 'Alawis (ca. 1666–1830). *Maghreb Review* 3:3–13.

————. 1981. Socio-Economic Structures and the Development of an Urban Bourgeoisie in Pre-Colonial Morocco. *Maghreb Review* 6:55–76.

Claisse, Alain. 1987. Makhzen Traditions and Administrative Channels. In *The Political Economy of Morocco*, ed. I. William Zartman.

Clément, Jean-François. 1986. Les révoltes urbaines de janvier 1984 au Maroc. *Réseau villes monde arabe*, bull. no. 5, pp. 3–46.

————. 1990. Maroc: Les atouts et les défis de la monarchie. In *Maghreb: Les années de transition*, ed. Bassma Kodmani-Darwish.

Clifford, James. 1983. On Ethnographic Authority. *Representations* 1:118–46.

Clifford, James, and George E. Marcus, eds. 1986. *Writing Culture: The Poetics and Politics of Ethnography*. Berkeley: University of California Press.

Combs-Schilling, Elaine. 1989. *Sacred Performances: Islam, Sexuality, and Sacrifice*. New York: Columbia University Press.

Cornell, Vincent. 1989. Mirrors of Prophethood: The Evolving Image of the Spiritual Master in the Western Maghrib from the Origins of Sufism to the End of the Sixteenth Century. Ph.D. dissertation, University of California, Los Angeles.

Cottart, Nicole. 1991. Malikiyya. EI^2. 6: 278–83.

Crapanzano, Vincent. 1973. *The Hamadsha: A Study in Moroccan Ethnopsychiatry*. Berkeley: University of California Press.

————. 1986. Hermes' Dilemma: The Masking of Subversion in Ethnographic Description. In *Writing Culture*, by Clifford and Marcus.

Crone, Patricia, and Martin Hinds. 1986. *God's Caliph: Religious Authority in the First Centuries of Islam*. New York: Cambridge University Press.

Dabashi, Hamid. 1989. *Authority in Islam: From the Rise of Muhammad to the Establishment of the Umayyads*. New Brunswick: Transaction Books.

Damis, John. 1983. *Conflict in Northwest Africa: The Western Sahara Dispute*. Stanford: Hoover Institution Press.

————. 1987. The Impact of the Saharan Dispute on Moroccan Foreign and Domestic Policy. In *The Political Economy of Morocco*, ed. Zartman.

———. 1990. Morocco and the Western Sahara. Current History 89:165–68, 184–86.

Daoud, Zakya. 1991. Le Maghreb, déchiré par la "nouvelle défaite arabe." Le Monde Diplomatique, April, p. 15.

Darnton, Robert. 1984. The Great Cat Massacre and Other Episodes of French Cultural History. New York: Basic Books.

Daure-Serfaty, Christine. 1992. Tazmamart: Une prison de la mort au Maroc. Paris: Stock.

Davis, Susan S. 1983. Patience and Power: Women's Lives in a Moroccan Village. Cambridge: Schenkman.

del Pino, Domingo. 1990. Marruecos entre la tradición y el modernismo. Granada: Universidad de Granada.

Dermenghem, Emile. 1954. Le culte des saints dans l'islam maghrébin. Paris: Gallimard.

Deshen, Shlomo. 1989. The Mellah Society: Jewish Community Life in Sherifian Morocco. Chicago: University of Chicago Press.

Dhaouadi, Zouhaier, and Amr Ibrahim. 1982. Documents—Maroc. Peuples Méditerranéens 21 (Oct.–Dec. 1982): 57–60.

Diouri, Moumen. 1972. Réquisitoire contre un despote: Pour une république au Maroc. Paris: Albatros.

———. 1987. Réalités marocaines: La dynastie alaouite de l'usurpation à l'impasse. Paris: L'Harmattan.

———. 1991. Chronique d'une expulsion annoncée. Paris: L'Harmattan.

———. 1992. A qui appartient le Maroc? Paris: L'Harmattan.

Douglas, Mary. 1966. Purity and Danger: An Analysis of Concepts of Pollution and Taboo. New York: Praeger.

Doutté, Edmond. 1909. La royauté marocaine, troisième conférence. Renseignements Coloniaux 9: 185–89.

Dresch, Paul. 1989. Tribes, Government, and History in Yemen. New York: Oxford University Press.

al-Dukkali, Abu Shuʿayb. 1914. Opinion de Bou Chaib Doukkali. Revue du Monde Musulman 29:362–67.

Dunn, Ross. 1977. Resistance in the Desert: Moroccan Responses to French Imperialism, 1881–1912. London: Croom Helm.

———. 1981. The Bu Himara Rebellion in Northeast Morocco: Phase 1. Middle Eastern Studies 17:31–48.

———. 1991. France, Spain, and the Bu Himara Rebellion. In Tribe and State, ed. E. G. H. Joffé and C. R. Pennell.

Dwyer, Daisy. 1978. Images and Self-Images: Male and Female in Morocco. New York: Columbia University Press.

Dwyer, Kevin. 1991. *Arab Voices: The Human Rights Debate in the Middle East.* Berkeley: University of California Press.

Eco, Umberto. 1992. Interpretation and History. In *Interpretation and Overinterpretation,* ed. Stefan Collini. New York: Cambridge University Press.

Eickelman, Dale. 1976. *Moroccan Islam: Tradition and Society in a Pilgrimage Center.* Austin: University of Texas Press.

———. 1985. *Knowledge and Power in Morocco: The Education of a Twentieth-Century Notable.* Princeton: Princeton University Press.

———. 1986. Royal Authority and Religious Legitimacy: Morocco's Elections, 1960–1984. In *The Frailty of Authority,* ed. Myron J. Aronoff, pp. 181–205. New Brunswick: Transaction Books.

———.1989. *The Middle East: An Anthropological Approach.* 2d ed. Englewood Cliffs: Prentice Hall.

Elboudrari, Hassan. 1985. Quand les saints font les villes: Lecture anthropologique de la pratique sociale d'un saint marocain du dix–septième siècle. *Annales-ESC* 40:489–508.

El Mansour, Mohamed 1981. Political and Social Developments in Morocco during the Reign of Mawlay Sulayman, 1792–1822. Ph.D. dissertation, SOAS, University of London.

———. 1990. *Morocco in the Reign of Mawlay Sulayman.* Cambridgeshire: MENAS Press. (*See* al-Mansur, Muhammad, in Bibliography A.)

Enayat, Hamid. 1982. *Modern Islamic Political Thought.* Austin: University of Texas Press.

Entelis, John. 1989. *Culture and Counterculture in Moroccan Politics.* Boulder: Westview.

———. 1992. U.S.-Maghreb Relations in a Democratic Age: The Priority of Algeria. *Middle East Insight* 8(3): 31–35.

Escallier, Robert. 1991. Démographie: Obsession du nombre et considérable rajeunissement de la population. In *L'état du Maghreb,* ed. Lacoste.

Etienne, Bruno. 1987. *L'islamisme radical.* Paris: Hachette.

al-Fassi, ʿAllal 1954. *The Independence Movements of North Africa.* Trans. Hazem Zaki Nuseibeh. Washington, D.C.: American Council of Learned Societies. (*See* al-Fasi in Bibliography A.)

Fernea, Elizabeth Warnock. 1976. *A Street in Marrakesh.* Garden City: Doubleday.

Freeman, Derek. 1983. *Margaret Mead and Samoa: The Making and Unmaking of an Anthropological Myth*. Cambridge: Harvard University Press.

Fuchs, H., and F. de Jong. 1989. Mawlid. EI² 6:895–97.

Geertz, Clifford. 1960. *The Religion of Java*. Chicago: University of Chicago Press.

———. 1966. Religion as a Cultural System. In *Anthropological Approaches to the Study of Religion*, ed. Michael Banton, 1–46. London: Tavistock Publications.

———. 1968. *Islam Observed: Religious Development in Morocco and Indonesia*. New Haven: Yale University Press.

———. 1972. Deep Play: Notes on the Balinese Cockfight. *Daedalus* 101:1–37.

———. 1973. *The Interpretation of Cultures*. New York: Basic Books.

———. 1979. Suq: the Bazaar Economy in Sefrou. In *Meaning and Order in Moroccan Society: Three Essays in Cultural Analysis*, by Clifford Geertz, Hildred Geertz, and Lawrence Rosen. New York: Cambridge University Press.

———. 1980. *Negara: The Theatre State in Nineteenth-Century Bali*. Princeton: Princeton University Press.

———. 1983. *Local Knowledge: Further Essays in Interpretive Anthropology*. New York: Basic Books.

Geertz, Clifford, Hildred Geertz, and Lawrence Rosen. 1979. *Meaning and Order in Moroccan Society: Three Essays in Cultural Analysis*. New York: Cambridge University Press.

Geertz, Hildred. 1979. The Meanings of Family Ties. In *Meaning and Order in Moroccan Society*, by Geertz, Geertz, and Rosen.

Gellner, Ernest. 1969. *Saints of the Atlas*. Chicago: University of Chicago Press.

———. 1981. *Muslim Society*. New York: Cambridge University Press.

Gendarmerie Royale de Kenitra. 1990. Procès-verbal d'enquête préliminaire. 12 Jan.

Ghaffari, Salman. 1975. *The Prayer*. 4th ed. Tehran: n.p.

Gibb, H. A. R., and J. H. Kramers. 1953. *Shorter Encyclopaedia of Islam*. Ithaca: Cornell University Press.

Goitein, Shlomo. 1968. *Studies in Islamic History and Institutions*. Leiden: E. J. Brill.

Gold, Daniel. 1991. Organized Hinduisms: From Vedic Truth to Hindu Nation. In *Fundamentalisms Observed*, ed. Marty and Appleby.

Goldfrank, Esther. 1945. Socialization, Personality and the Structure of Pueblo Society. *American Anthropologist* 47:516–39.

Gombrich, Richard, and Gananath Obeyesekere. 1988. Buddhism Transformed: Religious Change in Sri Lanka. Princeton: Princeton University Press.

Gouzi, Nabila Berrada. 1991. Le mystère de la grande mosquée. Afrique Magazine, Sept., 55–59.

Graham, William A. 1983. Islam in the Mirror of Ritual. In Islam's Understanding of Itself, ed. Richard G. Hovannisian and Speros Vryonis, Jr. Malibu: Undena Publications.

Grottanelli, Christiano. 1987. Kingship. The Encyclopaedia of Religion 8:312–17. New York: Macmillan.

Guillen, Pierre. 1967. L'Allemagne et le Maroc, 1870–1905. Paris: Presses Universitaires de France.

Haddad, Yvonne. 1983. Sayyid Qutb: Ideologue of Islamic Revival. In Voices of Resurgent Islam, ed. John L. Esposito, pp. 67–98. New York: Oxford University Press.

Hammoudi, Abdellah. 1981. Aspects de la mobilisation populaire à la campagne vus à travers la biographie d'un mahdi mort en 1919. In Islam et politique au Maghreb, ed. Ernest Gellner and Jean-Claude Vatin. Paris: CNRS.

———. 1988. La victime et ses masques. Paris: Seuil.

Harbi, Mohammed, ed. 1991. L'islamisme dans tous ses états. Paris: Arcantère.

Harrak, Fatima. 1989. State and Religion in Eighteenth-Century Morocco: The Religious Policy of Sidi Muhammad b. ʿAbd Allah, 1757–1790. Ph.D. dissertation, SOAS, University of London.

Hart, David M. 1976. The Aith Waryaghar of the Moroccan Rif: An Ethnography and History. Tucson: University of Arizona Press.

———. 1981. Dadda ʿAtta and His Forty Grandsons: The Socio-Political Organisation of the Ait ʿAtta of Southern Morocco. Cambridge: Middle East and North African Studies Press.

———. 1984. The Ait ʿAtta of Southern Morocco: Daily Life and Recent History. Cambridge: Middle East and North African Studies Press.

———. 1989. Rejoinder to Henry Munson, Jr., "On the Irrelevance of the Segmentary Lineage Model in the Moroccan Rif." American Anthropologist 91:765–69.

Hegland, Mary. 1983. Two Images of Husain: Accommodation and Revolution in an Iranian Village. In Religion and Politics in Iran, ed. Nikki R. Keddie. New Haven: Yale University Press.

Heilman, Samuel C., and Menachem Friedman. 1991. Religious Fundamentalism and Religious Jews: The Case of the Haredim. In *Fundamentalisms Observed*, Marty and Appleby.

Heusch, Luc de. 1987. *Ecrits sur la royauté sacrée*. Brussels: Editions de l'Université libre de Bruxelles.

Hobsbawm, Eric J., and Terence O. Ranger. 1983. *The Invention of Tradition*. New York: Cambridge University Press.

Hoisington, William A., Jr. 1984. *The Casablanca Connection: French Colonial Policy, 1936–1943*. Chapel Hill: University of North Carolina Press.

Holt, George Edmund. 1914. *Morocco the Bizarre: Or Life in Sunset Land*. New York: McBride, Nast.

Hopkins, J. H. F. 1971. Ibn Tumart. EI^2 3:958–60.

Hugeux, Vincent. 1992. Maroc, le défi au commandeur. *L'Express*, 24 Jan., 24–25.

Hume, David. [1757] 1976. *The Natural History of Religion*, ed. A. Wayne Oliver, and *Dialogues Concerning Natural Religion*, ed. John V. Price. Oxford: Oxford University Press.

Ibn Abi Zar', 'Ali. 1860. *Raoudh al-Qirtas: Histoire des souverains du Magreb et annales de la ville de Fès*, trans. Auguste Beaumier. Paris: Librairie Impériale.

Ibn Anas, Malik. 1989. *Al-Muwatta of Imam Malik ibn Anas: The First Formulation of Islamic Law*, trans. Aisha Abdurrahman Bewley. London: Kegan Paul International.

Ibn 'Askar. 1913. *Daouhat an-Nashir: Sur les vertus éminentes des chaikhs du Maghrib au dixième siècle*. *Archives Marocaines* 19 (entire volume).

Ibn Khaldun. 1958. *The Muqaddimah: An Introduction to History*, trans. Franz Rosenthal. New York: Pantheon (Bollingen Series XLIII).

Jamous, Raymond. 1981. *Honneur et baraka: Les structures sociales traditionnelles dans le Rif*. Paris: CNRS, and Cambridge: Cambridge University Press.

Joffé, E. G. H. 1991a. The Zawiya of Wazzan: Relations between Shurafa and Tribe up to 1860. In *Tribe and State*, ed. Joffé and Pennell.

————. 1991b. The Zawiya of Wazzan: Relations between Shurafa and Tribe at the Advent of Colonial Occupation. In *Jbala—histoire et société: Etudes sur le Maroc du nord-ouest*, ed. Ahmed Zouggari and Jawhar Vignet-Zunz. Paris: CNRS, and Casablanca: Wallada.

Joffé, E. G. H., and C. R. Pennell, eds. 1991. *Tribe and State: Essays in Honour of David Montgomery Hart*. Cambridgeshire: MENAS Press.

Juergensmeyer, Mark. 1990. What the Bhikku Said: Reflections on the Rise of Militant Religious Nationalism. *Religion* 20:53–75.

Julien, Charles-André. 1978. *Le Maroc face aux impérialismes, 1415–1956*. Paris: Jeune Afrique.

Kably, Mohamed. 1986. *Société, pouvoir et religion au Maroc à la fin du Moyen-Age*. Paris: Maisonneuve et Larose. (*See* al-Qabli, Muhammad in Bibliography A.)

Kamal, Abd al-Aziz. 1978. *The Prescribed Prayers*. Lahore: Islamic Publications.

Keddie, Nikki. 1981. *Roots of Revolution: An Interpretive History of Modern Iran*. New Haven: Yale University Press.

———, ed. 1972. *Scholars, Saints, and Sufis: Muslim Religious Institutions since 1500*. Berkeley: University of California Press.

Kenbib, Mohammed. 1984. Structures sociales et protections étrangères au dix-neuvième siècle. *Hespéris-Tamuda* 22:79–101.

Kepel, Gilles. 1991. *La revanche de Dieu: Chrétiens, juifs et musulmans à la reconquête du monde*. Paris: Seuil.

Kodmani-Darwish, Bassma, ed. 1990. *Maghreb: Les années de transition*. Paris: Masson.

Koentjaraningrat. 1985. *Javanese Culture*. Singapore: Oxford University Press.

Laabi, Abdellatif. 1982. *Le chemin des ordalies*. Paris: Denoël.

———. 1983. *Chroniques de la citadelle d'exil: Lettres de prison (1972–1980)*. Paris: Denoël.

Lacouture, Jean. 1961. *Cinq hommes et la France*. Paris: Seuil.

Lacouture, Jean, and Simonne Lacouture. 1958. *Le Maroc à l'épreuve*. Paris: Seuil.

Lahbabi, Mohamed. 1958. *Le gouvernement marocain à l'aube du vingtième siècle*. Rabat: Techniques nord-africaines.

Lahlou, Mehdi. 1991. Chômage et sous-emploi: Un phénomène de très grave ampleur. In *L'état du Maghreb*, ed. Lacoste.

Lambton, Ann. 1981. *State and Government in Medieval Islam*. Oxford: Oxford University Press.

Lamchichi, Abderrahim. 1989. *Islam et contestation au Maghreb*. Paris: L'Harmattan.

Laroui, Abdallah. 1977a. *The History of the Magrib: An Interpretive Essay*, trans. Ralph Manheim. Princeton: Princeton University Press.

———. 1977b. *Les origines sociales et culturelles du nationalisme marocain (1830–1912)*. Paris: Maspéro.

———. 1987. Islam in North Africa. *The Encyclopedia of Religion* 7:322–36. New York: Macmillan.

Laskier, Michael M. 1990. Developments in the Jewish Communities of Morocco 1956–76. *Middle Eastern Studies* 26:465–505.

Lawrence, Bruce B. 1989. *Defenders of God: The Fundamentalist Revolt against the Modern Age.* New York: Harper and Row.

Leveau, Rémy. 1987. Pouvoir politique et pouvoir économique au Maroc. *Les Cahiers de l'Orient* 6:31–42.

Levi Della Vida, G. 1978. Kharidjites. EI² 4:1074–77.

Lévi-Provençal, E. 1922. *Les historiens des chorfa: Essai sur la littérature historique et biographique au Maroc du seizième au vigtième siècle.* Paris: Emile Larose.

———. 1928. *Documents inedits d'histoire almohade.* Paris: Paul Geuthner.

Lévy, Elisabeth. 1991. Maroc: Les islamistes à l'assaut de l'université. *Jeune Afrique,* 15–21 May, 6–7.

Lewis, Bernard. 1984. *The Jews of Islam.* Princeton: Princeton University Press.

———. 1988. *The Political Language of Islam.* Chicago: University of Chicago Press.

Lewis, Oscar. 1951. *Life in a Mexican Village: Tepoztlán Restudied.* Urbana: University of Illinois Press.

Linton, Ralph. 1943. Nativistic Movements. *American Anthropologist* 45:230–40.

Loeffler, Reinhold. 1988. *Islam in Practice: Religious Beliefs in a Persian Village.* Albany: State University of New York Press.

Lyautey, Louis-Hubert-Gonzalve. 1953–58. *Lyautey l'Africain: Textes et lettres du Maréchal Lyautey,* ed. Pierre Lyautey. 4 vols. Paris: Plon.

MAE. See Ministère des Affaires Etrangères.

Maher, Vanessa. 1974. *Women and Property in Morocco.* Cambridge: Cambridge University Press.

Maitrot de la Motte Capron, A., and Trenga, 1936. Un correspondant de révolution (Journal d'un Israélite de Fès). *Bulletin de la Société de Géographie d'Alger et de l'Afrique du Nord,* pp. 1–62, 133–92, 261–315.

Maldonado, Edouardo. 1949. *El Rogui.* Tetuan: Instituto General Franco para la investigación hispano-arabe.

Mannheim, Karl. 1953. *Essays on Sociology and Social Psychology,* ed. Paul Kecskemeti. London: Routledge and Kegan Paul.

Marcus, Michael A. 1985. "The Saint Has Been Stolen": Sanctity and Social Change in a Tribe of Eastern Morocco. *American Ethnologist* 12(3): 455–67.

Martin, A. G. P. 1923. *Quatre siècles d'histoire marocaine.* Paris: Félix Alcan.

Martin, Vanessa. 1989. *Islam and Modernism: The Iranian Revolution of 1906.* Syracuse: Syracuse University Press.

Marty, Martin E. 1988. Fundamentalism as a Social Phenomenon. *Bulletin of the American Academy of the Arts and Sciences* 42 (Nov.): 15–29.

Marty, Martin E., and R. Scott Appleby, eds. 1991. *Fundamentalisms Observed.* Chicago: University of Chicago Press.

Merad, Ali. 1978. Islah. EI^2 4:141–63.

Mercier, Louis. 1906. Les mosquées et la vie religieuse à Rabat. *Archives Marocaines* 8:99–195.

Mernissi, Fatima. 1987. *Beyond the Veil: Male-Female Dynamics in a Modern Muslim Society.* Rev. ed. Bloomington: Indiana University Press.

Meyers, Allan R. 1974. The 'Abid al-Bukhari: Slave Soldiers and Statecraft in Morocco, 1672–1790. Ph.D. dissertation, Cornell University.

———. 1982. Patronage and Protection: The Status of Jews in Precolonial Morocco. In *Jewish Societies in the Middle East,* ed. Shlomo Deshen and Walter Zenner. Washington D.C.: University Press of America.

Michaux-Bellaire, Edouard. 1908. Une tentative de restauration idrisite à Fès. *Revue du Monde Musulman* 2(7): 393–423.

———. 1917. La légende idrisite et le chérifisme au Maroc. *Revue du Monde Musulman* 35:57–73.

Michon, Jean-Louis. 1969. *L'autobiographie du soufi marocain Ahmad Ibn 'Agiba (1747–1809).* Leiden: E. J. Brill.

———. 1973. *Le soufi marocain Ahmad ibn 'Ajiba et son Mi'raj.* Paris: Librairie Philosophique J. Vrin.

Middle East Watch. 1990. Morocco: Deaths in a Secret Detention Center. *News from Middle East Watch,* April.

———. 1991. Ex-Political Prisoners Barred from Leaving Morocco despite Liberalization of Passport Policies. New York: Middle East Watch. (This is a four-page report issued in Sept.)

Miller, Susan G. 1992. *Disorienting Encounters: Travels of a Moroccan Scholar in France in 1845–1846.* Berkeley: University of California Press.

Milner, A. C. 1983. Islam and the Muslim State. In *Islam in Southeast Asia,* ed. M. B. Hooker. Leiden: E. J. Brill.

Mimouni, Rachid. 1992. *De la barbarie en général et de l'intégrisme en particulier.* Belfond: Le Pré aux clercs.

Ministère des Affaires Etrangères (France) (MAE). 1907. *Documents diplomatiques 3: Affaires du Maroc (1906–1907).* Paris.

———. 1908. *Documents diplomatiques 4: Affaires du Maroc (1907–1908).* Paris.

Montagne, Robert. 1953. *Révolution au Maroc.* Paris: France-Empire.

Montbrial, Thierry de. 1986. Entretien de S. M. le roi Hassan ii du Maroc. *Revue des Deux Mondes,* April, 3–26.

el-Mossadeq, Rkia. 1987. Political Parties and Power-Sharing. In *The Political Economy of Morocco,* ed. Zartman.

Munson, Henry, Jr. 1981. The Mountain People of Northwest Morocco: Tribesmen or Peasants? *Middle Eastern Studies* 17:249-55.

———. 1984. *The House of Si Abd Allah: The Oral History of a Moroccan Family.* New Haven: Yale University Press.

———. 1986a. Geertz on Religion: The Theory and the Practice. *Religion* 16:19–32.

———. 1986b. The Social Base of Islamic Militancy in Morocco. *Middle East Journal* 40:267–84.

———. 1986c. Islamic Revivalism in Morocco and Tunisia. *Muslim World* 76 (July/Oct. 1986): 203–18.

———. 1988a. *Islam and Revolution in the Middle East.* New Haven: Yale University Press.

———. 1988b. Morocco. In *The Politics of Islamic Revivalism: Diversity and Unity,* ed. Shireen Hunter. Bloomington: Indiana University Press.

———. 1989. On the Irrelevance of the Segmentary Lineage Model in the Moroccan Rif. *American Anthropologist* 91:386–400.

———. 1990. Slash-and-Burn Cultivation, Charcoalmaking and Emigration from the Highlands of Northwest Morocco. In *Anthropology and Rural Development in North Africa and the Middle East,* ed. Muneera Salem-Murdock and Michael Horowitz. Boulder: Westview.

———. 1991a. Morocco's Fundamentalists. *Government and Opposition* 26:331–44.

———. 1991b. The Segmentary Lineage Model in the Jbalan Highlands. In *Tribe and State,* ed. Joffé and Pennell.

———. 1993. Rethinking Gellner's Segmentary Analysis of Morocco's Ait ʿAtta. *Man* 28(2).

———. In press. The Political Role of the Moroccan "Ulama" (1860–1912). In *Reform, Crisis, and Everyday Life in Nineteenth-Century Morocco,* ed. Abdellah Hammoudi, and Wilfrid Rollman. Cambridge: Harvard University, Center for Middle Eatern Studies.

Muratet, Roger. 1967. *On a tué Ben Barka.* Paris: Librairie Plon.

Nakamura, Mitsuo. 1983. *The Crescent Arises over the Banyan Tree.* Yogyakarta: Gadja Mada University Press.

Ockrent, Christine, and le Comte de Marenches. 1986. *Dans le secret des princes.* Paris: Stock.

Ouardighi, Abderrahim. 1985(?). *Un cheikh militant: Mohammed Belarbi el Alaoui, 1880–1964.* Rabat: Littoral.

Padwick, Constance E. 1961. *Muslim Devotions: A Study of Prayer-Manuals in Common Use.* London: SPCK.

Palazzoli, Claude. 1974. *Le Maroc politique: De l'indépendance à 1973.* Paris: Sindbad.

Parker, Richard B. 1990. La politique des Etats-Unis au Maghreb. In *Maghreb*, by Kodmani-Darwish. Paris: Masson.

Paul, Jim. 1984. States of Emergency: The Riots in Tunisia and Morocco. *MERIP Reports*, no. 127 (Oct.): 3–6.

Pédron, François. 1974. *Echec au roi: Du coup d'état de Skhirat au "suicide" d'Oufkir.* Paris: La Table Ronde.

Pennell, C. R. 1986. *A Country with a Government and a Flag: The Rif War in Morocco, 1921–1926.* Cambridgeshire: MENAS Press.

Perrault, Gilles. 1990. *Notre ami le roi.* Paris: Gallimard.

Pinon, René. 1904. *L'empire de la Méditerranée.* Paris: Perrin.

Prémare, A. L. de. 1985. *Sidi 'Abd-er-Rahman El-Mejdub: Mysticisme populaire, société et pouvoir au Maroc au seizième siècle.* Paris: CNRS, and Rabat: SMER.

————.1986. *La tradition orale du Mejdub: Récits et quatrains inédits.* La Calade: Edisud.

Preston, James J. 1987. Purification. *The Encyclopedia of Religion.* 12:91–100. New York: Macmillan.

al-Qabli, Muhammed. (*See* Kably above and Bibliography A.)

Rabinow, Paul. 1975. *Symbolic Domination: Cultural Form and Historical Change in Morocco.* Chicago: University of Chicago Press.

————. 1977. *Reflections on Fieldwork in Morocco.* Berkeley: University of California Press.

————. 1986. Representations Are Social Facts: Modernity and Post-Modernity in Anthropology. In *Writing Culture*, ed. Clifford and Marcus.

Rassam, Amal. 1980. Women and Domestic Power in Morocco. *International Journal of Middle East Studies* 12:171–79. (*See* Vinogradov.)

Reinhart, A. Kevin. 1990. Impurity/No Danger. *History of Religions* 30:1–24.

René-LeClerc, Charles. 1908. Les débuts du règne de Moulay Hafid. *Renseignements Coloniaux* 2 (Feb.): 41–44.

Reysoo, Fenneke. 1991. *Pèlerinages au Maroc: Fête, politique et échange dans l'islam populaire.* Paris: Maison des sciences de l'homme, and Neuchâtel:

L'Institut d'ethnologie.

Rhazaoui, Ahmed. 1987. Recent Economic Trends: Managing the Indebtedness. In *The Political Economy of Morocco*, ed. Zartman.

Ricklefs, M. C. 1983. Review of *Negara: The Theatre State in Nineteenth-Century Bali. Journal of Southeast Asian Studies* 14:184–85.

Roberts, Hugh. 1991. A Trial of Strength: Algerian Islamism. In *Islamic Fundamentalisms and the Gulf Crisis*, ed. James Piscatori. Chicago: Fundamentalism Project of the American Academy of Arts and Sciences.

Robertson Smith, William. 1927. *Lectures on the Religion of the Semites: The Fundamental Institutions*. 3d ed. London: Macmillan.

Rorty, Richard. 1992. The Pragmatist's Progress. In *Interpretation and Overinterpretation*, ed. Stefan Collini. New York: Cambridge University Press.

Rosen, Lawrence. 1970. A Moroccan Jewish Community during the Middle Eastern Crisis. In *Peoples and Cultures of the Middle East*, ed. Louise E. Sweet. Garden City: Natural History Press.

———. 1979. Social Identity and Points of Attachment: Approaches to Social Organization. In *Meaning and Order in Moroccan Society*, by Geertz, Geertz, and Rosen.

———. 1984. *Bargaining for Reality: The Construction of Social Relations in a Muslim Community*. Princeton: Princeton University Press.

Rouadjia, Ahmed. 1990. *Les frères et la mosquée: Enquête sur le mouvement islamiste en Algérie*. Paris: Karthala.

Sada, Hugo. 1990. Mission accomplie: Roland Dumas chez Hassan II. *Jeune Afrique*, 21–27 Nov., 25–26.

Saint-Aulaire, Comte de. 1953. *Confession d'un vieux diplomate*. Paris: Flammarion.

Saint Olon, François Pidou de. 1695. *Relation de l'Empire de Maroc*. Paris: Chez la veuve mabre Cramoisy.

Saint-René Taillandier. 1930. *Les origines du Maroc français*. Paris: J. Peyronnet.

Salmi, Ahmed. 1956. Le genre des poèmes de nativité (mauludiyyas) dans le royaume de Grenade et au Maroc du treizième au dix-septième siècle. *Hespéris* 43:335–435.

Santucci, Jean-Claude. 1985. *Chroniques politiques marocaines (1971–1982)*. Paris: CNRS.

Schimmel, Annemarie. 1975. *Mystical Dimensions of Islam*. Chapel Hill: University of North Carolina Press.

———. 1985. *And Muhammad Is His Messenger: The Veneration of the Prophet in*

Islamic Piety. Chapel Hill: University of North Carolina Press.

Schneider, David M. 1980. *American Kinship: A Cultural Account.* 2d ed. Chicago: University of Chicago Press.

Schroeter, Daniel J. 1988. *Merchants of Essaouira: Urban Society and Imperialism in Southwestern Morocco, 1844–1886.* New York: Cambridge University Press.

Schulte Nordholt, Henk. 1981. Negara: A Theatre State? *Bijdragen Tot de Taal-, Land- en Volkenkunde* 137:47–76.

Sebti, Abdelahad. 1986. Au Maroc: Sharifisme citadin, charisme et historiographie. *Annales ESC* 41:433–457.

Seddon, David. 1984. Winter of Discontent: Economic Crisis in Tunisia and Morocco. *MERIP Reports*, no. 127 (Oct.): 7–16.

Serfaty, Abraham. 1986. Face aux tortionnaires. *Les Temps Modernes* 41 (April): 1–27.

———. 1992. *Dans les prisons du roi: Ecrits de Kenitra sur le Maroc.* Paris: Messidor/sociales.

Shahin, Emad Eldin Ali. 1989. The Restitution of Islam: A Comparative Study of the Islamic Movements in Contemporary Tunisia and Morocco. Ph.D. dissertation, Johns Hopkins University.

Shinar, Pessah. 1977. Traditional and Reformist Mawlid Celebrations in the Maghrib. In *Studies in Memory of Gaston Wiet*, ed. Myriam Rosen-Ayalon. Jerusalem: Institute of Asian and African Studies, Hebrew University of Jerusalem.

———. 1983. *Essai de bibliographie sélective et annotée sur l'islam maghrébin contemporain: Maroc, Algérie, Tunisie, Libye (1830–1978).* Paris: CNRS.

Shokeid, Moshe. 1985. *The Dual Heritage: Immigrants from the Atlas Mountains in an Israeli Village.* 2d ed. New Brunswick: Transaction Books.

Sivan, Emmanuel. 1985. *Radical Islam: Medieval Theology and Modern Politics.* New Haven: Yale University Press.

Smith, Donald E. 1971. *Religion, Politics, and Social Change in the Third World: A Sourcebook.* New York: Free Press.

Smith, Jane Idleman, and Yvonne Yazbeck Haddad. 1981. *The Islamic Understanding of Death and Resurrection.* Albany: State University of New York Press.

Soudan, François. 1990a. Maroc: Des droits de l'état à l'état de droit. *Jeune Afrique*, 21 May, 4–5.

———. 1990b. Chronique d'une crise annoncée et contenue: Liaisons tumultueuses entre Rabat et Paris. *Jeune Afrique*, 21–27 Nov., 18–25.

———. 1991a. La longue marche de Abdessalam Yassin. *Jeune Afrique*, 17–23 April, 38–41.

———. 1991b. L'opposition entre le Golfe et le Sahara. *Jeune Afrique*, 8–14 May, 28–32.

———. 1991c. Hassan II–Mitterand: Logique de guerre. *Jeune Afrique*, 31 July–6 Aug., 30–33.

———. 1991d. Un roi en Amérique. *Jeune Afrique*, 16–22 Oct., 26–29.

Souhaili, Mohamed. 1986. *Les damnés du royaume: Le drame des libertés au Maroc*. Paris: Etudes et Documentation Internationales.

Sourdel, Dominique. 1978. Khalifa. *EI²* 4:937–47.

Souriau, Christiane. 1983. Notes d'information: Quelques données comparatives sur les institutions islamiques actuelles du Maghreb. In *Le Maghreb musulman en 1979*, ed. Christiane Souriau. Paris: CNRS.

Stillman, Norman. 1977. Muslims and Jews in Morocco. *Jerusalem Quarterly* 5:74–83.

———. 1978. The Moroccan Jewish Experience: A Revisionist View. *Jerusalem Quarterly* 9:111–23.

———. 1988. *The Language and Culture of the Jews of Sefrou, Morocco: An Ethnolinguistic Study*. Journal of Semitic Studies Monograph 11. Manchester: University of Manchester Press.

Stocking, George W., Jr. 1989. The Ethnographic Sensibility of the 1920s and the Dualism of the Anthropological Tradition. In *Romantic Motives: Essays on Anthropological Sensibility*, ed. George W. Stocking, Jr. History of Anthropology 6. Madison: University of Wisconsin Press.

Suleiman, Michael W. 1987. Attitudes, Values, and the Political Process in Morocco. In *The Political Economy of Morocco*, ed. Zartman.

Swearer, Donald K. 1991. Fundamentalistic Movements in Theravada Buddhism. In *Fundamentalisms Observed*, ed. Marty and Appleby.

Tambiah, Stanley J. 1976. *World Conqueror and World Renouncer: A Study of Buddhism and Polity in Thailand against a Historical Background*. Cambridge: Cambridge University Press.

———. 1985. *Culture, Thought, and Social Action: An Anthropological Perspective*. Cambridge: Harvard University Press.

Tapper, Nancy, and Richard Tapper. 1987. The Birth of the Prophet: Ritual and Gender in Turkish Islam. *Man* 22:69–92.

Tessler, Mark A. 1981. Politics in Morocco: The Monarch, the War, and the Opposition. Hanover: American Universities Field Staff, Africa, Report no. 47.

———. 1982. Morocco: Institutional Pluralism and Monarchical Dominance. In *Political Elites in North Africa*, ed. I. William Zartman, pp.

35–91. New York: Longman.

———. 1987. Image and Reality in Moroccan Political Economy. In *The Political Economy of Morocco*, ed. Zartman.

———. 1991. Anger and Governance in the Arab World: Lessons from the Maghrib and Implications for the West. *Jerusalem Journal of International Relations* 13(3): 7–33.

———. 1992. Youth in the Maghrib: Social Mobilization, Unrealized Expectations and Political Alienation. In *State and Society in Contemporary North Africa*, ed. I. William Zartman and Mark Habeeb. Boulder: Westview.

Tharaud, Jérôme, and Jean Tharaud. 1920. *Marrakech, ou les seigneurs de l'Atlas*. Paris: Librairie Plon.

Touati, Houari. 1989. Approche sémiologique et historique d'un document hagiographique algérien. *Annales ESC* 44:1205–28.

Tozy, Mohamed. 1983. Monopolisation de la production symbolique et hiérarchisation du champ politico-religieux au Maroc. In *Le Maghreb musulman en 1979*, ed. Souriau. Paris: CNRS.

———. 1984. Champ et contrechamp politico-religieux au Maroc. Thèse pour le Doctorat d'Etat en Science Politique. Université de Droit, d'Economie et des Sciences d'Aix-Marseille.

———. 1989. Islam et état au Maghreb. *Maghreb Machrek* 126:25–46.

Tozy, Mohamed, and Bruno Etienne. 1986. La Da'wa au Maroc: Prolégomènes théorico-historiques. In *Radicalismes islamiques*, ed. Olivier Carré and Paul Dumont, 2:5–32. Paris: L'Harmattan.

U.S. Congress. House. 1991. *Human Rights in the Maghreb and Mauritania*. Hearing before the Subcommittees on Human Rights and International Organizations and on Africa, Committee on Foreign Affairs, 102d Cong., 1st sess., 1991. Washington, D.C.: GPO.

Valls-Russell, Janice. 1990. A Place for Opponents: King Hassan's Secret Garden. *New Leader*, 29 Oct. 1990, 5–6.

van der Yeught, Michel. 1989. *Le Maroc à nu*. Paris: L'Harmattan.

Van Gennep, Arnold. 1960. *The Rites of Passage*. Chicago: University of Chicago Press.

Veronne, Chantal de la. 1974. *Vie de Moulay Isma'il, roi de Fès et de Maroc, d'après Joseph de Léon (1708–1728)*. Paris: Geuthner.

Vinogradov, Amal Rassam. 1974. *The Ait Ndhir of Morocco: A Study of the Social Transformation of a Berber Tribe*. Ann Arbor: Museum of Anthropology, University of Michigan, Anthropological Papers no. 55.

Violet, Bernard. 1991. *L'affaire Ben Barka*. Paris: Fayard.

Voll, John. 1982. *Islam: Continuity and Change in the Modern World*. Boulder: Westview.

Wallace, Anthony. 1956. Revitalization Movements. *American Anthropologist* 58:264–81.

Waltz, Susan. 1991. Making Waves: The Political Impact of Human Rights Groups in North Africa. *Journal of Modern African Studies* 29(3): 481–504.

Walzer, Michael. 1974. *Regicide and Revolution: Speeches at the Trial of Louis XVI*. New York: Cambridge University Press.

Waterbury, John. 1970. *The Commander of the Faithful: The Moroccan Political Elite, A Study in Segmented Politics*. London: Weidenfeld and Nicolson.

Weber, Max. [1922] 1963. *The Sociology of Religion*, trans. Ephraim Fischoff. Boston: Beacon Press.

Wehr, Hans. 1976. *Arabic-English Dictionary*, ed. Milton J. Cowan. Ithaca: Cornell University Press.

Weisgerber, Dr. Félix. 1947. *Au seuil du Maroc moderne*. Rabat: Les Editions la Porte.

Westermarck, Edward. 1914. *Marriage Ceremonies in Morocco*. London: Macmillan.

———. 1926. *Ritual and belief in Morocco*. 2 vols. London: Macmillan.

———. 1930. *Wit and Wisdom in Morocco: A Study of Native Proverbs*. London: George Routledge and Sons.

Woodward, Mark R. 1989. *Islam in Java: Normative Piety and Mysticism in the Sultanate of Yogyakarta*. Tucson: University of Arizona Press.

World Bank. 1989. *Social Indicators of Development 1989*. Baltimore: Johns Hopkins University Press.

Yasin, 'Abd as-Slam. 1982. *La révolution à l'heure de l'islam*. Marseille: n.p. (*See* Bibliography A.)

Zafrani, Haim. 1983. *Mille ans de vie juive au Maroc: Histoire et culture, religion et magie*. Paris: Maisonneuve et Larose.

Zartman, I. William. 1964a. *Destiny of a Dynasty: The Search for Institutions in Morocco's Developing Society*. Columbia: University of South Carolina Press.

———. 1964b. *Problems of New Power: Morocco*. New York: Atherton.

———. 1987a. King Hassan's New Morocco. In *The Political Economy of Morocco*, ed. Zartman.

———, ed. 1987b. *The Political Economy of Morocco*. New York: Praeger.

Index